QUESTIONS & ANSWERS:
Wills, Trusts & Estates

QUESTIONS & ANSWERS:
Wills, Trusts & Estates

SECOND EDITION

*Multiple Choice and Short Answer
Questions and Answers*

By

Thomas M. Featherston, Jr.
Mills Cox Professor of Law
Baylor Law School

Michael Hatfield
Professor of Law
Texas Tech University
School of Law

ISBN#: 9781422417454

> **NOTE TO USERS**
> To ensure that you are using the latest materials available in this area, please be sure to periodically check the LexisNexis Law School web site for downloadable updates and supplements at www.lexisnexis.com /lawschool

Editorial Offices
744 Broad Street, Newark, NJ 07102 (973) 820-2000
201 Mission St., San Francisco, CA 94105-1831 (415) 908-3200
701 East Water Street, Charlottesville, VA 22902-7587 (434) 972-7600
www.lexis.com

(Pub.3186)

About the Authors

Thomas M. Featherston, Jr. is the Mills Cox Professor of Law at Baylor Law School in Waco, Texas. He earned his J.D. with highest honors from Baylor Law School in 1972. After graduation, he entered private practice in Houston from 1972 through 1982. He is Board Certified in Estate Planning and Probate Law by the Texas Board of Legal Specialization (originally certified in 1979). He joined the Baylor Law School faculty in 1982, and in 1990, he was appointed to the Mills Cox Chair.

Professor Featherston was elected as an Academic Fellow of the American College of Trust and Estate Counsel in 1991 and a Fellow of the American Bar Foundation in 1993. He is active in both the State Bar of Texas and the American Bar Association. He is a past chair of the Real Estate, Probate, and Trust Law Section of the State Bar of Texas and currently serves on the governing council of the Real Estate, Probate, and Trust Law Section of the American Bar Association. He is also the Trusts and Estates Editor for *Probate and Property*, an ABA publication, and has co-authored *West's Texas Practice Guide — Probate* and *Drafting for Tax and Administration Issues*, an ABA publication. He is a frequent author and lecturer in the areas of trusts, estates, marital property, fiduciary administration, and other related topics, the subjects that he teaches at Baylor Law School.

Michael Hatfield is Professor of Law at Texas Tech University School of Law in Lubbock, Texas. He earned his J.D. with honors from New York University School of Law in 1996. After graduation, he entered private practice from 1996 through 2005, first in New York, New York, as an associate at Debevoise & Plimpton and Simpson, Thacher & Bartlett, and then in San Antonio, Texas, where he became a shareholder in Schoenbaum, Curphy & Scanlan, P.C. He is Board Certified in Estate Planning and Probate Law by the Texas Board of Legal Specialization (originally certified in 2005) and admitted to practice in New York, Texas, and before the U.S. Tax Court. He joined the Texas Tech University School of Law faculty in 2005 where he teaches wills and trusts, marital property, income taxation, and planning for small businesses.

Professor Hatfield's research has been published in the Baylor Law Review, the Lewis & Clark Law Review, the Notre Dame Journal of Law, Ethics & Public Policy, Topics in Philanthropy, and the Texas Tech Law Review. In 2006, he was named the Texas Tech University School of Law Outstanding Professor of the Year, and in 2007, he was awarded the New Faculty Award by the Texas Tech University Alumni Association.

PREFACE TO THE SECOND EDITION

The law governing Wills, Trusts, and Estates in the United States finds its origins primarily in the common law of England. Today, it is increasingly based on statutory law. It is also largely "state law" oriented. Each state has its own set of rules, procedures, statutes, and case law. While there are many common denominators, the law can and frequently will differ from state to state. Some of these differences are significant.

To address this reality, several assumptions about applicable law must be made, which are described below. However, in recognition of the differences in states' laws, answers will also explain how the result may differ in a state that does not follow the position taken by uniform codes or the "majority" case law approach. Regardless of the state law that the student has learned in class, the key issues are explained, and it is hoped that the relevant answer is made clear for each question.

A primary purpose of this book is to test the student's understanding of this area of the law. This book supplements the student's casebook and includes questions and answers in subject areas that correspond to basic topics covered in a typical Wills, Trusts, and Estates course. Although space does not allow for the coverage of every topic, the topics covered have been chosen with reference to popular case books and syllabi in use across the nation.

In order to determine applicable laws, and to focus questions on specific issues, the following questions and the suggested answers have been formed with several assumptions. Accordingly, unless otherwise instructed, the student should assume as follows:

- All states have adopted the Uniform Probate Code, the Uniform Trust Code, the American Bar Association's Model Rules of Professional Responsibility (and the American College of Trust and Estates Counsel's commentaries on those rules), and the common law as represented in the relevant Restatements of the Law. However, unless expressly directed do not consider Uniform Probate Code § 2-504 (or any "substantial compliance" rule in any jurisdiction that has not adopted the Uniform Probate Code).

- There are sufficient assets, and there are no expenses or creditors' claims. For example, if a question asks about the proper distribution of an intestate's estate, simply divide the assets described, assuming there are no estate administration expenses or debts of the decedent.

- There are no survivors relevant to determining a deceased's heirs other than those specifically identified. For example, if George is said to be survived by his daughter, Elena, assume that he has no other children or other descendants, and that he has no surviving spouse, parents, or siblings, unless they are expressly named.

- None of the property is community property. For example, if Mary and Ted are married, and Mary dies, assume her estate is wholly comprised of separate property. Unless expressly questioned, ignore Ted's homestead, exempt property, and family allowance rights. Also assume the state has abolished the common law doctrines of dower and curtesy.

- A deceased's will was valid and duly admitted to probate. If the question recites that Mary died testate, assume there are no problems with the will, unless the question directs your attention to a potential problem. Assume similarly for all deeds.

- All trusts are valid, irrevocable, and express. If the question describes a trust that Merwan has established for Nishan, assume the trust is irrevocable, valid, and express, unless the question directs your attention to the trust's validity, revocability, or an issue as to whether it is an express, constructive, or resulting trust.

- All schools, religious congregations, and hospitals are bona fide charities. Unless directly questioned, assume the charities are tax-exempt and non-profit and that donations are deductible for all relevant tax purposes.

- Individuals are unmarried, and are alive at all relevant times. For example, if the question states that Henri died, assume he was single. If the question states Henri was survived by his sister, Fran, assume that Fran is still living at all times relevant to any legal analysis involved in the question.

- For any question involving federal transfer taxes, assume the annual exclusion in effect for all years is $12,000.

Professor Thomas M. Featherston, Jr.
Baylor Law School
Waco, Texas

Professor Michael Hatfield
Texas Tech University School of Law
Lubbock, Texas
September, 2007

TABLE OF CONTENTS

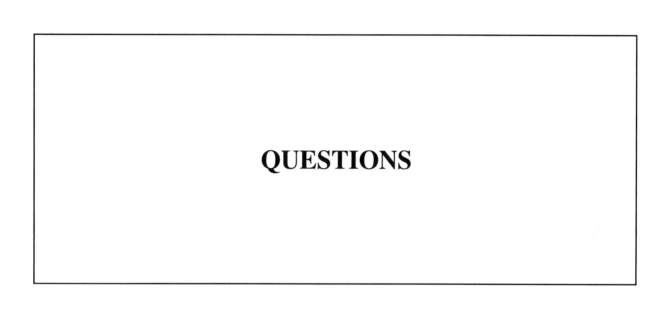

QUESTIONS

1. Felipe died. His will was drafted by his lawyer, Karen. His will names a local bank as executor. Felipe's will disinherited his youngest son, Raul. The will did not specify why Raul was being disinherited. Felipe and Karen had several discussions about disinheriting Raul in which Felipe explained why he wanted to disinherit Raul. Felipe was married to Tammy when the will was executed, as well as when he died. Tammy was not represented by Karen. Tammy was distressed to learn from the bank that Raul had been disinherited. Karen believes that, if Tammy knew the reasons for Raul's disinheritance, she would not be distressed. Karen and Felipe never discussed revealing the information after his death, and Karen does not believe Felipe would want her to reveal the information for any purposes.

    Which of the following is the best statement as to Karen's obligations with respect to the information?

    (A) So long as Felipe was living, Karen was obligated not to disclose confidential information. However, the lawyer-client relationship does not survive death, which means Karen can now use her professional discretion with respect to disclosing the information.

    (B) Since Raul is the object of the information, Raul may consent to the disclosure by Karen to Tammy. However, if Raul does not consent, Karen may not disclose the information.

    (C) Since Tammy was married to Felipe when the will was drafted, Tammy has the right to any information disclosed to Karen since spouses do not have the right to keep legally relevant information confidential from each other.

    (D) Since the bank is the personal representative of Felipe's estate, only the bank has the right to the information and the right to consent to Karen's disclosure of the information.

2. Jayashri is a solo practioner. Her primary practice area is in probate and estate planning. She has always worked alone and expects that she always will. Since she is concerned as to what would happen to her clients and their files when she dies, she has made arrangements with another solo practitioner, Tae, to review all of her files when she dies. Jayashri and Tae share office space, but they are not partners and do not consult with one another regarding their clients. None of Jayashri's clients have ever met Tae.

    Does this arrangement with Tae violate Jayashri's duty to preserve the confidentiality of her clients' information?

(A)   Yes, unless her clients have explicitly authorized the arrangement. She cannot disclose any confidential information unless she has explicit authorization.

(B)   No, unless her clients have explicitly prohibited her from making such an arrangement, she is authorized to make these arrangements since a reasonable client would approve the arrangement to safeguard his or her own interests.

(C)   Yes, because Tae is not a partner, associate, or employee of Jayashri.

(D)   No, unless (i) the client explicitly authorize the arrangement or (ii) the court approves the arrangement.

3.   Thelma makes an appointment with Pam. Pam is a lawyer and has never represented or met Thelma. Thelma provides Pam with her prior estate planning documents and detailed information of her assets. As Thelma begins discussing her plans for her estate, Pam becomes convinced that Thelma is very mentally ill. Thelma believes that terrorists are living in her apartment and are attempting to persuade her to leave her estate to them so that they can hasten a "glorious apocalypse." Thelma explains that the terrorists only allow her access to food or water when she agrees to leave them the estate and that she often has gone several days without eating or drinking. She then reveals the sides of her arms to Pam which appear to have been repeatedly cut with small scissors. Pam believes Thelma has done this to herself.

Which of the following is the best statement?

(A)   Based on what she has learned, Pam may initiate a guardianship or other appropriate protective court proceeding, or she may consult with appropriate third parties who may have the ability to protect Thelma without such a court proceeding, such as Thelma's family or social workers. Pam may disclose information she learned during discussions with Thelma to the extent necessary to protect Thelma's interests.

(B)   Thelma is Pam's client, and Pam may not disclose any of the information or use it in a guardianship or similar proceeding without Thelma's consent.

(C)   Pam may initiate a guardianship or other appropriate protective court proceeding with respect to Thelma only if the court approves the disclosure of the information and determines the extent to which disclosing it is necessary to protect Thelma's interests.

(D)   Based on what she has learned, Pam may initiate a guardianship or other appropriate protective court proceeding. However, she may not consult with any third parties other than the appropriate court. Pam may disclose information she learned during discussions only with the court, only in the context of a guardianship or other appropriate proceeding, and only to the extent necessary to the proceeding.

4.   Jolene is an attorney. She receives a phone call from Nancy. Nancy is Jolene's client on various matters, and Jolene knows her well. Nancy explains that her mother is in a nursing home in a persistent weakened and bedfast state but mentally aware. Nancy explains that her mother would like to update her will. Jolene makes an appointment

to visit with them at the nursing home. Nancy's mother's name is Martha, and she is unable to rise from bed or speak much above a whisper. Jolene is barely able to understand what Martha is saying, so she relies on Nancy to explain what Martha is saying about the changes she would like in her will. When Nancy explains something to Jolene, she turns to Martha and asks, "Mom, is that right?" and Martha invariably shakes her head that it is. Part of what Martha wants changed in her will relates to an ongoing litigation involving some real estate and distant family members. Through Nancy, Martha tells Jolene several facts that have not been revealed in the litigation but are prompting her to change her estate plan.

How does Nancy's presence during these discussions affect the applicability of the attorney-client evidentiary privilege?

(A) Since Nancy is a third party present during the disclosure of the information, there is no attorney-client privilege with respect to the information.

(B) Since both Nancy and Martha are Jolene's clients, the attorney-client privilege remains applicable to the information.

(C) Since Nancy's participation in the discussion between Jolene and Martha is necessary to Jolene's representation, the attorney-client privilege remains applicable to the information.

(D) Nancy's participation in the discussion has prevented the attorney-client relationship from being formed between Jolene and Martha. Thus, the attorney-client privilege is entirely inapplicable.

5. Andy and Helen are married. They make an appointment with an attorney, Bea, to discuss estate planning. Andy, Helen, and Bea discuss the estate planning in detail but never discuss Bea's legal representation as such.

In the absence of an agreement otherwise, what is the result?

(A) Bea is presumed to represent Andy and Helen jointly.

(B) Bea is presumed to represent Andy and Helen separately.

(C) Bea is presumed to represent Andy and Helen jointly and separately.

(D) Bea does not represent either Andy or Helen until they discuss her representation.

6. Refer to Question 5. What should Bea explain to them about the ethical rules and jointly representing a husband and wife in estate planning?

ANSWER:

7. Refer to Question 5. After Bea begins working on Andy's and Helen's estate plans, Helen comes in to see Bea. In the course of their meeting, Helen mentions to Bea that she committed adultery three years before. Helen tells Bea not to tell Andy, of course.

Does Bea have a duty to disclose this information to Andy?

(A) Yes, because she must disclose to each of them the content of all communications with the other.

(B) No, if she concludes the communication is not relevant to the legal representation.

(C) No, because it is confidential information provided by her client.

(D) Yes, unless Andy has waived his right to be provided information Helen gives Bea.

8. Refer to Question 5. Andy's and Helen's estate plans involve coordinating their non-probate and probate assets. In order to minimize Bea's fees, Andy and Helen agreed with Bea that they would each be responsible for making any changes necessary with respect to their respective non-probate assets and that she would have no responsibility with respect to the non-probate assets. Their largest assets are their respective individual retirement accounts. They have agreed under their wills to leave all of their probate assets to Andy's children from a prior marriage. At a meeting of the three of them on Monday, Andy and Helen each report that, as previously planned, they have completed the paper work to name the other as the respective retirement account beneficiary. Having the non-probate assets in place as planned, Bea prepares their wills to leave their probate assets to Andy's children. On the day before the wills were to be executed, Andy calls Bea and tells her that he changed his retirement account so as to benefit his children rather than Nancy. He tells Bea not to tell Helen.

What should Bea do with respect to this information?

(A) As Andy is her client and instructed her to keep it confidential, she must not reveal it to Helen.

(B) She should discuss with Andy her need to disclose this information or withdraw from the representation unless he discloses it.

(C) She should withdraw from representation and refuse to discuss the matter any further with either Andy or Helen.

(D) Andy, Helen, and Bea agreed that Bea would have no responsibility for the non-probate assets, only for drafting the wills. Thus, Bea has no responsibility to disclose any information related to the non-probate assets.

9. Maria is the executor of Kurt's estate. Maria hires an attorney to assist her during the estate administration. Absent any agreement otherwise, who is the attorney's client?

(A) Maria.

(B) Kurt's estate.

(C) The beneficiaries of Kurt's estate.

(D) The creditors and beneficiaries of Kurt's estate.

10. Cheryl is Manny's client. Manny has been her attorney for many years. Each year on Manny's birthday, Cheryl gives him a gift.

    Is it ethical for Manny to accept such gifts?

    (A) No, because lawyers may not accept gifts from clients.

    (B) Yes, so long as Manny does not suggest the gift or engage in any type of undue influence to obtain the gift.

    (C) No, because it is presumptively fraudulent.

    (D) Yes, because there are no restrictions on social gifts or other activities between lawyers and their clients.

11. Refer to Question 10. When Manny is drafting Cheryl's will, Cheryl tells him that she would like for his birthday gifts to continue in the event she predeceases him. She instructs him to set aside $50,000 in a trust with her daughter as trustee. Her daughter is to be directed to buy a birthday gift for Manny each year so that he will always remember Cheryl and her appreciation for his loyal services over the decades. Manny tells her that this is not necessary, but Cheryl insists. Can Manny draft this provision?

ANSWER:

12. Josh is Lilly's client. Lilly drafts a will for Josh. After the will is executed, Lilly asks if Josh would like to keep the will in Lilly's vault for safekeeping.

    Is it proper for Lilly to keep the will?

ANSWER:

13. Henry created an irrevocable trust for the benefit of Beto. Darren is the trustee. Darren hires an attorney, Penelope, to assist in the administration of the trust.

    Who is Penelope's client?

    (A) Henry.

    (B) Darren.

    (C) Beto.

    (D) Darren and Beto.

14. Barry hires an attorney, Henrietta, to draft his will. Since Henrietta becomes so familiar with Barry's estate during the estate planning process, Barry asks her to serve as executor of his estate.

Is it ethical for Henrietta to draft a will naming herself as the executor of the estate?

(A)   Yes, so long as while serving as executor she does not charge the estate for being both the executor and the executor's attorney.

(B)   No, because she cannot draft a will in which she receives any substantial interest.

(C)   Yes, but she should make sure he understands there is no necessity of her being named and discuss with him what her fees would be, including any fees as attorney and not just as executor.

(D)   No, unless the will requires that she serve as executor without compensation.

15.   Refer to Question 14. Assume that Barry would like Henrietta to serve as a trustee under his will. If the will contains an exculpatory clause for trustees, will a court enforce it if Henrietta serves as trustee?

ANSWER:

16. Nolan died partially intestate. Six hundred shares of stock are to be distributed under the intestacy statute. His will contained a provision that read "my brother Trevor is not to receive any of my property." Nolan was survived by Trevor; Trevor's three children, Cora, Lara, and Tyra; and Alan who was the sole surviving child of Nolan's deceased sister, Dalia. Dalia's widower, Frank, is also living.

    How is the stock to be distributed?

    (A) Trevor takes 300 shares; Frank takes 300 shares.

    (B) Alan takes 300 shares; Cora, Lara, and Tyra each take 100 shares.

    (C) Alan, Cora, Lara, and Tyra each take 150 shares.

    (D) Cora, Lara, and Tyra each take 200 shares.

17. Camila and Orlando have not divorced. However, due to court filings initiated by Orlando upon his discovery of Camila's adultery, a court has issued a legal decree of separation. Orlando dies intestate. Camila and Orlando have one son, Gerald, who is unmarried and has no descendants. Neither Camila nor Orlando has any other surviving descendants. Both of Orlando's parents, Hugo and Avery, are living.

    How is Orlando's estate to be distributed?

    (A) Camila takes the estate.

    (B) Gerald takes the estate.

    (C) Camila takes the first $200,000 plus ¾ of the balance of the intestate estate; Gerald takes the remaining ¼ of the estate.

    (D) Camila takes the first $200,000 plus ¾ of the balance of the intestate estate; Hugo and Avery each take ⅛ of the remaining estate.

18. Refer to Question 17. Assume Gerald had predeceased Orlando and that Orlando had no surviving descendants.

    What, if any, part of the estate would Camila take?

ANSWER:

19. Refer to Question 17. Assume Camila had a daughter, Andrea, from a prior marriage.

    What, if any, part of the estate would Camila take?

ANSWER:

20. Refer to Question 17. Assume Orlando had a daughter, Jen, from a prior marriage.

    What, if any, part of the estate would Camila take?

ANSWER:

21. Angel and Madeline were married. Neither had any children. Madeline died intestate two years ago. She was survived by her father, Ted, and her mother, Claire. Angel has now died intestate. He is survived by a brother, Joe, and his mother, Rosa.

    How is Angel's estate to be distributed?

    (A) Ted and Claire each take ¼; Rosa takes ½.

    (B) Ted, Claire, Rosa, and Joe each take ¼.

    (C) Rosa and Joe each take ½.

    (D) Rosa takes the estate.

22. Refer to Question 21. How would your answer differ if Rosa duly filed an effective disclaimer?

ANSWER:

23. Refer to Question 21. How would your answer differ if both Rosa and Joe had predeceased Angel, and he was survived only by his great-grandfather, Horacio?

ANSWER:

24. Tony dies intestate. He is survived by his sister, Marla, and his great-grandfather, Luis. Three days after Tony's death, Marla dies intestate. She has no living descendants, but she does have a husband, Chuck.

    Who receives Tony's estate?

(A) Marla did not survive for 120 hours after Tony's death. Thus, she is deemed to have predeceased him, which means that Luis will take the estate.

(B) Marla did not survive for 120 hours after Tony's death. Thus, she is deemed to have predeceased him, which means that the state will take the estate.

(C) Marla took Tony's estate. As her surviving spouse, Chuck will take Marla's estate, which now indirectly includes Tony's.

(D) Marla took Tony's estate, but since she died intestate, his estate is distributed to Luis.

25. Victor is a widower. Victor dies intestate. He had two children, Alejandro and Jorge. Alejandro, however, predeceased his father, Victor, leaving one child, Eduardo. Jorge also predeceased his father, Victor, leaving two children, Olivia and Serena. Olivia survived her father, Jorge, but she predeceased her grandfather, Victor, leaving two children, Nina and Miranda. Thus, Victor is survived by Eduardo (his grandson; Alejandro's son), Serena (his granddaughter; Jorge's daughter), Nina (his great-granddaughter; Olivia's daughter), and Miranda (his great-granddaughter; Olivia's daughter). How is Victor's estate to be distributed?

(A) Eduardo, Serena, Nina, and Miranda each take ¼.

(B) Eduardo takes ⅓; Serena takes ⅓; Nina takes ⅙; and Miranda takes ⅙.

(C) Eduardo takes ½; Serena takes ¼; Nina takes ⅛; and Miranda takes ⅛.

(D) Eduardo takes it all.

26. Refer to Question 25. Would the result differ if the jurisdiction had a modern per stirpes system of representation in effect?

ANSWER:

27. Refer to Question 25. Assume that Victor had a third child, Christopher, who predeceased Victor. Also assume that Serena has a child, Tina. So Victor is survived by Eduardo (his grandson; Alejandro's son), Serena (his granddaughter; Jorge's daughter), Nina (his great-granddaughter; Olivia's daughter), Miranda (his great-granddaughter; Olivia's daughter), and Tina (his great-granddaughter; Serena's daughter). How is VictorÖs estate to be distributed?

ANSWER:

28. Aaron is a widower who was predeceased by his parents. He died intestate. He was survived by his brother, Booker. However, he was predeceased by his brother, Cameron, his brother, Doug, and his half-sister, Elisa. Cameron's daughter, Faye, survived Aaron.

Doug's daughter, Gabby, survived Aaron, but Doug's sons, Hank and Ivan, predeceased Aaron. Aaron was survived by Hank's three children: his son, Leo, and his daughters, Michelle and Nell. Aaron was also survived by Ivan's son, Odell, and Elisa's son, Jerry. However, Elisa's son, Kenton, predeceased Aaron, though Kenton's daughter, Patty, survived Aaron. Thus, Aaron was survived by Booker (his brother), Faye (his niece; Cameron's daughter), Gabby (his niece; Doug's daughter), Jerry (his nephew; Elisa's son), Leo (his grand-nephew; Hank's son), Michelle (his grand-niece; Hank's daughter), Nell (his grand-niece; Hank's daughter), Odell (his grand-nephew; Ivan's son) and Patty (his grand-niece; Kenton's daughter).

How is Aaron's estate to be distributed?

(A)   Booker takes $\frac{1}{4}$; Faye, Gabby, and Jerry each take $\frac{1}{8}$; Leo, Michelle, Nell, Odell, and Patty each take $\frac{3}{40}$.

(B)   Booker and Faye each take $\frac{1}{4}$; Jerry and Patty each take $\frac{1}{8}$; Gabby and Odell each take $\frac{1}{12}$; Leo, Michelle, and Nell each take $\frac{1}{36}$.

(C)   Booker, Faye, Gabby, Jerry, Leo, Michelle, Nell, Odell, and Patty each take $\frac{1}{9}$.

(D)   Booker takes the estate.

29.   Delmar, a single man, dies intestate. He is survived by his mother, Corine. His brother, Bart, predeceased Delmar, but Delmar is survived by Bart's two sons, Shawn and Terrell. His sister, Odessa, also survives Delmar.

How is Delmar's estate to be distributed?

(A)   Corine takes $\frac{1}{2}$; Odessa takes $\frac{1}{2}$.

(B)   Corine takes $\frac{1}{2}$; Odessa takes $\frac{1}{4}$; Shawn and Terrell each take $\frac{1}{8}$.

(C)   Corine, Odessa, Shawn, and Terrell each take $\frac{1}{4}$.

(D)   Corine takes the estate.

30.   Lennon's biological mother is Dacey, and his biological father is Baird. Dacey and Baird have never been married. Lennon has been adopted by his mother's husband, Alan. Baird has never provided any support for Lennon.

Explain the effect of the adoption on Lennon's inheritance rights and the rights of other family members to inherit through Lennon.

ANSWER:

31.   Adam died intestate. He was survived by his wife, Beryl, and his three daughters from a prior marriage, Cassandra, Daphne, and Electra. Adam's probate estate is valued at $190,000. During his lifetime, he advanced $50,000 to Cassandra and $10,000 to

Daphne. These gifts were memorialized in writing declaring the intention that the gifts be treated as advancements.

How should Adam's probate estate be distributed?

(A) $190,000 to Beryl.

(B) $100,000 to Beryl; $0 to Cassandra; $45,000 to Daphne; and $45,000 to Electra.

(C) $100,000 to Beryl; $0 to Cassandra; $20,000 to Daphne; and $70,000 to Electra.

(D) $150,000 to Beryl; $0 to Cassandra; $15,000 to Daphne; and $25,000 to Electra.

32. Kenton, a single man who was a resident of the state Michiana, died intestate in Michiana. He was survived by several members of his family residing in several different states. Kenton owned household furnishings, jewelry, clothing, and other personal effects located in a rented apartment in Michiana, as well as an automobile registered and located there. He owned a checking account at a local Michiana branch of a national bank, shares of stock in a corporation incorporated in the state of Westphalia, and other items of tangible personal property located at his parents' house in the state of Newberg.

How is succession to the described assets to be determined?

(A) Federal law will determine who succeeds to the ownership of the described personal property.

(B) The law of Michiana determines the succession to the tangible personal property located in Michiana; federal law determines the succession of the bank account; the law of Westphalia governs the succession of the shares of stock; and the law of Newberg governs the succession of the tangible personal property located in Newberg.

(C) The law of Michiana governs not only the succession of the tangible personal property located in Michiana but also the checking account; the law of Westphalia will govern the succession of the shares of stock; and the law of Newberg will govern the succession of the tangible personal property located in that state.

(D) The law of Michiana will determine who succeeds to the ownership of all of the described assets.

33. Refer to Question 32. Assume Kenton owned the fee simple title to three tracts of land, one tract located in each of the states of Michiana, Westphalia, and Newberg.

How is succession to the tracts of land to be determined?

(A) The law of Michiana governs the succession of all three tracts.

(B) The law of Michiana governs the succession of the land in Michiana; the law of Westphalia will govern the succession of the land in Westphalia; and the law of Newberg will govern the succession of the land in Newberg.

(C)   Federal law governs the succession of the three tracts to the extent of any inconsistencies existing among the laws of Michiana, Westphalia, and Newberg.

(D)   Federal law governs the succession of all three tracts of land because Kenton and the heirs resided in different states.

34. What is the difference between undue influence, duress, and fraud? What effect do they have on the execution of a will by a testator?

ANSWER:

35. Mitt was an electrical engineer for a start-up company that produced cutting-edge products for personal computers. On Monday morning, he came into his attorney's office to execute his will. During their initial meeting, he and his attorney discussed his friends and family and to whom he wanted to give his property. His attorney had told him to be sure to review the nature and extent of his assets in connection with his estate planning. On the Friday before the will execution, Mitt prepared a detailed spreadsheet describing all of his assets and their value. The total net value of his assets was $175,432. Unknown to Mitt, while he was on his way to the attorney's office, a much larger company made a public attempt to purchase his company, which had a dramatic impact on the value of Mitt's assets since he owned many shares of stock in his company and options to buy more. The value of his assets on Monday at the time he executed his will was $3,520,895. However, at that time, Mitt believed his assets were worth only $175,432.

Given that he did not know the actual nature and extent of his property, did Matt have the capacity to execute the will?

(A) No. A testator must know the nature and extent of his property in order to have the requisite mental capacity to execute a valid will.

(B) No. While a testator need not know the exact nature and extent of his property in order to have the requisite mental capacity to execute a valid will, Mitt made a substantial mistake with respect to his property's value. He lacked the requisite mental capacity.

(C) Yes. The test for mental capacity does not refer to a testator's property since a testator's property has nothing to do with his or her mental state when the will is being executed.

(D) Yes. A testator must only be capable of knowing and understanding in a general way the nature and extent of his or her property in order to have the requisite mental capacity. Clearly, Mitt had the capability to know his assets' value and understood what his assets were in a general way.

36. Robert is a very elderly and physically weak resident in a nursing home. Though he is mentally alert, he is in tremendous pain and not expected to live much longer. His

15

family members have begun to visit him in anticipation of his death. He is aware that his death is imminent, but he has resolved to do what he can to continue living until he has seen all of his children and grandchildren again. He has asked his attorney to prepare his will and to bring it to him on Thursday to be executed. On Wednesday, on their drive to visit him, one of his sons, his daughter-in-law, and their four-year-old son were killed in a tragic automobile accident. The remaining family members have decided not to tell Robert of their deaths since they are concerned it would weaken his resolve to live and make his last days more miserable than they otherwise might be. On Thursday, he executed his will, which made gifts to his son, his daughter-in-law, and their four-year-old son.

Did his ignorance of their deaths affect his capacity to execute the will?

(A)   Yes. Robert did not have actual knowledge as to his family members.

(B)   Yes. Robert was acting under a substantial mistake with respect to his family members, and such a mistake may have affected his testamentary plans.

(C)   No. The test for mental capacity does not refer to a testator's family members since they have nothing to do with his or her mental state when the will is being executed.

(D)   No. A testator must only be capable of knowing about his family members in order to have the requisite mental capacity.

37.   Refer to Questions 35 and 36. How would the result differ if the testators had been executing revocable inter vivos trusts as will substitutes?

ANSWER:

38.   Refer to Questions 35 and 36. Assuming the wills were executed in compliance with the statutory formalities, if the wills were contested on the grounds of lack of capacity, who would have the burden of proof?

ANSWER:

39.   Celine suffers from a substantial psychotic disorder. She often suffers from severe delusions and both audible and visual hallucinations. She has rarely been physically threatening to others or herself during such delusions, and her family has always been able to admit her into a care facility where additional medication and attention relieves her disorder by stopping the delusions and hallucinations. Lately, Celine's family has become more concerned about her condition because the time period required for the medication to relieve the disorder has been lengthening and the time periods between her acute need for hospitalization have been shortening. Celine has a very modest estate in terms of value, owning only some household furnishings, personal effects, and other

items of tangible personal property. However, she has expressed very specific desires as to whom each item should be left. She has also asked that an attorney prepare a will to memorialize her desires. As a result of a mental health crisis on Tuesday evening, Celine was hospitalized. The usual medications were administered, but they did not begin to have their effect for twenty-six hours, though in the past the medication never took longer than eight hours to become effective. Because her physicians were concerned, they decided to keep her hospitalized for observation for a full week. On the following Sunday, her attorney visited her in the hospital. While her attorney visits with her, she was lucid when discussing her property, her family, and the wishes for her family. She executed the will.

Did she have the capacity to execute the will?

(A) Yes. Even though she was hospitalized for mental health issues, since she was not adjudicated as incapacitated, she had the mental capacity to execute the will.

(B) No. Given the totality of the circumstances at the time the will was executed, she did not have the mental capacity to execute the will.

(C) Yes. Even though she was hospitalized for mental health issues, since she had a lucid interval during which to execute the will, she had the mental capacity to execute the will.

(D) No, unless her attending physician attests to her mental capacity.

40. Harold suffers from Alzheimer's and has become unable to manage his financial and personal affairs. His daughter, Loraine, petitioned a court of proper jurisdiction to declare him incapacitated and appoint her as his guardian and conservator, which the court did.

What is the effect of the court's declaration and appointment on Harold's mental capacity to execute a will?

(A) Having been declared incapacitated, Harold, by definition, does not have the mental capacity to execute a will.

(B) Having been declared incapacitated raises a rebuttable presumption that Harold does not have the mental capacity to execute a will.

(C) The legal standard for incapacity for the appointment of a conservator or guardian is different than the legal standard for testamentary capacity. The adjudication is not necessarily determinative of testamentary capacity.

(D) Since she has been appointed his conservator, Lorraine, rather than Harold, now has the legal authority to execute a will for Harold.

41. Serge is married to Ava. He executed a will several years ago that left his estate to his wife, Ava, and their son, Jas. Jas later died unexpectedly. After his son's death, Serge became socially and emotionally withdrawn from his friends and family, including Ava. He spends most of his days browsing the World Wide Web investigating claims

that alien life forms are attempting communication with humans. Serge increasingly became convinced that not only are aliens attempting to communicate with humans generally, they were specifically communicating with him. Despite his bizarre belief about alien communication, Serge continued to tend his professional and personal obligations and exhibited no unusual behavior. Ava found Serge dead in his home study. He had committed suicide. He left behind a lengthy note explaining that he has gone forward to prepare a place for Ava on a particular alien plant. He assured her that all will be well, that Jas is already awaiting their reunion there and has urged Serge to "make the transition." He left behind a holographic will revoking his prior will that left his estate to Ava and Jas and, instead, leaving his entire estate to Ava.

What effect did Serge's beliefs about alien communications have on his capacity to execute the holographic will?

(A)   While his beliefs are eccentric, nothing about Serge's beliefs impaired his testamentary capacity to leave a holographic will.

(B)   Serge's beliefs were so against the evidence and reason to the contrary that he was suffering an insane delusion. The result is that the holographic will is invalid.

(C)   Serge's beliefs were so against the evidence and reason to the contrary that he was suffering an insane delusion. However, since his delusion is unconnected with the disposition of his property in the will, the holographic will is valid.

(D)   Serge's beliefs were so against the evidence and reason to the contrary that he was suffering an insane delusion. However, if he wrote the holographic will during a lucid interval, the will is valid.

42.   Marcus was a 97-year-old socially-isolated widower with no living family. He relied on his housekeeper and his accountant to tend to all of his affairs. At his accountant's suggestion, he hired Louisa as his attorney. Marcus did not know Louisa before the accountant introduced them. Louisa prepared a will for Marcus. Under the terms of the will, his estate passed to Louisa. In his prior estate plans, Marcus had left his estate to the Bay Ridge Cardiology Research Hospital. Marcus died, and the hospital is prepared to contest the will.

Which of the following is the best statement as to the burden of proof?

(A)   Since Louisa and Marcus had an attorney-client relationship, Louisa has the burden of proving she did not exert undue influence over Marcus.

(B)   As the contestant, the Bay Ridge Cardiology Research Hospital has the burden of proving Louisa exerted undue influence over Marcus.

(C)   Even though Louisa and Marcus had an attorney-client relationship, Louisa does not have the burden of proving she did not exert undue influence over Marcus because there are no suspicious circumstances surrounding the will.

(D)   Bay Ridge Cardiology Research Hospital has the burden of proving Louisa exerted undue influence over Marcus, but, since Louisa and Marcus had an attorney-client relationship, Louisa has the burden of proving there are no suspicious circumstances surrounding the will.

43. Pearl, an elderly widow, suffered from severe arthritis, and cardiovascular problems. She could not take care of her own physical needs such as feeding, bathing, or dressing herself. Pearl's daughter, Maggie, had not visited Pearl in over twenty-five years, and when Pearl contacted her, Maggie refused to help. Pearl had no other family members. Pearl's next-door neighbor, Rachel, and her husband, Theo, took Pearl into their home and cared for her during the last year of her life. Pearl had no significant contact with anyone outside of her neighbor's home during that final year as she was essentially bedridden. Theo was an attorney, and a few weeks before Pearl died, she asked Theo to prepare a will for her that would leave her entire estate to Rachel. Theo told Pearl that he could not prepare the will for her, but he recommended another attorney, Donna, who specialized in trusts and estates and was willing to visit Pearl in her bedridden state. Donna met with Pearl privately and subsequently prepared a will to leave Pearl's entire estate to Rachel. Pearl has died. Maggie alleges that Theo and Rachel exerted undue influence over Pearl.

Which of the following is the best statement?

(A) Maggie has the burden of proof.

(B) Rachel has the burden of proof because Theo and she are married and Theo and Pearl had an attorney-client relationship.

(C) Rachel has the burden of proof because, as Pearl's caregiver, she was in a confidential relationship with Pearl.

(D) Rachel has the burden of proof because of the suspicious circumstances surrounding the execution of the will.

44. Hal is a widower who has three children: Uma, Leo, and Nick. Hal has never executed a will. Hal retained Barry as his attorney to prepare a will that would leave his estate in equal shares to Uma and Leo. Hal wanted to totally disinherit Nick because Nick is a drug addict. Barry prepared a will that left the residue of Hal's estate in two equal shares to Uma and Leo and also provided that Barry would receive a $100,000 pecuniary bequest. Barry told Hal that the will was prepared in accordance with his directions. Though he had the time and ability to do so, Hal did not review the will but rather executed it based on Barry's description. Hal has died.

Assuming Uma, Leo, and Nick would be his intestate heirs, which of the following is the best statement?

(A) Since Hal was fraudulently induced to execute the new will, the new will is invalid. Uma, Leo, and Nick will inherit the estate as his intestate heirs.

(B) Since Hal had complete testamentary capacity and the ability and opportunity to review the will, the will was valid as executed even if Hal was mistaken as to what the will provided.

(C)   Since Hal was fraudulently induced to execute the new will, the portion of the will procured by the fraud is invalid. Thus, Barry's $100,000 gift is invalid, and Uma and Leo will inherit the estate in equal shares.

(D)   The will is invalid because Hal did not review it.

45.   Refer to Question 44. What if Hal had instructed Barry to provide a no contest clause in Hal's will, and Barry did. The clause clearly provides that any person who challenges "all or any part" of the will's validity will not be entitled to receive any benefit under the will. Are Uma and Leo risking their shares of the estate by challenging the part of the will that gives Barry $100,000?

ANSWER:

46.   Refer to Questions 44 and 45. Assume Barry did not fraudulently insert the $100,000 bequest to himself. Instead, he drafted Hal's will so as to disinherit Nick and to provide a no-contest clause.

       Would the no-contest clause provide an incentive for Nick not to contest the will?

ANSWER:

47. Mario is injured in a car accident. Both of his arms are broken, and he can use neither one. Two neighbors, Jo and Keith, visit him in his living room at his home where he is recuperating. He asks them to witness his will, and they agree to sign as witnesses after he signs. Since he is unable to sign his name, he asks Jo to sign his name for him. Looking for a good surface to write on, Jo takes the will from the living room into the kitchen and signs Mario's name. Mario cannot see Jo sign though both Mario and Keith know that she has stepped into the kitchen to do so. When the telephone in the kitchen rings, Mario asks Jo to answer it and take a message. She immediately returns from the kitchen and shows Mario the will on which she has signed his name. Mario nods his head in approval. Jo places the will on a coffee table and the three of them discuss the previous night's ball game. Jo and Keith leave without any further discussions with Mario about the will. They leave without signing the will as witnesses. The next morning, Jo receives a phone call from Mario's wife who tells her that Mario died unexpectedly during the night. She tells Jo that she is relieved to know that Mario's will was executed because she expects considerable litigation over Mario's estate between her and his adult children from a prior marriage. After Jo hangs up, Keith and she discuss the fact that neither of them signed the will as witnesses as Mario had asked. They forgot. Knowing that Mario's wife did not have a good relationship with Mario's adult children from the prior marriage, Jo and Keith are scared about the litigation risk, so they return to Mario's home and sign the will, which was still on the coffee table.

Does Jo's signature on Mario's behalf count as Mario's signature?

(A) No. She did not sign in Mario's physical presence even though she did sign at his direction.

(B) No. She did not sign in Mario's line of sight even though she did sign at his direction.

(C) Yes. She signed in Mario's conscious presence and at his direction.

(D) Yes. She signed at Mario's direction. There is no requirement that she also do so in his presence or line of sight.

48. Refer to Question 47. Did Mario "acknowledge" the will?

(A) No. Keith did not actually watch Jo sign the will for Mario.

(B) Yes. Mario acknowledged the will to Keith and Jo.

(C) No. Mario did not acknowledge the will to Keith and Jo.

(D) No. While Mario acknowledged the will, Mario did not acknowledge the signature to Keith and Jo.

49. Refer to Question 47. Are the signatures of Jo and Keith effective?

(A) Yes. They signed in a reasonable time after Jo signed on Mario's behalf.

(B) No. They did not sign in Mario's presence.

(C) No. Mario was dead when they signed.

(D) Yes. They signed within the statutorily prescribed 24 hour period.

50. Jorge sits down at his dining table to execute his will in the presence of two witnesses, Wendy and Chayah. Attached to his will is a self-proving affidavit. While seated at Jorge's dining table, Wendy and Chayah sign as witnesses one after the other, and then Jorge signs. However, each of them mistakenly only signed the self-proving affidavit rather than the will. Dalia is a notary public who is present and who affixes her signature and seal to the self-proving affidavit after she takes the three's oaths.

Was Jorge's will duly executed?

(A) No. The will was not signed by the Jorge, Wendy, and Chayah.

(B) Yes. Jorge, Wendy, and Chayah signed the self-proving affidavit.

(C) No. Only the self-providing affidavit, not the will, was notarized.

(D) No. Wendy and Chayah signed before Jorge.

51. Explain the effects of a self-proving affidavit in contrast to an attestation clause.

ANSWER:

52. Shelly has died. Her parents, Bob and Luz, were divorced when she was a young child. Pursuant to her will, her mother receives her entire estate. Though Shelly's sister, Nina, does not receive a gift, she is appointed as executor. Luz and Nina witnessed Shelly's will. There were no other witnesses. Bob and Luz are Shelly's heirs.

Which of the following is the best statement?

(A) Since Luz was an interested witness, she is not competent to witness the will's execution, so the will is void.

(B) Each of Luz and Nina are competent to witness the will's execution. However, Luz's gift will be limited to what her share would be as an intestate heir of Shelly.

(C) Although Luz and Nina are competent to witness the will's execution, the gift to Luz and the appointment of Nina are void because each of them were interested witnesses.

(D) Although Luz and Nina are competent to witness the will's execution, the gift to Luz is void because she was an interested witness, but the appointment of Nina is unaffected by her being a witness.

(E) Both Luz and Nina are competent to witness the will's execution. Neither Luz's gift nor Nina's appointment are affected by their role as witnesses.

53. Stanton buys a pre-printed will form from a national bookstore chain. The form reads as follows:

I am _____ of _____ County, _____. This is my Last Will and Testament. I am of sound mind and moral character. I leave all of my real property to _____, and I leave all of my personal property to _____. I name _____ as the executor of my estate. Signed on this _____ day of _____, _____ by _____. At the request of the testator, and in the testator's presence, each of us have subscribed as witnesses to this will on this _____ day of _____, _____: _____ _____.

Alone at home, he uses a pen to complete the form by handwriting his name and place of domicile in the first sentence's blanks. In the next three blanks, he names Herman Huber to receive his real property, Gloria Washington to receive his personal property, and Janet Dava to serve as his executor. He then dates and signs the will. He dies that night of an unexpected heart attack, and is found the next morning by a friend. The will was located on his night stand.

Is the will valid?

(A) No. The will was not attested.

(B) Yes, but only because material portions of the will are in the testator's handwriting and it is signed by the testator.

(C) Yes, but only because material portions of the will are in the testator's handwriting and it is signed and dated by the testator.

(D) No, because unattested wills are not valid.

(E) No, insofar as the pre-printed form language is necessary to the will.

54. Asma is literate in both English and Urdu. After many consultations, her lawyer has drafted Asma's will just as Asma told the lawyer to do. Asma goes to her lawyer's office where the lawyer's two legal assistants are present to witness her execute the will. Upon final review, Asma changes her mind about one provision on the fourth of the will's twenty-two pages. Asma strikes out the provision and rewrites it in Urdu. The remainder of the will is in English. Asma then executes the will — signing only at the end of the will. The lawyer and the legal assistants are not literate in Urdu and have no idea what the change means. The legal assistants sign as witnesses below Asma's signature.

Which of the following is the best statement?

(A) The will is void because it is not written entirely in English.

(B)   The will was not validly executed because the witnesses cannot competently testify in court as to the testamentary intentions reflected in the Urdu handwriting.

(C)   The portion of the will handwritten in Urdu is void unless it qualifies as a holographic codicil.

(D)   The portion of the will handwritten in Urdu is void because the testator and witnesses did not sign on the changed page as well as the final page of the will.

(E)   The will is valid, including the portion of the will handwritten in Urdu.

55.   Joe was a very elderly man who lived alone on the third floor of a walk-up apartment house. His neighbors saw him come and go on a daily basis. His neighbor Sasha realized that she had not seen Joe come or go for more than a week. Sasha went to his door and knocked, but he did not answer. She found the door unlocked, opened it, and discovered Joe dead on his kitchen floor. When the authorities removed his body, they noticed the following etched into the vinyl flooring with a steak knife found nearby: "I leave my entire estate to my brother and nothing to my son." Joe's brother had this portion of the vinyl flooring removed and offered for probate by having several witnesses testify that the writing on the floor was certainly in Joe's handwriting.

       Should the will be admitted to probate?

(A)   No. Vinyl flooring cannot be probated.

(B)   Yes. It is entirely in the testator's handwriting.

(C)   No. It was neither signed nor dated.

(D)   No. It was not signed.

(E)   No. Since no one witnessed it being etched into the vinyl, there is no legal certainty as to how it got there.

56.   Though mentally competent, Jo is gravely ill in the hospital. Her lawyer has drafted a will for her to reflect her intention of leaving her estate to her husband, Jim. Her lawyer has brought the will to Jo's hospital room. Jo's husband, neighbor, priest, and doctor are in the hospital room. Her lawyer invites two legal assistants into the room to sign as witnesses to the will. Jo sits in bed and reads the will aloud to everyone in the room, and then she adds, "I can go peacefully now, since this will leaves everything to my husband when I am gone, which is what I have always wanted." She asks the two legal assistants to come to her bed side to sign as witnesses as soon as she signs. She begins to sign the will but unexpectedly dies after only partially completing her signature. The witnesses never sign the will. If she dies intestate, her heirs would include her estranged father who had abandoned her as a child. Jo's mother is deceased.

       Assuming Jo is in a jurisdiction with a provision similar to both Uniform Probate Code §§ 2-502 and 2-503, is Jo's will valid?

(A) No. It was not signed and attested as required by Uniform Probate Code § 2-502.

(B) Yes. It substantially complies with Uniform Probate Code § 2-502.

(C) Yes. It qualifies as a holographic will under Uniform Probate Code § 2-502.

(D) Yes. There is clear and convincing evidence that Jo intended the document to be her will even though it does not substantially comply with Uniform Probate Code § 2-502.

57. On Monday, Sonja meets with her lawyer to execute the will the lawyer had drafted for her. Sonja signs, followed by two witnesses signing. In the will, Sonja leaves her entire estate to her sister Noelle. On Tuesday, Noelle and Sonja have an argument over lunch. She handwrites a note to her lawyer that reads: "My sister Noelle has changed. I learned that today. I don't want that will I signed yesterday anymore. I will come back next week when I'm not so mad and decide what to do next. Yesterday's will is void." She signed the note and mailed it on Tuesday night. The lawyer received the note on Thursday morning, and then the lawyer wrote "VOID" across each page of the Monday will and through Sonja's signature. Sonja died on Sunday.

What is the status of the Monday will?

(A) The Monday will is valid because the lawyer did not write "VOID" in Sonja's presence.

(B) The Monday will was revoked when the lawyer wrote "VOID" across the top pursuant to the note.

(C) The Monday will is valid because neither Sonja's note nor the lawyer's writing "VOID" changed the fact that the Monday will was duly executed.

(D) The Monday will was revoked when Sonja handwrote and signed the note to the lawyer.

(E) The Monday will is still valid because the note did not include Sonja's new dispositive wishes.

58. Refer to Question 57. Assume the facts are the same except that the signed note Sonja sent her lawyer was printed by a computer rather than in her own handwriting.

(A) The Monday will is valid because the doctrine of dependent relative revocation applies.

(B) The Monday will was revoked when the lawyer wrote "VOID" across the top pursuant to the note.

(C) The Monday will is valid because neither Sonja's note nor the lawyer's writing "VOID" changed the fact that the Monday will was duly executed.

(D) The Monday will was revoked when Sonja signed the note to the lawyer.

(E) The Monday will is still valid because the note did not include Sonja's new dispositive wishes.

59. Seth's 2000 will was duly signed and witnessed and read as follows:

I, SETH HAIMS, do make this my Will on January 17, 2000. I give $10,000 in cash to my friend ANNA CROOKS; all my household effects to my friend JULIO PALACIA; and my residuary estate to my friend PRADEEP GANATRA.

In   2005, Seth executed a new will that was duly signed and witnessed and read as follows:

I, SETH HAIMS, do make this my Will on June 19, 2005. I give $10,000 in cash to my friend ANNA CROOKS; $15,000 in cash to my friend MARIA PALACIA; and my household effects to my friend FRANKLIN HUBER.

Assuming each named individual survives and that the probate estate is more than sufficient to make all the gifts described, which of the following is the best statement?

(A)   Anna receives $20,000 in cash; Maria receives $15,000 in cash; Franklin receives the household effects; and Pradeep receives the residue.

(B)   Anna receives $10,000 in cash; Maria receives $15,000 in cash; Franklin receives the household effects; and Pradeep receives the residue.

(C)   Anna receives $10,000 in cash; Maria receives $15,000 in cash; Julio receives the household effects; and the residuary estate is distributed to Pradeep.

(D)   Anna receives $20,000 in cash; Maria receives $15,000 in cash; Julio receives the household effects; and the residuary estate is distributed to Pradeep.

(E)   Anna receives $10,000 in cash; Maria receives $15,000 in cash; Franklin and Julio each receive one-half of the household effects; and the residuary estate is distributed one-half to Pradeep and one-half to the intestacy heirs.

60. Refer to Question 59 above. Assume the same facts except that Seth intends to revoke the 2005 will by tearing-up the 2005 will, which he does.

Explain the revival and revocation issues of Seth's intention and action.

ANSWER:

61. Refer to Question 59 above. Assume the facts are the same except that the 2005 will is duly signed and witnessed and reads as follows:

I, SETH HAIMS, do make this my Will on June 19, 2005. I give $10,000 in cash to my friend ANNA CROOKS; $15,000 in cash to my friend MARIA PALACIA; my household effects to my friend FRANKLIN HUBER; and my residuary estate to my friend JOLENE KOSLOWE.

Assuming each named individual survives and that the probate estate is more than sufficient to make all the gifts described, which of the following is the best statement?

(A)   Anna receives $10,000 in cash; Maria receives $15,000 in cash; Julio receives the household effects; and Pradeep receives the residue.

(B)   Anna receives $10,000 in cash; Maria receives $15,000 in cash; Franklin receives the household effects; and Pradeep receives the residue.

(C)   Anna receives $10,000 in cash; Maria receives $15,000 in cash; Franklin receives the household effects; and Jolene receives the residue.

(D)   Anna receives $10,000 in cash; Maria receives $15,000 in cash; Franklin and Julio each receive one-half of the household effects; and the residuary estate is distributed one-half to Pradeep and one-half to Julio.

62.   Refer to Question 59 above. Assume the same facts except that Seth intends to revoke the 2005 will by tearing-up the 2005 will, which he does.

Which of the following is the best statement?

(A)   The 2000 will is revived.

(B)   The 2000 will is not revived.

(C)   The presumption is that the 2000 will is revived.

(D)   The presumption is that the 2000 will is not revived.

63.   Refer to Question 59 above. Assume the same facts except that Seth intends to revoke the 2005 will, which he does by executing a duly witnessed document that reads "On this the 17th day of June, 2007, I, SETH HAIMS, do hereby revoke my Will executed on June 19, 2005."

Which of the following is the best statement?

(A)   The 2000 will is revived, unless there is evidence extrinsic to the 2007 will that the testator did not intend to revive the 2000 will.

(B)   The 2000 will is not revived since nothing in the text of the 2007 will evidences an intention to revive the 2000 will.

(C)   The 2000 will is not revived unless there is evidence extrinsic to the 2007 will that the testator intended to revive the 2000 will.

(D)   The 2000 will is revived to the extent it is consistent with the 2007 will since the 2007 will is to be read as a codicil to the 2000 will. On these facts, the 2000 and the 2007 will are consistent.

64.   Frank invited his friends, Kristyn and Gina, to his house to witness his will. Using his word processor, he had printed out a short one page will that gave his estate to his mother. There was no space on the single page will for his signature or their signature. Frank folded the single page over and placed it into an envelope. On the back of the envelope, he dated and signed his name, and Kristyn and Gina signed as witnesses.

On the front of the envelope he wrote "FRANK'S WILL SIGNED AND WITNESSED ON DECEMBER 2, 2004."

Which of the following is the best statement?

(A)   The will was not validly executed and attested because the signatures appear on the envelope rather than on the will.

(B)   The will was not validly executed and attested because the signatures do not appear on a page containing a dispositive or other substantive provision.

(C)   The will was not validly executed and attested unless the execution and attestation are covered by the "harmless error" standard of Uniform Probate Code § 2-503.

(D)   The will was validly executed and attested because the single page and the envelope are integrated, and the will is comprised of both writings.

65.   On September 12, 2003, Victor's will is validly executed. The will appoints Sara as executor, provides that $10,000 in cash is to be paid to the "individuals named in a letter addressed to my executor and kept in my safe deposit box #5357 at High Mountain Savings," and leaves the residue of his estate to his father. On November 4, 2005, Victor's codicil is validly executed. The codicil appoints Avinash to serve as co-executor with Sara but makes no other changes. On January 7, 2006, Victor dies. The only letter in the safe deposit box is signed by Victor and dated September 13, 2003. The letter names Bob and Marianne to each receive $5,000 in cash.

Are Bob and Marianne entitled to the cash gifts?

(A)   Yes, if the letter was signed by the testator and either validly attested or written entirely in the testator's own handwriting.

(B)   No, because the letter was not in existence on September 12, 2003, when the will referring to it was executed.

(C)   No, because writings separate from the will that identify bequests can only dispose of items of tangible personal property other than cash.

(D)   Yes, because it was in existence on or before January 7, 2006, when the codicil was executed.

66.   Marjorie validly executes her will. The will provides that each of her household effects should be distributed to the person whose name is affixed to the piece of property. After executing her will, she spends the next several months placing the names of her children and grandchildren on the bottom of pieces of furniture, appliances, and other tangible personal property in her house. She places the name of a child or a grandchild on a piece of tape that is then put onto the property.

When she dies, should the property be distributed to those individuals whose named is taped onto it?

(A) No. Even though a will may dispose of property with reference to acts that occur before or after the will's execution so long as these acts have "independent significance," these do not.

(B) Yes. A will may dispose of property with reference to acts that occur before or after the will's execution so long as these acts have "independent significance," which these do.

(C) No because a will may only dispose of property with reference to acts that occur before or at the will's execution, and these acts occur afterwards.

(D) Yes because Uniform Probate Code § 2-513 allows separate writings to dispose of items of tangible personal property other than money regardless of whether or not the writings were in existence when the will was executed, and these taped names qualify for such purposes.

67.   With respect to joint and mutual wills, which of the following is *not* true?

(A) A joint will is one instrument executed by two persons as the will of both.

(B) Mutual wills are separate wills of two or more persons that contain reciprocal provisions.

(C) Not all joint wills are mutual wills, and not all mutual wills are joint wills.

(D) A joint and mutual will may only be revoked by the agreement of both testators.

68. Zane died testate. His will devised to his brother, Fred, a tract of real estate described as "LOT 11 BLK C GARDEN OAKS SEC 2, STILLWATER, WESTPHALIA." There were no other specific gifts. The residue of Zane's estate is to be distributed to Short Creek College. The lawyer for Short Creek College has discovered that Zane never owned a tract by the exact description used in the will. Instead, Zane owned a Lot 11 in "BLK D GARDEN OAKS SEC 2." Between the time Zane executed his will and his death, he had begun to build a house on this lot in Block D. The lawyer for Short Creek College insists that the college should be distributed the house and the lot as part of the residue because the specific devise to Fred was of a tract in another block.

Which of the following is the best statement?

(A) The only evidence of Zane's intention that the court should consider is the language he used in his will. He specifically devised the tract he intended to devise, and if he did not own the tract when he died, then Fred should not receive the property.

(B) The description of the devised tract does not fit any property that Zane ever owned. His ownership of a similarly described tract that was not devised to anyone else and his building the house on that tract show by a preponderance of the evidence that Zane intended to give the tract he did own to Fred. Thus, the devise should be construed so as to effect the gift to Fred.

(C) The description of the devised tract does not fit any property that Zane ever owned. His ownership of a similarly described tract that was not devised to anyone else and his building the house on that tract show with clear and convincing evidence that Zane intended to give the tract he did own to Fred. Thus, the devise should be construed so as to effect the gift to Fred.

(D) Ambiguities are always resolved in favor of the residuary beneficiaries because testators identify these beneficiaries to receive whatever is not otherwise specifically gifted. Thus, as the chosen residuary beneficiary, Short Creek College should take the tract.

69. Dawn died testate. Article II of her Will provided that "I give my antique bracelet to my cousin, Julia." The executor of Dawn's estate determines that Dawn owned three antique bracelets. The bracelets were worth $250, $1,500 and $6,000. Dawn owned all three bracelets when she executed the will. The executor interviewed Julia, Dawn's friends and family, and Dawn's attorney who drafted the will and reviewed all of Dawn's correspondence, diaries, and other papers. However, there is no evidence of any kind that would tend to establish which bracelet Dawn intended to give to Julia. Julia's attorney insists that she should be given the $6,000 bracelet though he agrees there is

31

no evidence that would show Dawn's intention to give that specific bracelet. The residuary beneficiary is Dawn's other cousin, Ella. Ella's attorney insists that, since there is no evidence as to Dawn's intention, the gift to Julia should fail, and Ella should receive all three bracelets.

Assuming there is no evidence as to which bracelet Dawn intended to give, what is the appropriate solution of last resort for construing the provision?

(A) An ambiguous provision that cannot be resolved fails. Thus, Ella should receive all three bracelets.

(B) The provision should be construed to refer to the bracelet of highest value. Since Dawn intended to give Julia one of the three bracelets and did not specifically devise a bracelet to anyone else, it is only reasonable to construe the provision as referring to the most valuable bracelet. Thus, Julia should receive the $6,000 bracelet.

(C) The provision should be construed to refer to the bracelet of middle value. Clearly, Dawn intended to give Julia one of the three bracelets. However, since there is no evidence that she intended to give her the one of least value and equally no evidence that she intended to give her the most valuable one, the provision should be construed to refer to the $1,500 bracelet. Thus, Julia should receive the $1,500 bracelet.

(D) The provision should be construed to refer to the bracelet of the lowest value. Since Dawn intended to give Julia one of the three bracelets, at the least, she intended to devise the one of lowest value. Thus, Julia should receive the $250 bracelet.

70. Refer to Question 69. Assume Dawn had two cousins named "Julia," and they were each first cousins. Assuming there is no evidence as to which Julia Dawn intended to benefit, what is the appropriate solution of last resort for construing the provision?

ANSWER:

71. Abel died testate. Abel's will bequeathed a certain tract of land to "my nephew Darryl Wilson and his wife Juanita Wilson of Bay Ridge, Westphalia." When the will was executed, Darryl was married to Bea, not Juanita. Juanita was Darryl's former wife, who had remarried, taken her new husband's surname, and was no longer living in Bay Ridge when the will was executed, but rather, she was living with her new husband, Marcus Bard, in Cabot, Westphalia. Juanita Bard insists that she should receive a one-half undivided interest in the tract since she is the only person once named "Juanita Wilson" when married to Darryl. Bea Wilson insists that she should receive a one-half undivided interest in the tract because she was married to Darryl when the will was executed, and she was living in Bay Ridge unlike Juanita. The drafting attorney will testify that Abel intended to benefit Darryl's then current wife, Bea, and was confused when he gave the name of Darryl's former wife, Juanita.

Which of the following is the best statement?

(A) Since the language used does not precisely fit either woman, extrinsic evidence, such as the attorney's testimony, should be considered to determine whom Abel intended to benefit.

(B) Since the text of the provision is not ambiguous on its face, no extrinsic evidence such as the attorney's testimony, should be considered to determine whom Abel intended to benefit. Thus, the gift must fail.

(C) Since the text of the provision is not ambiguous on its face, no extrinsic evidence, such as the attorney's testimony, should be considered to determine whom Abel intended to benefit. Thus, the provision should be construed to benefit Juanita because the proper name "Juanita" is the only unique description in the provision since both women at one time or another were Darryl's wife, surnamed "Wilson," and lived in Bay Ridge.

(D) Since the text of the provision is not ambiguous on its face, no extrinsic evidence, such as the attorney's testimony, should be considered to determine whom Abel intended to benefit. The provision should be construed to benefit Bea because Abel's will "speaks" at the moment of Abel's death, and at that time, Bea was Darryl's wife, surnamed "Wilson," and living in Bay Ridge.

72. Bud died testate. Article II of his will provides several pecuniary gifts. Section 2, Paragraph (e) of Article II gives "$5,000 to my son, Wayne." However, Section 2, Paragraph (f) of Article II gives "$25,000 to my son, Wayne."

   Should extrinsic evidence be introduced as to Bud's intent?

ANSWER:

73. Hersh died testate. His will provides for a gift of "$10,000 to Anna." The executor of Hersh's estate soon learns that there are two women who claim this gift. One Anna is Hersh's niece. The second Anna is Hersh's neighbor. Both women visited Hersh often, and both exchanged small gifts with Hersh on birthdays and other gift-giving events.

   Assuming there is no evidence as to Hersh's actual intention, to which Anna should the executor distribute the gift?

(A) Both women should share the gift equally.

(B) Each woman should receive $10,000.

(C) Anna the niece is to be preferred because she is a family member.

(D) Anna the neighbor is to be preferred because the other Anna was a niece and was not referenced as a family member, so the preferred construction is that the non-family member Anna should take.

74.   Refer to Question 73. Assume that both Annas are family members. Anna Casto is the adopted daughter of Hersh's whole blooded brother, Ron. Anna Thurber is the biological granddaughter of Hersh's half-blooded brother, Zeke.

Assuming there is no evidence as to Hersh's actual intention, to which Anna should the executor distribute the gift?

(A)   Both women should share the gift equally because each is a family member.

(B)   The construction that benefits Anna Casto should be preferred because Anna Thurbur is related through a half-blood brother.

(C)   The construction that benefits Anna Thurber should be preferred because Anna Casto is related through adoption.

(D)   The construction that benefits Anna Casto should be preferred because she is the daughter of a brother, and Anna Thurber is the granddaughter of a brother.

75.   Gerald died testate. His will provides for a gift of "$1,000 to my brother, Harold." The executor of Gerald's estate uncovers correspondence between Gerald and the attorney who drafted Gerald's will. The correspondence indicates that Gerald intended to give $10,000, not $1,000, to his brother. The executor contacts the drafting attorney, who confirms a mistake was made in the drafting.

Which of the following is the best statement?

(A)   Since there is no ambiguity as to the amount of the gift or the beneficiary, Harold should receive $1,000.

(B)   There is an ambiguity as to the amount of the gift, so a court should construe the gift in a manner that reflects Gerald's actual intentions. If there is a preponderance of the evidence that Gerald intended to give $10,000 rather than $1,000, the construction for the $10,000 gift should be preferred.

(C)   If there is a preponderance of the evidence that Gerald intended to give $10,000 rather than $1,000, the court should reform the will to correct the mistaken expression of Gerald's intention.

(D)   If there is clear and convincing evidence that Gerald intended to give $10,000 rather than $1,000, the court should reform the will to correct the mistaken expression of Gerald's intention.

76.   Refer to Question 75. Assume at the time Gerald executed his will, he did intend to give $1,000 to Harold. However, after executed, he decided he should give Harold $10,000 instead. He called his attorney and told him that he intended for Harold to receive $10,000 instead of $1,000. On his way to the attorney's office to execute a codicil reflecting his new intention, Gerald is killed in a traffic accident. Assuming that the evidence is clear and convincing that Gerald intended Harold to receive $10,000 and not merely $1,000, should a court reform Gerald's will?

ANSWER:

77. Harlan died testate. The residuary of his estate is to be distributed one-half to his friend Nick and one-half to his friend Marie. Harlan's only intestate heirs are his two surviving children, Opal and Pete. Marie survived Harland but died within 24 hours of him.

Which of the following best describes the distribution of the residuary estate?

(A) Nick receives 100%.

(B) Nick receives 50%, Opal 25%, and Pete 25%.

(C) Opal receives 50% and Pete receives 50%.

(D) Nick receives 50% and Marie's estate receives 50%.

78. Refer to Question 77. Would the result differ if, instead of being Harlan's friend, Marie had been his niece and was survived by her daughter, Wanda?

ANSWER:

79. Refer to Question 78. Would the result differ if, instead of being Harlan's friends, Nick was his nephew, Marie was his niece, and the gift of the residue was to be made "one-half to my nephew, Nick, if he survives me, and one-half to my niece, Marie, if she survives me."

ANSWER:

80. Jose died testate. His will made a gift of "$100,000 to my son, Alfonso, if he is living at my death, but if he is not then living, to his children." Alfonso had two daughters, Pamela and Jessica. Jessica had two sons, Luis and Nick. Both Alfonso and Jessica predeceased Jose, and both died testate. Pamela, Luis, and Nick survived Jose by more than 120 hours.

What should be the effect on the $100,000 gift?

(A) Since Alfonso died testate, the $100,000 should be distributed to his estate to pass under his will.

(B) Pamela should receive $50,000, and Jessica's estate should receive $50,000 to be distributed under Jessica's will.

(C) Pamela should receive $100,000.

(D) Pamela should receive $50,000, Luis $25,000, and Nick $25,000.

81. Tina died intestate. Tina owned a painting entitled "Los Muertos" by a famous painter known as Diagur. Article II of her will provided that "I give the painting Los Muertos by Diagur to my daughter, Isabel." However, three years before Tina died and some six years after executing her will, Tina donated the painting to a local art museum. The painting was worth $500,000. Isabel insists that the executor of Tina's estate should give her a cash gift of $500,000 since the painting was not owned by Tina when she died.

    Should the executor make this cash gift?

    (A) Yes. The beneficiary of a specific gift is entitled to the cash value of the property described in the will whenever the testator dies without owning it.

    (B) Yes. It was Tina's intention that Isabel receives a gift of $500,000. Although in her will she made the gift in the form of the painting, since she did not own the painting at death, the gift must take some other form; otherwise, Tina's intention will be frustrated.

    (C) No. Under the identity theory of ademption, since Tina did not own the painting when she died, Isabel receives nothing.

    (D) No. Tina's deliberate act of giving away the painting is a fact and circumstance indicating that ademption of the gift was intended. In the absence of persuasive evidence to the contrary, Isabel is not entitled to receive the value of the painting.

82. Refer to Question 81. Would the result differ if, instead of donating the painting to a museum, a burglar had stolen the painting from Tina's home?

ANSWER:

83. Elias died testate. Article II of his will provided a gift of "100 shares of Halco, Inc. stock to my daughter, Monica." Two months after he executed his will, Halco, Inc. split its stock four-for-one. This meant Elias owned 400 shares of stock in the company. Two years later, the company declared a stock dividend issuing one share of stock for each 10 shares owned, which means Elias then owned 440 shares of Halco stock. One year later, Halco declared a cash dividend of $2 per share, which meant Elias received a total of $880. The executor of his estate determined that Elias continued to own 440 shares of Halco, Inc. when he died. The executor also discovered that Elias had placed the $880 cash dividend in a specific account in which he made no additional deposits and from which he made no withdrawals. Because of the interest accrued, the total balance in the account was $970 when Elias died.

    Which of the following should you advise the executor to do with respect to the shares?

    (A) Distribute 100 shares to Monica.

    (B) Distribute 400 shares to Monica

(C) Distribute 440 shares to Monica

(D) None of the above.

84. Refer to Question 83. Which of the following should you advise the executor to do with respect to the cash in the special dividend account?

(A) None of the cash should be distributed to Monica.

(B) $880 should be distributed to Monica.

(C) $970 should be distributed to Monica.

(D) $90 should be distributed to Monica.

85. Aaron and Diane had been married 16 years when Aaron died. Aaron and Diane had no children together although Aaron had a son, Tony, and a daughter, Jasmine, from a prior marriage. Under his will, he gave all of his probate estate to his son, Tony. At the time he executed his will, he also executed a revocable inter vivos trust that made a $100,000 transfer to Jasmine when he died. Aaron made no other nonprobate transfers. He made no nonprobate transfers to Diane. Aaron's probate estate was valued at $300,000.

If Diane's assets have a value of $200,000, what is her elective share amount under the Uniform Probate Code?

ANSWER:

86. Christopher died testate, survived by his wife, Emily. During the marriage, Christopher acquired real and personal property, which was titled in Christopher's name. Christopher's original will left all of Christopher's property equally to Emily and Madison, Christopher's daughter by prior marriage. However, Christopher revoked the described will shortly before he died and executed a new will leaving all of his property to Ava, his girlfriend.

Which answer best describes the most likely disposition of the described assets?

(A) Ava succeeds to the assets.

(B) Emily takes her elective share, Madison takes an intestate share, and Ava inherits the balance.

(C) Emily takes her elective share, and Ava inherits the balance.

(D) Madison takes an intestate share, and Ava inherits the balance.

87. Haskell died recently. He was survived by his wife, Candace, and their two minor children, Aiken and Jenna. Haskell's will, which was executed after Haskell married Candace but before the births of Aiken and Jenna, leaves all of Haskell's property to

Candace. It was also executed before the birth of Matthew, a child born of an extramarital affair of Haskell and Lola; Matthew also survived Haskell.

Which answer best describes the most likely disposition of Haskell's estate?

(A)   The entire estate passes to Candace.

(B)   The entire estate passes to Aiken, Jenna, and Matthew.

(C)   Aiken, Jenna, and Matthew will be entitled to an intestate share of the estate, and the balance of the entire estate passes to Candace.

(D)   Matthew will be entitled to an intestate share of the estate, and the balance of the entire estate passes to Candace.

88. Identify six common will substitutes.

ANSWER:

89. Abe transferred property to Naomi, in trust, to pay Abe the income for life, and to distribute the trust estate to Helena on Abe's death. Abe retained the power to revoke or amend the trust. Abe died intestate, survived by Helena. Helena is not Abe's intestate heir. The trust instrument was not witnessed and was not otherwise executed in compliance with the statutory formalities for a will.

Which of the following best describes the distribution of the trust estate at Abe's death?

(A) Abe's trust is valid even though the instrument was not executed in compliance with the statutory formalities required for a will. Helena's beneficial interest became possessory when Abe transferred property to Naomi, in trust. A settlor's power to revoke or amend a trust does not include the right to revoke or amend beneficial interests after the trust is funded. Thus, the gift to Helena was completed during Abe's lifetime and there is no need for the trust estate to pass through the probate system.

(B) Abe's trust is valid even though the instrument was not executed in compliance with the statutory formalities required for a will. However, in order for Helena's interest to become possessory at Abe's death, the trust estate must pass through the probate system.

(C) Abe's trust is invalid. Since the instrument was not executed in compliance with the statutory formalities required for a will, it cannot transfer any property interest to Helena at Abe's death. Since the trust cannot be admitted to probate, the trust estate must pass through the probate system which means that the trust estate passes to Abe's intestate heirs.

(D) Abe's trust is valid even though the instrument was not executed in compliance with the statutory formalities required for a will. Helena's future interest becomes possessory at Abe's death, which means that the trust estate passes to Helena outside of the probate system.

90. Would the result in Question 89 be different if Abe had declared himself to be the trustee of the property rather than transferring it to a third party as trustee?

ANSWER:

91. Abe took out a life insurance policy on himself. The policy named Naomi as the beneficiary to receive the proceeds on Abe's death. Under the terms of the policy, (i) Naomi must survive Abe to be entitled to the proceeds and (ii) Abe had the power to change the beneficiary any time. After he took out the policy, Abe signed and delivered to the insurance company the company's change-of-beneficiary form in which Abe named Helena rather than Naomi as the primary beneficiary. Neither of the beneficiary forms were witnessed or otherwise executed in compliance with the statutory formalities for a will. Abe has died intestate, survived by both Naomi and Helena. Neither Naomi nor Helena is an intestate heir of Abe.

Which of the following best describes the proper disposition of the insurance proceeds?

(A) Since neither the initial beneficiary designation nor the change-of-beneficiary form were executed in compliance with the statutory formalities for a will, the policy proceeds are payable to Abe's intestate heirs.

(B) The initial beneficiary designation conferred a contract right on Naomi to the proceeds of the policy subject to the requirement that she survive Abe and that Abe not change the beneficiary to someone else before he died. However, the change-of-beneficiary form negated Naomi's contract rights and conferred on Helena the same rights subject to the same conditions. Neither the initial beneficiary designation nor the change-of-beneficiary form needs to be executed in compliance with the statutory formalities for a will. The policy proceeds are payable to Helena.

(C) The initial beneficiary designation conferred a contract right on Naomi to the proceeds of the policy subject to the requirement that she survive Abe and that Abe not change the beneficiary to someone else before he died. However, the change-of-beneficiary form did not negate Naomi as the beneficiary because it was not executed in compliance with the statutory formalities for a will. Change-of-beneficiary forms must comply with the statutory formalities for a will since their sole purpose is to transfer property rights upon the owner's death. The policy proceeds are payable to Naomi.

(D) The initial beneficiary designation conferred a contract right on Naomi to the proceeds of the policy subject to the requirement that she survive Abe. The change-of-beneficiary form negated neither Naomi's contract right nor the requirement that she survive Abe. The policy proceeds are payable to Naomi.

92. Refer to Question 91. How would the results differ if Abe had validly executed a will that clearly provides that the life insurance proceeds are to be paid to the Gowanus Canal Academy "regardless of such person who may, from time to time, be named on any beneficiary designation form on file with the life insurance company." The terms of the policy did not provide that beneficiaries could be changed by will. Would Abe's dying testate affect the result?

ANSWER:

93. Mina owned and lived on the family farm. Her grandson Nathan operated the farming activities. Mina wanted Nathan to have the farm after she died because she believed he would continue to operate the farm as her husband had. To encourage Nathan, she conveyed the farm to Nathan in a deed reserving a life estate for herself, but giving the remainder to Nathan. She assumed Nathan would outlive her, but he did not. He died before Mina. Under the terms of his will, he left his entire estate to his wife, Rebecca. Since Nathan died, Mina executed a will leaving the farm to her other grandson, Dawson. Assuming both Rebecca and Dawson are living when Mina dies, who gets the farm?

    (A) Dawson because Nathan did not survive Mina's life estate.

    (B) Dawson because Mina's will revoked the earlier gift.

    (C) Rebecca because she inherited Nathan's remainder interest in the farm.

    (D) Dawson, unless the deed was executed in compliance with the statutory formalities for wills, in which case, Rebecca.

94. Anthony is an obstetrician. He has recently read several books on avoiding probate. These books describe probate as a corrupt system whose primary beneficiaries are lawyers. The books insist that any reasonable person would want to avoid probate and that there are never any benefits to property passing through the system. Anthony has retained you as his lawyer and has informed you that you are to draft a "living trust" (*i.e.*, a fully funded revocable inter vivos trust) so that his estate avoids probate. When you ask Anthony why he is so insistent on avoiding probate, his response is simply that "only suckers and fools" subject their estates to probate. Provide an outline for giving Anthony a more balanced understanding of the potential advantages and disadvantages of probate compared to "living trusts."

ANSWER:

95. Anthony died on June 15. On January 15, Anthony had executed a will and a revocable inter vivos trust instrument. The will provided that Anthony's estate shall be distributed to the trustee of the trust, which it clearly identified. The will did not provide for any alternative dispositions of property. The trustee is directed to hold any property received from Anthony's probate estate in trust for his son, Henry. On March 15, Anthony had amended the trust terms to direct the trustee to hold any property received from his probate estate for his grandson, Leonard. Despite Anthony's intention to avoid probate by transferring all of his assets into the trust, between January 15 and June 15, no assets were ever transferred.

    Which of the following best describes the distribution of Anthony's probate estate?

    (A) The trust was not valid because no assets were transferred to the trust during Anthony's lifetime. Thus, the gift to the trust under the will fails. Since no alternative provision was made, the estate passes to Anthony's intestate heirs.

(B)   Even though wills may provide gifts to "unfunded" trusts, the terms of the trust must be established on or prior to the will's execution. Thus, the estate is to be held by the trustee in trust for Henry in compliance with the terms of the trust on the date of the will's execution.

(C)   Even though wills may provide gifts to "unfunded" trusts, the terms of the trust must be established on or prior to the will's execution. Thus, the gift to the trust fails since the trust terms that were in existence on the date of the will's execution were thereafter changed. Since no alternative provision was made, the estate passes to Anthony's intestate heirs.

(D)   Neither the trust being "unfunded" nor the trust terms being amended after the execution of the will is legally relevant. The gift is valid and to be held by the trustee in trust for Leonard.

96.   Buddy and Madge were married in 2000. Madge has no descendants, but Buddy has a 6 year-old daughter, Caroline. In 2001, Madge took out a life insurance policy on herself. The policy named Caroline as the beneficiary to receive the proceeds on Madge's death. The policy also provided that Park Slope Hospital would be the alternate beneficiary in the event that Caroline did not survive Madge. In 2002, Buddy and Madge divorced. Madge has died.

Which of the following best describes the disposition of the proceeds?

(A)   Caroline is entitled to receive the proceeds because Madge did not file a change of beneficiary form to negate Caroline's rights under the insurance policy. The divorce has no effect on the life insurance policy.

(B)   Caroline is not entitled to receive the proceeds because Madge divorced Buddy, which statutorily revoked Caroline's being named the beneficiary of the policy. Thus, Park Slope Hospital is entitled to receive the proceeds.

(C)   Caroline is entitled to receive the proceeds. Even though Madge divorced Buddy, there is no statutory revocation of Caroline's being named the beneficiary of the policy because Caroline is a minor child of a divorced parent.

(D)   Unless the property settlement agreement between Buddy and Madge or the divorce decree divested Caroline of her rights under the insurance policy, she will be entitled to receive the proceeds because Madge did not file a change of beneficiary form.

97.   Louise loaned cash to Hal in exchange for a promissory note. The terms of the note required Hal to repay the loan in annual installments at a fixed rate of interest. The terms also provided that if Louise died before Hal repaid the loan, Hal was to repay the balance owing to Louise's daughter, Jen. Hal and Jen later developed a romantic relationship. Louise has died, and there is one payment left to be made on the note. Louise's other daughter, Nan, has been appointed the executor of Louise's estate. Under the terms of Louise's will, all of her property was to be distributed in equal shares to Nan and Jen. Jen has told Hal that she will forgive his debt under the note.

Is Nan entitled to the final payment?

(A) Yes. As executor of Louise's estate, Nan has the right to demand payment from Hal on behalf of the estate. Nan and Jan will be entitled to share the payment.

(B) Yes. As executor of Louise's estate, Nan the right to demand payment from Hal on behalf of the estate. However, only Jen will be entitled to receive the payment.

(C) No. Under the terms of the note, Jen received the right to be paid. The note passed as a non-probate asset to Jen.

(D) Yes, unless the note were executed with the statutory formalities for wills. If it were so executed, the note passed as a non-probate asset to Jen, which means Jen received the right to be paid.

98. Frieda and Hass are married. They have two sons, Coyt and Gary. Frieda takes out a life insurance policy on herself. The beneficiary designation is "to Hass, if he survives me, otherwise, to my children." No alternative beneficiary was provided. Hass and Gary predeceased Frieda. However, Gary was survived by his daughter, Ava. Freida has died. Which of the following best describes the proper disposition of the proceeds at Frieda's death?

(A) Coyt is entitled to receive the proceeds under the terms of the beneficiary designation.

(B) Coyt and Ava are entitled to receive the proceeds. The antilapse statute applies such that Ava is entitled to receive Gary's share.

(C) Coyt and Ava are entitled to receive the proceeds. The antilapse statute applies such that Ava is entitled to share one-half of the proceeds to which Coyt is entitled as she is one generation removed from Coyt.

(D) The proceeds will be paid to Freida's probate estate because the beneficiary designation is no longer applicable because it did not provide an alternative if one or more of her children were not living.

99. Refer to Question 98. If Frieda had a joint checking account with Coyt and Gary and the account provided for rights of survivorship, who would have been entitled to the account at Frieda's death?

(A) Coyt.

(B) Coyt and Ava.

(C) Frieda's probate estate.

(D) The bank.

100. Harriet and David divorced one another. Under the terms of their divorce agreement, Harriet received the home, a car, and various securities. David received a car, various other securities, and his company pension plan. His company pension plan was governed

by ERISA, and he had named Harriet as his designated beneficiary when they got married. David's job required him to travel extensively, and he was out of the country for several months after his divorce and did not file any change-of-beneficiary forms with his pension plan administrators as required by ERISA. After returning from one of his trips, he became violently ill and died very unexpectedly. His sole intestate heir was his seven-year-old daughter from a prior marriage, Candace.

Which of the following best describes the proper disposition of the benefits?

(A) Harriet is entitled to the pension plan. She was the designated beneficiary. Divorce has no effect on nonprobate transfers.

(B) Harriet is entitled to the pension plan. Even though the divorce revoked her designation under state law, as a federal law, ERISA's requirements that a change-of-beneficiary form be filed pre-empt state law.

(C) Candace is entitled to the pension plan. Harriet's designation was revoked by the divorce. Thus, the pension plan passes through probate to Candace as David's sole intestate heir.

(D) Candace is entitled to the pension plan. Even though Harriet was the designated beneficiary, a resulting trust will be imposed on Harriet in Candace's favor to prevent Harriet's unjust enrichment. Enriching Harriet with the proceeds would be unjust in light of the divorce decree.

101. Tae and Ron have a joint savings account at a local bank. Tae has contributed $1,000 to the account. Ron has contributed $500. There has been $100 in interest paid. The current balance in the account is $1,600. There have not been any withdrawals from the account. Which of the following is the best statement as to the ownership of the account during Tae's and Ron's life?

(A) Tae and Ron own the account jointly and equally. Thus, they each own $800 of the account.

(B) Tae and Ron own the account jointly in proportion to their net contributions and pro rata share of the interest. Thus, Tae owns $1,066.66 and Ron owns $533.33 of the account.

(C) Tae and Ron own the account jointly in proportion to their net contributions but equally with respect to the interest. Thus, Tae owns $1,050 and Ron owns $550.

(D) Tae owns the account and Ron owns $500.

102. Refer to Question 101. If Ron dies, what is Tae's ownership in the account?

ANSWER:

103. Refer to Question 101. Assume that Ron, Ron's wife, Lori, and Tae had been the parties to the account. Lori had made no contributions or withdrawals. Would the result differ from Question 102 if Ron died survived by Tae and Lori?

ANSWER:

104. Refer to Question 103. Assume that Ron and Lori were not married. Would the result differ if Ron died survived by Tae and Lori?

ANSWER:

105. Refer to Question 104. What would Lori own when Tae dies?

ANSWER:

106. Refer to Question 104. Assume RonÖs probate estate is insufficient to pay his estateÖs debts, taxes, and expenses of administration. Is this account subject to those claims?

ANSWER:

107. Lila opens a bank account and designates that it should pay on death to Penny. Lila has deposited $5,000 in it, and it has earned $200 in interest. The total balance is $5,200. What are Penny's rights to the account before and after Lila's death?

ANSWER:

108. Sal and Tad are brothers. They own a tract of investment real estate as joint tenants. Under Sal's will, his entire probate estate passed to his wife, Opal. Sal dies.

      Which of the following best describes the proper disposition of the land?

(A) Opal receives Sal's interest in the real estate. However, it is subject to the claims of Sal's creditors.

(B) Opal receives Sal's interest in the real estate free and clear of Sal's creditor's claims.

(C) Tad receives Sal's interest in the real estate. However, it is subject to the claims of Sal's creditors.

(D) Tad receives Sal's interest in the real estate free and clear of Sal's creditor's claims.

109. Darla has died. She was a widow. During her life, she owned the following assets. She owned a life estate in her family farm but she had conveyed the remainder to her sister, Carla. She and Carla owned a joint savings account, though Darla is the only one who has made any deposits to it. She also owned a savings account, which she designated to pay on her death to her son, Stephen. She was the sole owner of a securities account at a national brokerage firm. She was the sole owner of her home. She also owned her car, furnishings, and various other items of tangible personal property. She had a valid will leaving her entire estate to Stephen.

  If her brother, Richard, serves as executor of her estate, which assets will he have a duty to administer?

  (A) Darla's interest in the family farm; both savings accounts; the securities account; the home; and her car, furnishings, and various other items of tangible personal property.

  (B) Darla's interest in both savings accounts; the securities account; the home; and her car, furnishings, and various other items of tangible personal property.

  (C) Darla's interest in the securities account; the home; and her car, furnishings, and various other items of tangible personal property.

  (D) None of the assets listed.

110. Refer to Question 109. Assume the home had been owned as a joint tenancy with Carla. Also, assume that Darla had owned a life insurance policy on herself with Carla named as the beneficiary, and that Darla was the sole beneficiary of a "QTIP" trust set up by her deceased husband when he died. Under the terms of the QTIP trust, Stephen receives the trust estate at Darla's death.

  If her brother, Richard, serves as the executor of her estate, which additional assets will he have a duty to administer?

  (A) Darla's interest in the home; the QTIP trust; and the life insurance proceeds.

  (B) Darla's interest in the home and the QTIP trust.

  (C) The life insurance proceeds.

  (D) The home.

  (E) None.

111. Refer to Questions 109 and 110. Which of the assets not included in Darla's *probate* estate are included in her *gross* estate for federal tax purposes.

ANSWER:

112. Refer to Question 109. Assume Darla was an attorney. A former client brings a malpractice suit against Darla's estate thirteen months after her death. Is the claim barred?

   (A) Yes.

   (B) Yes, but only if notice of an impending nonclaim period was mailed to the former client.

   (C) Yes, if the former client was given constructive notice by publication of the impending nonclaim period. It is not necessary that the notice be mailed.

   (D) No.

113. Refer to Question 109. Richard has hired you to advise him with respect to the administration of Darla's estate.

   What do you advise him to do in order to bar as many creditors' claims as quickly as possible?

   (A) Publish notice for three successive weeks in a general circulation newspaper announcing that claims must be presented within 60 days. This limits the claim period for creditors' claims to 60 days rather than one year.

   (B) Mail notice to all known creditors informing them that claims must be presented within 60 days. This limits the claim period for creditors' claims to 60 days rather than one year.

   (C) Publish notice for three successive weeks in a general circulation newspaper announcing that claims must be presented within four months. However, on the date of the first notice by publication, also mail notice to all known creditors informing them that their claims must be presented within 60 days. All claims will be barred at four months rather than one year.

   (D) Publish notice for three successive weeks in a general circulation newspaper announcing that claims must be presented within four months. However, on the date of the first notice by publication, also mail notice to all known creditors informing them that their claims must be presented within 60 days. Those creditors receiving notice will be subject to the 60 day period, and all other creditors will be subject to the four month period. No creditor will be entitled to the one year period.

114. Refer to Question 109. Under what circumstances would Richard, as the executor, be entitled to recover any part of the multi-party account with Carla to pay Darla's creditors?

(A) The multi-party account is not subject to the claims of Darla's creditors.

(B) The multi-party account is not subject to the claims of Darla's creditors unless Darla's probate estate is insufficient to satisfy the creditor's claims and the creditor has made a written demand to Richard as executor.

(C) The multi-party account is not subject to the claims of Darla's creditors, unless the creditor has made a written demand to Richard as executor and Richard begins a proceeding to collect from the account within one year of Darla's death.

(D) The multi-party account is not subject to the claims of Darla's creditors, unless Darla's probate estate is insufficient to satisfy the creditor's claims, the creditor has made a written demand to Richard as executor, and Richard begins a proceeding to collect from the account within one year of Darla's death.

115. Refer to Question 109. How long after Darla's death may her will be probated?

ANSWER:

116. Refer to Question 109. Assume Darla had another son, Joe, who was not mentioned in her will. Assuming an informal probate has been instituted by Richard for Darla's estate, what is Joe's time limit to file a formal testacy petition to determine the validity of Darla's will?

ANSWER:

117. Refer to Question 109. Assuming Darla's will does not address the powers of the executor, if Richard is serving as the executor, which of the following powers is expressly granted to him under the Uniform Probate Code?

(A) The power to make extraordinary repairs; to borrow money; to hold securities in the name of a nominee; and the power to set his own reasonable compensation for serving as executor.

(B) The power to make extraordinary repairs; to borrow money; to hold securities in the name of a nominee; but not the power to set his own reasonable compensation for serving as executor.

(C) The power to borrow money; but not the power to make extraordinary repairs; to hold securities in the name of a nominee; to set his own reasonable compensation for serving as executor.

(D) None of the following: the power to make extraordinary repairs; to borrow money; to hold securities in the name of a nominee; the power to set his own reasonable compensation for serving as executor.

118.   Refer to Question 117. What duties limit the powers given to Richard as executor?

ANSWER:

119.   Refer to Question 117. If Richard serves as executor of Darla's estate, what will be his principal responsibilities?

ANSWER:

120. What are four common uses of trusts in estate planning?

ANSWER:

121. On June 2, Niles recorded an executed deed by which he conveyed a rental house he owned as an investment to his sister, Samantha, as trustee. In the deed, he and Samantha agreed that she would pay all of the net income each year to him for his life. They further agreed that when he died, Samantha would distribute the rental house free-of-trust to Samantha's daughter, Amy.

As of June 2, which of the following describes the legal relationships of the parties concerning real property?

(A) Samantha has fee simple title.

(B) A constructive trust in favor of Amy was duly created.

(C) A resulting trust in favor of Amy was duly created.

(D) An express trust enforceable in favor of Amy was duly created.

122. Bo, a widower, executed a written declaration of trust. Pursuant to the terms of the trust, Bo held all of his personal property in trust for himself so long as he would live, but after his death, the trust was to continue for the exclusive benefit of his daughter, Liane, with his friend, Harvey, serving as trustee. Bo has died intestate. His only other child, his daughter, June, has demanded that Liane and she share his personal property as his sole intestate heirs. Harvey and Liane insists that Bo's personal property was held in trust. Bo's primary personal property was $100,000 worth of publicly traded securities. When Bo died, the securities account was still in his individual name. In fact, title to the personal property was never transferred out of Bo's name.

Which of the following best describes the disposition of the personal property?

(A) Harvey holds the personal property in constructive trust for Liane.

(B) Harvey holds the personal property in constructive trust for both Liane and June.

(C) Since the property was never transferred from Bo's name, the property passes to Liane and June as his intestate heirs.

(D) Harvey holds the personal property in an express trust for Liane.

123. Refer to Question 122. Assume that Bo had not declared himself as trustee, but instead, Bo and Harvey executed a written trust agreement naming Harvey as the sole initial trustee. The other terms of the trust document are the same. Would the result differ?

ANSWER:

124. Dusan has died. His will disposes of his residuary estate as follows: "the residue of my estate shall be held in trust for the life of wife, Ivana, who shall be entitled to all of the income from the trust during her life, and upon Ivana's death, the remaining trust assets shall be distributed to my granddaughter, Kate." Although Dusan's intention to create the trust for his wife is clear, he did not name a trustee.

      What is the result?

      (A) Ivana takes the residue free-of-trust.

      (B) Ivana takes a life estate in the residue with Kate entitled to the remainder.

      (C) As the sole current beneficiary, Ivana is also the sole trustee since Dusan did not specify otherwise.

      (D) A valid trust was created, but the court will need to appoint a trustee.

125. Huan executed a deed conveying one of his real estate investments to his friend, Lim. He delivers the deed to Lim along with a letter stating, "Lim, enclosed please find the deed to the property at Duval and Main. Sell it and split the proceeds equally between Guan-yin and Mei lien." Lim is willing and able to follow Huan's instructions.

      Has a valid express trust been created?

      (A) Yes.

      (B) No, unless the deed expressly conveyed the property to Lim as trustee.

      (C) No, unless Lim executes a written instrument specifying the terms and acknowledging that he is trustee.

      (D) No, because neither term "trust" nor "trustee" nor any similar term was used.

126. Carl and Marge were married. When Carl died, he left his estate in a testamentary trust for Marge for life, remainder to their son, Doug, if he is living, otherwise, to Doug's then living descendants. Marge is a wealthy woman independently of what her husband left her in trust. Under her will, Doug will inherit the entire estate. As part of his own estate plan, Doug executes and delivers a deed conveying Doug's remainder interest in the trust established by his father along with whatever property he ultimately receives from his mother's estate. The grantee of the deed is his friend, Earl, as trustee for the benefit of Doug's children.

Which of the following best describes the effect of Doug's conveyance?

(A) Doug has created a trust funded with his contingent remainder interest in the trust created by his father and the right to whatever property, if any, he becomes entitled to receive from his mother's estate.

(B) Doug has created a trust funded with his contingent remainder interest in the trust created by his father.

(C) Doug has created a trust funded by his right to whatever property, if any, he becomes entitled to receive from his mother's estate.

(D) Doug has failed to create a trust.

127. Wallace is not married and has no children. However, he hopes someday to be married and have children. He conveys his family farm to his friend, Nancy, to hold as trustee. Under the terms of a written trust instrument, he instructs that the farm is to be held for the benefit of his first-born child until the child becomes an adult, at which time it is to be delivered to the child.

Which of the following is the best statement?

(A) Wallace has failed to create a valid trust. Since he has no children, there is no trust because there are no beneficiaries. If he dies with children however, a court would impose a constructive trust on Nancy with respect to the farm. If he dies without children, Nancy holds the farm, free of trust.

(B) Wallace has created a valid trust even though he does not currently have any children. However, if he dies without any children, Nancy will hold the family farm, free of trust.

(C) Wallace has failed to create a valid trust. Since he has no children, there is no trust because there are no beneficiaries. If he dies with children however, a court would impose a constructive trust on Nancy with respect to the family farm. If he dies without children, Nancy will hold the family farm for Wallace's heirs and/or devisees.

(D) Wallace has created a valid a trust even though he does not currently have any children. However, if he dies without any children, Nancy will hold the family farm in trust for Wallace's heirs and/or devisees.

128. Armen owned an 800-acre corn farm. Armen was in his eighties and unable to tend to the farm as he once could. On August 1, he executed and recorded a deed conveying his farm to Idra. Idra has recently moved onto the farm next to Armen. On September 3, Armen told his grandson, Ohan, that when he conveyed the farm to Idra, Idra and he had orally agreed that Idra would manage the farm until Armen died, paying him all the net income each year. He said they had agreed that when he died, Idra would convey the farm to Ohan. Armen had one child, Elma, who is Ohan's mother. Armen died intestate on October 11. Idra denies that Armen and she had any agreement concerning what she was to do with the property.

Assuming Elma is Armen's only intestate heir, which answer best describes the most likely disposition of the farm now that Armen has died?

(A)   Idra retains the farm since the oral express trust is invalid.

(B)   Ohan can have the court enforce the terms of the oral express trust.

(C)   Elma will have the court impose a resulting trust on Idra in favor of Elma since her father's attempt to create an express trust failed.

(D)   Ohan will have the court impose a constructive trust on Idra in favor of Ohan because Idra breached the oral agreement.

129.   Refer to Question 128. Assume Idra admits that Armen and she had the oral agreement, but she is relying on her lawyer's advice that she is not bound by the agreement.

Which answer best describes the most likely disposition of the farm?

(A)   Ohan can have the court enforce the terms of the oral express trust.

(B)   Elma will have the court impose a resulting trust on Idra in favor of Elma since Armen's attempt to create an express trust failed.

(C)   Idra retains the farm since the oral express trust is unenforceable.

(D)   Ohan will have the court impose a constructive trust on Idra in favor of Ohan because Idra breached the oral agreement.

130.   Refer to Question 129, but assume that Idra was Armen's pastor.

Which answer best describes the most likely disposition the farm?

(A)   Elma will have the court impose a constructive trust on Idra in favor of Elma.

(B)   Idra retains the farm since the oral express trust is unenforceable.

(C)   Ohan will have the court impose a constructive trust on Idra in favor of Ohan.

(D)   Ohan will ask the court to enforce the terms of the oral express trust.

131.   Refer to Question 128, but assume that June and Hector were sitting in a café with Ohan and Idra as they discussed the transfer. Also assume that the property involved was not real property but rather a boat. Of course, the boat generated no income, but there were no expenses either.

Which answer best describes the most likely disposition of the boat upon Armen's death?

(A)   Ohan will have the court enforce the terms of the oral express trust.

(B)   Ohan will have the court impose a constructive trust on Idra in favor of Ohan because Idra breached the oral agreement.

(C)   Elma will have the court impose a resulting trust on Idra in favor of Elma because Armen's attempt to create an express trust failed.

(D)   Idra retains the boat since the oral express trust is unenforceable.

132.   Refer to Question 128, but assume that June and Hector were sitting in a café with Ohan and Idra as they discussed the transfer.

If the deed conveyed the farm to "Idra, as trustee," which answer best describes the most likely disposition of the farm?

(A)   Ohan will have the court enforce the terms of the oral express trust.

(B)   Ohan will have the court impose a constructive trust on Idra in favor of Ohan because Idra breached the oral agreement.

(C)   Idra will retain the farm since the oral express trust is unenforceable.

(D)   Elma will have the court impose a resulting trust on Idra in favor of Elma because Armen's attempt to create an express trust failed.

133.   Refer to Question 128, but assume there is no evidence of the terms of any discussion between Armen and Idra but that the deed conveyed the farm to "Idra, as trustee for Ohan."

Which answer best describes the most likely disposition of the farm?

(A)   Fee simple title is vested in Elma.

(B)   Idra owns the legal interests, and Ohan owns the equitable interests.

(C)   Fee simple title is vested in Ohan.

(D)   Idra owns the legal title, and Elma owns the equitable interests.

134.   Refer to Question 128, but assume that there was a writing signed by Armen and Idra setting out the trust terms. However, a creditor of Idra has a judgment against her and is seeking to satisfy the judgment by attaching the farm.

Which answer best describes the legal advice that should be given to Idra?

(A)   You can convey the farm to Ohan pursuant to your agreement with Armen notwithstanding the judgment against you.

(B)   You can convey the farm to Ohan pursuant to the agreement with Armen, but the creditor will have it set aside as a transfer in fraud of creditors.

(C)   You can allow the creditor to attach the farm notwithstanding your agreement with Armen.

(D)   The creditor can attach the farm regardless of what you decide to do.

135.   On February 14, Steven and his brother, Victor, entered into a written trust agreement signed by each of them. Following the execution of the trust agreement, Steven conveyed an apartment complex to Victor by a duly recorded deed. Under the terms of the trust

agreement, Victor is to manage the complex until Steven's death, and at that time, Victor is to convey the complex to Steven's only grandchild, Tabitha. Tabitha was the daughter of Steven's only child, Harvey. However, on February 13, Tabitha had died with a will leaving all of her property to her husband, Andy, though neither Steven nor Victor knew it. Tabitha was survived by Andy and their one child, Danny. On November 23, Steven died intestate, survived by his only child, Harvey, who was his only intestate heir.

Which answer best describes the most likely disposition of the properties by reason of Steven's death?

(A)   Andy will ask the court to enforce the terms of an express trust as Tabitha's successor in interest.

(B)   Danny will ask the court to impose a constructive trust on Victor in favor of Danny.

(C)   Harvey will ask the court to impose a constructive trust on Victor in favor of Harvey.

(D)   Harvey will ask the court to impose a resulting trust on Victor in favor of Harvey.

136.   Bao died recently, survived by his son, Chan, and his granddaughter, Jin, who is the child of Bao's daughter, Chow, who predeceased Bao. Bao's will has been admitted to probate. It devised his vacation home to Chan "with the request that Chan deliver the home to Jin if Jin graduates from college"; the rest, residue, and remainder of Bao's estate is devised to Rockingham Academy for Gifted Children. Jin was eighteen at the time of Bao's death and had not yet graduated from high school.

Which answer best explains the likely disposition of the shares of stock upon Bao's death?

(A)   Chan owns the vacation home.

(B)   Jin will have the court impose a constructive trust on Chan in favor of Jin to avoid unjust enrichment.

(C)   The charity will have the court impose a resulting trust on Chan in favor of Jin since Bao's attempt to create a private express trust failed.

(D)   Chan is the trustee of an express trust for the benefit of Jin.

137.   Refer to Question 136, but assume that Bao's will devises the vacation home to "Chan to be delivered to Jin when Jin graduates from college."

Which answer best explains the likely disposition of the shares of stock upon Bao's death?

(A)   Chan is the trustee of an express trust for the benefit of Jin.

(B)   Jin will have the court impose a constructive trust on Chan in favor of Jin to avoid unjust enrichment.

(C)   The charity will have the court impose a resulting trust on Chan in favor of Jin since Bao's attempt to create a private express trust failed.

(D)   Chan owns the vacation home.

138.   Refer to Question 137, but assume Jin died after the will was executed by Bao but before Bao died. Jin had enrolled in college.

Which answer best explains the likely disposition of the vacation home upon Bao's death.

(A)   Rockingham Academy for Gifted Children owns the vacation home.

(B)   Chan is the trustee of an express trust for the benefit of Jin's heirs.

(C)   Rockingham Academy for Gifted Children will have the court impose a resulting trust on Chan in favor of it since Bao's attempt to create an express trust failed.

(D)   Chan owns the vacation home.

139.   Karmil died intestate recently. Karmil was survived by his daughter, Dana, and grandson, Jiri, who is Dana's son. Prior to Karmil's death, Karmil told Ayce and Nona that he was holding the family farm as trustee for the benefit of Jiri, and when Jiri reached age 21, Karmil was going to convey legal title to Jiri. Record legal title then and now is in Karmil's name. There is no written evidence of Karmil's stated intent. When Karmil died, Jiri was only age 13. Dana now claims the family farm as Karmil's sole intestate heir. Assuming the statute of frauds does not require a trust of real property to be in writing and that Dana is Karmil's sole intestate heir, what is the most likely disposition of the family farm upon Karmil's death?

ANSWER:

140.   Refer to Question 139, but assume that the property was a valuable painting.

Which answer best explains the most likely disposition of the painting?

(A)   The court should appoint a successor trustee of the express trust to hold the painting until Jiri attains age 21.

(B)   The trust is unenforceable; the painting passes to Dana.

(C)   Jiri will have the court impose a constructive trust on Dana to avoid unjust enrichment by Dana.

(D)   The personal representative of Karmil's estate should retain the painting until Jiri attains age 21 and then deliver it to Jiri.

141.   Refer to Question 139, but assume a signed letter from Karmil to Ayce has been discovered. The letter explains Kirmil's intentions regarding the farm.

Which answer best describes the most likely disposition of the family farm upon Karmil's death?

(A)   Jiri will have the court impose a constructive trust on Dana to avoid unjust enrichment by Dana.

(B)   The trust is unenforceable; the family farm passes to Dana.

(C)   The court should appoint a successor trustee of the express trust to manage the family farm until Jiri attains age 21.

(D)   The personal representative of Karmil's estate should retain the family farm until Jiri attains age 21 and then deliver the family farm to Jiri.

142.   Refer to Question 141, but assume that, shortly prior to Karmil's death, Karmil had conveyed the family farm as a gift to his cardiologist, Phan. Phan was unaware of the trust.

Which answer best describes the legal advice you would give to Jiri?

(A)   That's life; there's nothing you can do.

(B)   You should file suit against Karmil's estate for breach of fiduciary duty.

(C)   You should have the court impose a constructive trust on Phan because Karmil breached a fiduciary duty.

(D)   You should file suit against Phan for conspiring with Karmil to breach a fiduciary duty.

143.   Andrew died last week. On May 13, 2003, he typed and signed a letter to his cousin, Keith. In the letter, Andrew said the family farm was henceforth to be held in an irrevocable trust; he declared that he was serving as the trustee of the family farm; and that he would continue to manage the farm as long as he could, paying himself all the income from the farm each year. However, the letter explained that, if he were ever unable or unwilling to continue as trustee, Keith would serve as trustee until Andrew died and was to pay Andrew any income the farm produced. At Andrew's death, the terms of the letter direct Keith, as trustee, to convey the family farm to himself, personally. Also on May 13, 2003, Andrew executed his will, which has now been admitted to probate. Under the terms of the will, Andrew's estate is devised to his only grandchild, his grandson, Derrick. Derrick, it happens, was the only child of Andrew's only child, Billy. Despite the letter, record title to the farm remained in Andrew's name, personally. Both Billy and Derrick survived Andrew.

Which answer best describes the most likely disposition of the family farm after Andrew's death?

(A)   The family farm passes to Derrick under Andrew's will because the letter was not duly witnessed.

(B)   The family farm passes to Billy as Andrew's intestate heir, since the letter was not duly witnessed.

(C)   At Andrew's death, the family farm passed to Keith as a non-probate asset.

(D)   Keith, as trustee, can convey legal title to himself, individually.

144.   Refer to Question 143, but assume that the terms of the letter provide that the trust
was revocable by Andrew at any time prior to Andrew's death. There is no evidence
that Andrew ever intended to revoke the trust.

Which answer best describes the most likely disposition of the family farm after
Andrew's death?

(A)   The family farm passes to Derrick under Andrew's will because the letter was not
duly witnessed.

(B)   The family farm passes to Billy as Andrew's intestate heir, since the letter was not
duly witnessed.

(C)   At Andrew's death, the family farm passed to Keith as a non-probate asset.

(D)   Keith, as trustee, can convey legal title to himself, individually.

145.   Refer to Question 143, but assume Keith died shortly before Andrew with a valid will
that has been admitted to probate and devises all of Keith's property to Keith's parents,
Ivan and Wanda. Before Keith died, he had been managing the family farm for Andrew
for several months due to Andrew's poor health. Keith did not have any descendants
who survived him.

Which answer best explains the most likely disposition of the family farm after Andrew's
death?

(A)   The family farm passes under Andrew's will to Derrick.

(B)   The family farm passes to Bill as Andrew's sole heir under the intestacy statute.

(C)   The family farm passes to Ivan and Wanda under Keith's will.

(D)   The family farm passes to Ivan and Wanda under the terms of the trust.

146.   Three years ago, Doug executed a written trust declaration, which declared that he was
the trustee of the "DK Living Trust." Under the terms of the DK Living Trust, Doug
could use the income and principal of the trust for his own maintenance and support
during his lifetime. At his death, the trust terms provided that any real property remaining
in the trust was to go to Doug's granddaughter, Angelica, and any personal property
remaining in the trust was to go to his other granddaughter, Janessa. The DK Living
Trust declaration also reserved to Doug the right to revoke the trust, though he never
considered doing so. The trust also provided that if Doug was ever unable or unwilling
to act, Westtown Savings and Trust was named as the successor trustee. When Doug
executed the document, he attached a ten-dollar bill to it. However, no other assets were
ever transferred to the trust during Doug's lifetime. A week after executing the
declaration, Doug executed a will devising his entire estate to Westtown Savings and
Trust as trustee under the DK Living Trust declaration. Doug has died. He was survived
by two children, Bobby and Carlie, and two grandchildren, Angelica and Janessa. The

significant assets of Doug's estate at the time of his death were his home (fair market value, $250,000) and stock in General Motors (fair market value $75,000). Neither the will nor the trust document addresses the payment of Doug's debts following his death, but there were unsecured debts of $185,000 at the time of his death.

What is the most likely disposition of the home and the stocks after Doug's death?

ANSWER:

147. Refer to Question 146, but assume that Doug was married to Ramona at the time he executed the DK Living Trust declaration and his will and also at the time of his death. Also, assume that prior to Doug's death, he transferred to himself, as trustee of the DK Living Trust, $100,000 cash still held in trust at his death.

Which answer best describes the legal advice you should give to Ramona after she explains to you that she has been apparently disinherited by Doug?

(A) The trust agreement and will are void.

(B) You are entitled to your marital share of the $100,000, the home, and the stocks.

(C) You are entitled to your marital share of the home and the stocks.

(D) You are entitled to your marital share of the home.

148. In 2004, Haskell, an aging and wealthy single man, created a trust by executing an irrevocable trust agreement with his aunt, Candace. The assets of the trust consist of real and personal property; title is in Candace's name, as trustee. The beneficiaries are Candace's adult children, Aiken and Jenna. Aiken is entitled to all of the income for the rest of Aiken's lifetime; at Aiken's death, Candace is to deliver the trust estate to Jenna. After creating the trust, Haskell became very ill and could not work. During his illness, he fell significantly behind on the payment of many of his debts. Consequently, one of Haskell's creditors has recently obtained a judgment against Haskell and is trying to attach the assets of the trust.

Which answer best describes the legal advice you would give to Candace?

(A) The trust estate is not reachable by Haskell's creditors unless they are tort creditors.

(B) The trust estate is not reachable by Haskell's creditors.

(C) The trust estate may be reached by Haskell's creditors.

(D) The trust estate is reachable by Haskell's creditors.

149. Refer to Question 148, but assume that the trust agreement by its own terms was revocable by Haskell.

Assuming that Haskell has never evidenced any intention to revoke the trust, which answer best describes the legal advice you would give to Candace?

(A) The trust estate is not reachable by Haskell's creditors.

(B) The trust estate is not reachable by Haskell's creditors unless they are tort creditors.

(C) The trust estate is reachable by Haskell's creditors.

(D) The trust estate may be reached by Haskell's creditors.

150. Refer to Question 149, and also assume that Haskell had just died and that the judgment was obtained by Haskell's creditor against Haskell's personal representative.

Which answer best describes the legal advice you would give to Candace?

(A) The trust estate is not reachable by Haskell's creditors.

(B) The trust estate is reachable by Haskell's creditors.

(C) The trust estate is not reachable by Haskell's creditors unless they are tort creditors.

(D) The trust estate may be reached by Haskell's creditors.

151. Refer to Question 148, but assume that the trust agreement was pursuant to an oral understanding between Haskell and Candace.

Which answer best describes the legal advice you would give to Candace under the circumstances?

(A) The trust estate may be reached by Haskell's creditors.

(B) The trust estate is not reachable by Haskell's creditors.

(C) The trust estate is reachable by Haskell's creditors.

(D) The trust estate is not reachable by Haskell's creditors unless they are tort creditors.

152. Refer to Question 148, but assume that the creditor was a creditor of Candace, not Haskell, and has obtained a judgment against Candace arising out of a situation totally unrelated to the trust property.

Which answer best describes the legal advice that you would give to Candace in view of these circumstances?

(A) The trust estate is not reachable by your creditors unless they are tort creditors.

(B) The trust estate may be reachable depending upon the facts and circumstances.

(C) The trust estate is reachable to satisfy your creditors.

(D) The trust estate is not reachable by your creditors.

153. Refer to Question 152, but assume that the trust agreement was pursuant to an oral agreement between Haskell and Candace, and Candace wishes to protect the interests of Aiken and Jenna.

What legal advice would you give to Candace?

ANSWER:

154. Refer to Question 150, but assume that the creditor is a creditor of Aiken, not Haskell. The creditor is a former business associate of Aiken and has obtained a judgment against Aiken related to a business transaction.

Which answer best describes the legal advice you would give to Candace under the circumstances?

(A) The trust estate can be attached to satisfy the debt.

(B) Trust income can be attached to satisfy the debt.

(C) Trust income can be attached if the creditor is a tort creditor.

(D) The trust estate cannot be attached to satisfy the debt.

155. Refer to Question 154, but assume that the trust agreement only authorizes Candace to distribute to Aiken as much income as Candace, in her discretion, determines is appropriate.

Which answer best describes the legal advice you would give to Candace under the circumstances?

(A) The trust estate can be attached to satisfy the debt.

(B) Trust income can be attached to satisfy the debt.

(C) Trust income can be attached if the creditor is a tort creditor.

(D) The trust estate cannot be attached to satisfy the debt.

156. Refer to Question 154, but assume that Candace, according to the terms of the trust agreement, can only distribute to Aiken such amounts of income as are necessary for Aiken's health, education, maintenance, or support.

Which answer best describes the legal advice you would give to Candace under the circumstances?

(A) The trust estate can be attached to satisfy the debt.

(B) Trust income can be attached to satisfy the debt.

(C) Trust income can be attached if the creditor is a tort creditor.

(D) The trust estate cannot be attached to satisfy the debt.

157. Refer to Question 156, but assume the creditor is a hospital that provided medical services to Aiken.

Which answer best describes the legal advice you would give to Candace under the circumstances?

(A) The trust estate cannot be attached to satisfy the debt.

(B) The trust estate can be attached to satisfy the debt.

(C) Trust income estate can be attached to satisfy the debt.

(D) Trust income can be attached only if the creditor has exhausted Aiken's individual assets.

158. Refer to Question 150, but assume that the creditor is a creditor of Jenna, not Haskell, and has a judgment against Jenna.

Which answer best describes the legal advice that should be given to Candace under the circumstances?

(A) The trust estate can be attached to satisfy Jenna's debt.

(B) Jenna's interest in the trust estate can be attached to satisfy Jenna's debt.

(C) The trust estate must be sold in order to pay the debt.

(D) The trust estate cannot be attached.

159. Refer to Questions 154 and 158. How would your answers differ if the trust agreement included a provision stating that the beneficiaries' interests in the trust could not be attached in order to satisfy any debt of a beneficiary?

ANSWER:

160. Refer to Question 158, but assume that the only provision in the trust agreement relating to creditors of beneficiaries is one that provides that if a creditor of Aiken ever attempts to attach Aiken's interest, the interest terminates and passes to Jenna and that if a creditor of Jenna ever attempts to attach the interest of Jenna, the interest terminates and passes to a charity.

Which answer best describes the legal advice you would give Candace under those circumstances?

(A) The provision is valid; terminate the trust by delivering the property to the charity.

(B) The provision is valid; terminate the trust by delivering the property to Aiken.

(C) The provision is valid; Jenna's interest has passed to the charity.

(D) The provision is not valid; the creditor can attach Jenna's interest in the trust.

161. What is a spendthrift provision, and how does it affect a beneficiary's right to transfer his or her beneficial interest?

ANSWER:

162.   How does conditioning a beneficiary's interests on his or her survival or limiting it to
        his or her lifetime affect the beneficiary's right to transfer the interest?

ANSWER:

163. Consider the differences in the following two deeds. First, Kyla conveys property in trust for Damian for life and then to Alondra. Second, Kyla conveys property in trust for Damian for life and then to Alondra, if Alondra survives Damian.

With respect to the transferability of Alondra's interest, and assuming Alondra predeceased Damian, what difference is there between the first and second deeds?

ANSWER:

164. Penny's parents died when Penny was very young. She was raised by her aunt, Cindi, who was her mother's sister. Cindi had another sister, Donna, who had two children, Alice and Sam. Cindi also raised Alice and Sam, as Donna was periodically homeless due to a drug addiction. Penny married a very wealthy man, Joe. In recognition of Penny's fondness for her aunt and cousins, Joe created a trust with Penny as trustee three years ago. Under the terms of the trust, Penny pays all the income to Cindi. At Cindi's death, Penny is directed to distribute the remaining trust estate to Alice and Sam. Two years ago, Alice died. Alice's will devised all of her property to her husband, Ted. Cindi died yesterday.

Who is entitled to the trust estate?

(A) Sam.

(B) Ted and Sam.

(C) Ted and Joe.

(D) Sam and Joe.

165. Refer to Question 164, but assume that Alice was also survived by a six year old son, Michael. Which answer best describes who will succeed to the trust estate upon Cindi's death?

(A) Sam.

(B) Sam and Joe.

(C) Ted and Sam.

(D) Michael and Sam.

166. Refer to Question 164, but assume that the terms of the trust directed Penny to deliver the remaining trust estate to "Donna's children" at Cindi's death and that Donna had

another child, Nancy, one year prior to Cindi's death. Since Cindi has died, who is entitled to the trust estate?

ANSWER:

167.   Refer to Question 166. Would the result differ if Donna was pregnant at the time of Cindi's death?

(A)   No.

(B)   The "child in embryo" succeeds to a remainder interest.

(C)   If born alive, the "child in embryo" succeeds to a remainder interest.

(D)   Joe will decide whether "the child in embryo" receives an interest in the trust estate.

168.   Refer to Question 164, but assume that the trust agreement directed Penny to distribute the trust estate at Cindi's death equally to each of Alice and Sam, who survive Cindi, or all to the survivor of them who survived Cindi.

Which answer best describes who succeeds to the trust estate upon Cindi's death?

(A)   Sam and Nancy.

(B)   Sam.

(C)   Ted and Sam.

(D)   Joe and Sam.

169.   Refer to Question 167, but assume that the trust terms require Penny to deliver the trust estate to Donna's children *who survive* their aunt Cindi's death.

Which answer best describes who succeeds to the trust estate when Cindi dies?

(A)   Sam and Nancy.

(B)   Ted, Sam, and Nancy.

(C)   Sam, Nancy, and the "child in embryo."

(D)   Sam, Nancy, and, if born alive, the "child in embryo."

170.   Refer to Question 167. Would the result differ if Penny learned that Donna intended to have at least one other child in addition to the "child in embryo?"

(A)   No.

(B)   No, unless Donna did in fact have an additional child; in that case, that child would partially divest all of the other children who had already received the trust estate.

(C)   No, unless Donna did in fact have an additional child; in that case, that child would partially divest only the "child in embryo."

(D)   No, unless Donna did in fact have an additional child; in that case, that child would partially divest all of the other children who had already received the trust estate, assuming that child was born before the statute of limitations had run.

171.   In 1962, Luis and Miranda were married. In 1963, their one and only child, Olivia, was born. In 1984, Olivia's only child, Savannah, was born. Luis died in 2001. Under his 1999 will, he devised the family farm to his wife, Miranda, if she was living, but otherwise to Olivia for life, remainder to Savannah. The residue of his estate was also devised to his wife, Miranda, but only if she was living, otherwise, it was devised to his alma mater, Barclay University. Miranda died in 2000. Savannah died in 2003, survived by her husband, Diego, her children, Andrea and Julian, and her mother, Olivia. Savannah's 2000 will devised all of her property to her husband, Diego.

Which answer best describes who succeeds to the future interest in the family farm that Savannah owned at her death?

(A)   Barclay University.

(B)   Olivia.

(C)   Diego.

(D)   Andrea and Julian.

172.   Refer to Question 171. How would the result differ if the family farm had been devised by Luis to Olivia for life, remainder to Savannah "if Savannah survives Olivia?"

(A)   My answer would not change.

(B)   Olivia.

(C)   Barclay University.

(D)   Andrea and Julian.

173.   Refer to Question 171. How would the result differ if Savannah had predeceased Luis?
ANSWER:

174.   Refer to Question 171. How would the result differ if the family farm had been devised to Sofia in trust with directions for Sofia to pay the income from the farm to Olivia for life and at Olivia's death to distribute the farm to Savannah?

(A)   The result would not change.

(B)   Olivia would receive the farm.

(C)   Barclay University would receive the farm.

(D)   Andrea and Julian would receive the farm.

175.   Caleb married his high school sweet heart, Adrianna. They had one daughter, Sofia, and one grandchild, Martin, when Adrianna passed away at age 83 ten years ago. Caleb died five years ago, survived by both Sofia and Martin. Under his will, he devised his home to Sofia, for life, remainder to Martin if Martin attains age 21. The rest of his estate passed to St. Jerome's Church. At the time of Caleb's death, Martin was only 14. Sofia has just died, and Martin is now 19.

Which answer best describes the disposition of Caleb's home upon Sofia's death?

(A)   Sofia's heirs and devisees succeed to fee simple title.

(B)   Sofia's heirs and devisees are entitled to possession until Martin attains age 21, *if he attains age 21.*

(C)   St. Jerome's Church succeeds to fee simple title.

(D)   St. Jerome's Church is entitled to possession until Martin reaches age 21, *if he attains age 21.*

176.   Ana was a family practice physician in a small community, Smokey Valley. She was a widow with only one child, her daughter, Natalia. Natalia had only one child, her daughter, Lily. Ana's will provided that the mountain vacation home was to go to Natalia for life, remainder to Lily, but if Lily is not survived by children, to Ana's alma mater, Bergman College. Ana devised the residue of her estate to the hospital where she had spent most of her career, the Smokey Valley Memorial Hospital. Ana has died, survived by both Natalia and Lily. After Ana's will was probated, Lily died. She was survived her husband, Jordan, and her son, Victor. Natalia, too, is still living. Under Lily's will, she devised her estate to Jordan. Her will has now been admitted to probate in the same court in which Ana's will was admitted to probate.

Which answer best describes the effect of Lily's death on the ownership of the vacation home?

(A)   Bergman College acquired the remainder interest.

(B)   Smokey Valley Memorial Hospital acquired the remainder interest.

(C)   Lily's interest passed to Jordan.

(D)   Lily's interest passed to Victor.

177.   Refer to Question 176. How would the result differ if Lily and Victor died in an automobile accident, and there is no evidence as to who survived whom?

(A)   The result would not change.

(B)   Bergman College acquired the remainder interest.

(C)   Smokey Valley Memorial Hospital acquired the remainder interest.

(D)   Lily's interest passed to Victor.

178.   Maya died in 2000. Maya's will devised her beach home to her daughter, Jade, for life, then to Jade's children, but if Jade is not survived by children, to Flint Hills Community College. The rest, residue, and remainder of Maya's estate was devised to Rolling Plains Memorial Hospital. Maya was survived by her daughter, Jade, and Jade's children, Mario and Eduardo. After Maya's death, Jade had another child, Gabriel, but Jade's son, Eduardo, died. Eduardo was survived by his wife, Olivia, and their son, Jonas. Eduardo's will devised his entire estate to Olivia, if she was living, otherwise to Jonas.

Which answer best describes the effect of Eduardo's death on the beach home?

(A)   Mario and Gabriel own the remainder interest.

(B)   Mario owns the remainder interest.

(C)   Eduardo's interest passed to Olivia.

(D)   Eduardo's interest passed to Olivia subject to divestment if none of Jade's children survive her.

179.   Refer to Question 178. How would the result differ if Maya's will devised the beach home to Jade for life, then to such of Jade's children who survive her, but if none survive her, to Easterwood College?

(A)   The result would not change.

(B)   Mario and Gabriel own the remainder interest.

(C)   Mario owns the remainder interest.

(D)   Eduardo's interest passed to Jonas.

180.   Axel died on Monday. His wife, Ruth, died several years ago. Axel was survived by his only child, Sadie, and her two children, 3-year-old Naomi and 2-year-old Aaron. Although she was hoping to have more children, Sadie was not pregnant when her father died. Axel's will devised his cattle ranch to his grandchildren, and the rest, residue, and remainder of his estate to the Boyarin Academy.

Who acquired ownership of the ranch when Axel died?

ANSWER:

181.   Refer to Question 180, but assume Sadie did not have any children at the time of Axel's death but was pregnant.

Which answer best explains the ownership of the ranch upon Axel's death?

(A)   The child in embryo owns fee simple title.

(B)   Boyarin Academy acquires fee simple title subject to divestment upon the birth of Sadie's first child, who will acquire fee simple title.

(C)   Boyarin Academy acquires fee simple title subject to divestment upon the birth of Sadie's first child, who will acquire fee simple title subject to partial divestment if Sadie has any more children.

(D)   Boyarin Academy owns fee simple title.

182.   Refer to Question 181, but assume that Sadie did not have any children and was not pregnant at the time of Axel's death.

Who acquired ownership of the ranch upon Axel's death?

ANSWER:

183.   State the common law rule against perpetuities.

ANSWER:

184.   What are the two basic purposes of the rule against perpetuities?
ANSWER:

185.   Explain both the "wait and see" approach to reforming the rule against perpetuities and the "reformation" approach.
ANSWER:

186.   Refer to Question 185. Explain the Uniform Probate Code's approach.
ANSWER:

187.   Natalie was a beloved classics professor at her alma mater, Hancock College. She died on Monday at the age of 72. The primary assets of her estate are the idyllic family farm located next to Hancock College and a $3,000,000 stock portfolio. Under Natalie's 1993 will, she devised the family farm to her grandchildren who are alive 100 years after her death and the rest, residue, and remainder of her estate to Hancock College. Natalie's only child, Evan, died in 2000. He had two children living at his death: Maria and Brian. Who owns the family farm as a result of Natalie's death?

   (A)   Hancock College owns fee simple title.

   (B)   Hancock College owns fee simple title subject to divestment if Maria and Brian are both alive on the one-hundredth anniversary of Natalie's death.

   (C)   Hancock College owns fee simple title subject to divestment if either Maria or Brian is alive on the one-hundredth anniversary of Natalie's death.

71

(D)   Hancock College owns fee simple title subject to divestment if any descendant of Evan is alive on the one-hundredth anniversary of Natalie's death.

188.   Aiden's wife, Martha, inherited a very large and valuable farm from her father, Ezra. Martha died in 2002. Under her will, she devised the farm to her husband, Aiden. Aiden died this past week survived by his only child, Oscar, and Oscar's two children, Angelina and Trevor, ages 18 and 19, respectively. Aiden's will devised Martha's family farm to his first grandchild who reaches age 25 and the rest, residue, and remainder of his estate to the John Brown Academy.

Who owns the family farm as a result of Aiden's death?

ANSWER:

189.   Refer to Question 188, but assume Angelina and Trevor were ages 24 and 26, respectively, at the time of Aiden's death.

Which answer best explains the ownership of the farm?

(A)   John Brown Academy owns fee simple title.

(B)   Trevor owns fee simple title.

(C)   Trevor owns fee simple title subject to partial divestment if Angelina reaches age 25.

(D)   Angelina owns fee simple title subject to partial divestment if any other children reach age 25.

190.   Refer to Question 188, but assume that Aiden's will devised the farm to his "grandchildren who reach age 21."

Which answer best explains the ownership of the family farm?

(A)   John Brown Academy owns fee simple title.

(B)   John Brown Academy owns fee simple title subject to divestment if Angelina or Trevor reaches age 21.

(C)   John Brown Academy owns fee simple title subject to divestment if any child of Oscar's reaches age 21.

(D)   Oscar owns fee simple title.

191.   Refer to Question 188, but assume that Aiden's will devised the farm to his "grandchildren who reach age 25" and that Oscar had predeceased Aiden by one day. Oscar's wife, Madeline, was pregnant at the time of the deaths of both Aiden and Oscar. Which answer best describes the ownership of the family upon Aiden's death?

(A)   John Brown Academy owns fee simple title.

(B)   John Brown Academy owns fee simple title subject to divestment if Angelina or Trevor reaches age 25.

(C)   John Brown Academy owns fee simple title subject to divestment if Angelina, Trevor, or the child in embryo reaches age 25.

(D)   John Brown Academy owns fee simple title subject to divestment only if all of Oscar's children, including the child in embryo, reach age 25.

192.   Kaden was a retired realtor. His wife, Camila, had passed away a few years ago, and Kaden spent much of his time thinking about real estate, his family, and what he should do with his home when he died. One day, he made a decision. Using a deed form from his desk drawer, he prepared a deed that conveyed his home to his first grandchild who reaches age 21. After preparing the deed, he duly executed and recorded it in the county records. On his drive back to home from the court house, while thinking about how to change his will, he was killed in a car accident. He was survived by one child, Avery, and two grandchildren, Claire and Omar, ages 8 and 9, respectively. His will, which was a decade old, devises all of his property to the Rockingham Valley State Hospital, if his wife was not living at the time of his death, which, of course, she was not.

Who acquired ownership of the home due to Kaden's conveyance and death?

ANSWER:

193.   Alan was the first and long time president of a small community college, Mays County Community College. At his death, Alan owned a very valuable beach home, which his family had enjoyed for decades, and a much more valuable stock portfolio. Alan's wife died many years ago, as did one of his children, Harold. Harold died without leaving any descendants. Alan's sole surviving child was Nolan, age 85, and one grandchild, Dalia, age 65. Alan's will devises the beach home to his children for their lifetimes with a remainder to his grandchildren. The rest, residue, and remainder of his estate passes to May County Community College.

Which best describes ownership of the beach home upon Alan's death?

(A)   Nolan has a life estate, and Dalia owns the remainder interest.

(B)   Nolan has a life estate, and Dalia and any other children Nolan might have in the future own the remainder interest.

(C)   May County Community College owns fee simple title.

(D)   Nolan has a life estate, and May County Community College owns the remainder interest.

194.   Refer to Question 193, but assume that, several years before Alan's death, he conveyed his beach home to his children for their lifetimes with a remainder to his grandchildren. His will devised his entire estate to the May County Community College.

Who acquired the ownership of the beach home due to the conveyance and his death?

ANSWER:

195.   Ali was married to Fatima. He died in 2005, leaving his entire probate estate to Fatima. Part of Ali's probate estate was a rental home that Fatima inherited. Fatima has recently died. She was survived by Yasmin (her only child), age 60, and Yasmin's children, Amira, Malik, and Jamal, ages 25, 27, and 30, respectively; each child is the parent of a child. Under her 2006 will, Fatima devised the rental home to Asia in trust with directions for Asia to pay Fatima's daughter, Yasmin, the income for the rest of Yasmin's life and then to pay the income to Yasmin's children for the rest of their lifetimes; upon the death of Yasmin's last surviving child, Asia is to deliver the trust estate to Yasmin's grandchildren.

Does all or any part of the disposition of the rental home devise violate the rule against perpetuities?

ANSWER:

196.   Orlando died Monday. He owned very little of value, except his home. Orlando was survived by his 38-year-old son, Hugo, and Hugo's thee young children, Lara, Tyra, and Gerald. Hugo is married to Cora, who is 36 years old. Lara, Tyra, and Gerald are all single, and have no children. Orlando's will devised his home to his son, Hugo, for life, then to Hugo's widow for her remaining lifetime, and the remainder to Hugo's children who survive his widow.

Does all or any part of the disposition of the homestead violate the rule against perpetuities?

ANSWER:

197.   Describe three different ways in which perpetual trusts have been effectively authorized in some jurisdictions.

ANSWER:

198.   Your client Geraldo has been reviewing a publication from a bank in a jurisdiction that has abolished the rule against perpetuities. The publication promotes its "Generational Endowment Trust" and leaves Geraldo with the impression that such trusts are likely suitable for almost everyone who cares for his family and has the means to provide for more than one following generation. Geraldo has asked you to give him both tax and non-tax advice regarding these perpetual trusts. Explain to Geraldo what the primary tax-motivation for perpetual trusts are, as well as some of the practical issues the trusts raises.

ANSWER:

199. Cyrus owns an importing business, which, with the help of his brother, Armen, and his son, Mark, he has expanded into a multi-state operation. In 2004, on the advice of his lawyer, Cyrus funds an irrevocable trust with the ownership interests in the business. The terms of the trust require Armen, as trustee, to pay the income to Mark for his lifetime, and at Mark's death, to deliver the trust estate to such of Mark's children as he appoints by will. In default of appointment, Armen is to deliver the trust estate to the New London Academy. In 2004, when his father created the trust, Mark executed a will appointing the trust estate to his only two children, Kyle and Uma. However, in 2005, Mark's third child, Erica, was born.

Which answer best describes the current beneficiaries of the trust?

(A) Mark.

(B) Mark, Kyle, and Uma.

(C) Mark and the New London Academy.

(D) Mark, Kyle, Uma, and the New London Academy.

200. Refer to Question 199. Mark has recently died, survived by his wife, Tina, and his three children, Kyle, Uma, and Erica. Which answer best describes who is likely to succeed to the trust estate by reason of Mark's death?

(A) New London Academy.

(B) Kyle and Uma.

(C) Kyle, Uma, and Erica.

(D) Tina, Kyle, Uma, and Erica.

201. Refer to Question 200. Assume Mark's will cannot be admitted to probate because it was not duly witnessed and no part of it was in Mark's own handwriting. What is the most likely disposition of the trust estate?

ANSWER:

202. Refer to Question 200. Assume Mark's had been in his own handwriting and admitted to probate as a holographic will, but also assume that the will does not make any reference to his power of appointment or to the trust estate. His will simply devises all of his property to his children. To whom should Armen distribute the property?

ANSWER:

203. Refer to Question 200. assume Mark never executed a will and died intestate.

      Which answer best describes the most likely disposition of the trust estate?

      (A) Armen should distribute it to the New London Academy.

      (B) Armen should distribute it to Kyle and Uma.

      (C) Kyle, Uma, and Erica will have the court impose a constructive trust on the charity
           to avoid unjust enrichment.

      (D) Kyle and Uma will have the court impose a constructive trust on the charity to avoid
           unjust enrichment.

204. Tammy divorced Leonard in 1988. Under their property settlement agreement, she
      received the home in which their only child, their daughter, Myra, had grown up. In
      1992, Tammy executed a will devising the home to Myra for life, remainder to such
      person or persons as Myra appoints by will, including Myra's estate, and in default
      of appointment, to the Highland County Clinic, which was the local hospital. Tammy
      died in 2004. Myra died recently survived by her husband, Peter, and their son, Diego.
      Myra's 2005 will was admitted to probate. It did not refer to her power of appointment
      but specifically devised the home to Diego and the rest, residue, and remainder of her
      estate to Peter. The home had a fair market value of $100,000 at the time of Myra's
      death; the value of Myra's property exceeded one million dollars.

      Which answer best describes the most likely disposition of the home?

      (A) It passes to Highland County Clinic.

      (B) It passes to Diego.

      (C) It passes to Diego subject to Peter's marital share.

      (D) It passes to Highland County Clinic subject to Peter's marital share.

205. Refer to Question 204. Assume Myra's will devised "all of my property to Diego."
      There is no specific reference to the home or to her power of appointment. Which answer
      best describes the most likely disposition of the home upon Myra's death?

      (A) It passes to Diego.

      (B) It passes to Diego subject to Peter's marital share.

      (C) It passes to the Highland County Clinic.

      (D) It passes to the charity subject to Peter's marital share.

206. Refer to Question 205, but assume Myra's will, instead, devised "all of my property, including any property over which I have a power of appointment, to Diego." What is the most likely disposition of the home?

ANSWER:

207. Refer to Question 206, but assume Diego predeceased Myra and was survived by Diego's spouse, Launa, and his child, Alec. Which answer best explains the most likely disposition of the home upon Myra's death?

   (A) It passes to Alec.

   (B) It passes to Launa.

   (C) It passes to Peter.

   (D) It passes to the Highland County Clinic.

208. Refer to Question 207, but assume Myra's will expressly exercised the power of appointment in favor of Diego and then devised all of Myra's property to Peter. Which answer best describes the most likely disposition of the home upon Myra's death?

   (A) It passes to Alec.

   (B) It passes to Launa.

   (C) It passes to Peter.

   (D) It passes to the Highland County Clinic.

209. Refer to Question 206, but assume that at the time of Myra's death Myra's liabilities exceeded her assets. Explain the rights of Myra's creditors, if any, in and to home.

ANSWER:

210. Harley left his job as a human resources manager and began day trading securities ten years ago. At that time, on the advice of his former college roommate, who had become a lawyer specializing in asset protection trusts, Harley created an irrevocable, express trust by declaring himself trustee of about half of his securities investments. Harley's friendly lawyer told him the best time to engage in asset protection planning is before any creditors' claims arise, and, he did. When the trust was funded, Harley was solvent. The terms of the written trust instrument authorize Harley to distribute to himself as much income and/or principal as he needs for his health, support, education, or maintenance. In addition, Harley may appoint any part of the trust estate to any one or more of his children by deed during his lifetime or at his death by will. At the time of Harley's death, the successor trustee is to distribute any remaining trust assets to

the Crabapple Cove College. Harley has never made any distributions from the trust, since he did not fund the trust with all of his assets, and has been able to live comfortably with the income from other assets. Unfortunately, late last year, due to some over-aggressive trading, Harley lost almost all of his investments that were not in the trust, and he has stopped paying his bills as they become due. A creditor of Harley is seeking your legal advice about attaching the trust estate.

Which answer best describes the legal advice you should give the creditor?

(A)   You cannot reach any part of the trust estate.

(B)   You may be able to reach whatever assets Harley may distribute to his children.

(C)   You may be able to attach only what Harley distributes to himself.

(D)   You can attach all or any part of the trust estate.

211.   Refer to Question 210. How would your answer differ if the trust described would have been a "spendthrift" trust? Would your answer differ if Harley's parent had created and funded the trust?

ANSWER:

212. Walls Hospital is a hospital that is organized as a nonprofit corporation. However, Walls Hospital charges substantial fees for its hospital services. Tim is considering an irrevocable trust that will make annual distributions to Walls Hospital each year for whatever specific purposes that Mary, as trustee, may choose.

    Is this a charitable trust?

    (A) No, unless the terms of the trust require the income to be used only to provide economic assistance for the benefit of those who otherwise would not be able to pay for the hospital services.

    (B) No, unless the fees charged by the hospital are so much less than those charged by for-profit hospitals.

    (C) Yes, because the trust will support the hospital's promotion of health, and it is irrelevant that the hospital charges fees for its services.

    (D) Yes, as long as the trust fund is not used to compensate the officers, directors, doctors, or other private individuals employed by the hospital.

213. Refer to Question 212. Rather than limiting the annual distributions to Walls Hospital each year, Tim is considering a trust that would allow Mary, as trustee, to make annual distributions for whatever charitable purposes she may choose.

    Is this a charitable trust?

    (A) No. The terms of a charitable trust must be specified irrevocably when it is created.

    (B) No. This creates a power of appointment in the trustee rather than a charitable trust.

    (C) Yes, as long as the court approves the trustee's choices as charitable.

    (D) Yes. The settler may delegate to the trustee the ability to select the charitable purposes or recipients.

214. Refer to Question 213. Last year Mary did not use the trust for a charitable purpose but rather made distributions to her church's summer camp in order to pay her children's tuition. Does Tim have standing to bring a cause of action against Mary for breach of trust?

    (A) Yes. As settlor of the trust, Tim has a statutory right to enforce it.

    (B) No. Once a trust is created, the settlor has no legal rights with respect to the trust.

    (C) No, unless the terms of the trust expressly authorize Tim to bring such a proceeding.

(D)   No. Only the state attorney general or other appropriate public authority has the standing to enforce a charitable trust.

215.   Assume a charitable trust is valid under state law, which of the following best describes its status under federal tax law?

(A)   All charitable trusts are entitled to federal income tax exemption and to receive deductible charitable contributions.

(B)   Some charitable trusts are entitled to federal income tax exemption, but all charitable trusts exempt from the income tax are entitled to receive deductible charitable contributions.

(C)   Some charitable trusts are entitled to federal income tax exemption, and some charitable trusts exempt from the income tax are entitled to receive deductible charitable contributions.

(D)   All charitable trusts are entitled to receive deductible charitable contributions, and some are also entitled to exemption from federal income tax.

216.   Harvey dies. His will purports to create a testamentary trust. The trust will be funded with Harvey's residuary estate. The trustees appointed in the will by Harvey are to use Harvey's home as a museum open to the public. The museum is to display Harvey's collection of his own artwork and of other artists he has collected over the years.

   Is this a charitable trust? If not, is it a private express trust?

(A)   Yes, it is a charitable trust.

(B)   Yes, as long as the museum does not charge admission.

(C)   No, unless the trustee can prove that the artwork has objective artistic merit or there is some other public interest in the museum. If not, the trust fails as a private express trust for lack of an identifiable beneficiary.

(D)   Yes, so long as the state attorney general consents to the trustee's operation of the museum as a charity.

217.   Refer to Question 216. If the trust fails as both a charitable trust and a private express trust, how should Harvey's residuary estate be distributed?

ANSWER:

218.   Nina establishes an irrevocable trust. The sole purpose is to provide college scholarships for the education of the children of her deceased sister. After the youngest living niece or nephew attains the age of 25, the trustee is directed to deliver the remaining trust estate to Barclay University's general scholarship fund.

Is this a charitable trust?

(A) Yes, because it advances education.

(B) Yes, as long as her nieces and nephews are objectively evidenced to be in financial need.

(C) No, because the initial beneficiaries are her nieces and nephews.

(D) No, unless the trustees impartially choose, on objective and reasonable grounds, which nieces and nephews shall receive the scholarship.

219. Claudia established an irrevocable trust with the following terms. The priest of St. Joseph's Parish in Claudia's hometown is to serve as trustee. On the day before Easter each year, the priest is to divide the income accumulated in the trust since the prior Easter among each of the children of the parish who are between ten and twelve years of age.

Is this a charitable trust?

(A) Yes, because the trust promotes the advancement of religion.

(B) Yes, because the trust is benevolent.

(C) No, because the distributions are not limited to those in financial need or otherwise restricted to ensure a charitable purpose.

(D) No, because the advancement of religion is not a charitable purpose since enforcing the trust would require state action.

220. Avi dies. Under his will, his residuary estate funds an irrevocable trust to promote health by encouraging the research for a cure for a specific rare blood disorder. Several years after his death, a cure is discovered for this blood disorder. The trust instrument does not mention termination nor otherwise contemplate that the disorder might ever be cured. Avi's intestate heirs demand that the trust terminate and the remaining assets be distributed to them since the purpose of the trust is fulfilled. The trustees of the trust insist that the court should modify the trust to provide it a new specific charitable purpose.

What is the status of the trust?

(A) Since the trust was established without a termination date, it violates the rule against perpetuities, and thus, should be terminated and distributed to Avi's intestate heirs.

(B) The court should apply the *cy pres* doctrine and specify a new charitable purpose for the trust consistent with the settlor's intent.

(C) The court should apply the *cy pres* doctrine and specify a new charitable purpose for the trust consistent with the settlor's intent only if it can be proven that the settlor had a *general* charitable intention for the trust.

    (D)   Since the charitable purpose of the trust has become impractical, impossible to achieve, or wasteful, the trust terminates and should be distributed to Avi's intestate heirs.

221.   Refer to Question 220. Assume that the trust instrument provided that if the blood disorder were ever cured, then the trust would terminate and the remaining assets would be distributed to Avi's intestate heirs. If the blood disorder is cured twenty-five years after Avi's death, should the court apply the *cy pres* doctrine and specify a new charitable purpose?

ANSWER:

222.   Eli establishes an irrevocable trust to relieve poverty, advance education, and promote health and other benefits to the community by providing financial support for the Libertarian party in his state.

    Is this a charitable purpose?

    (A)   No, because funding a political party is not charitable even if the party achieves public benefits.

    (B)   Yes, because the purpose is charitable.

    (C)   No, unless the Libertarian party limits its political goals to achieving charitable objectives.

223. Frank is the settlor of an irrevocable trust for the benefit of Deborah. Henry and Gordon are co-trustees. Henry has breached a duty to Deborah.

Assuming the suit does not seek the removal of Henry as trustee, who has standing to bring suit for damages against Henry for breaching the duty?

(A) Frank.

(B) Deborah.

(C) Frank or Gordon.

(D) Deborah or Gordon.

(E) Frank, Deborah, or Gordon.

224. Assume the same facts as in Question 223 above except that Henry has committed a serious breach of trust, and the suit will seek his removal. Who has standing to bring suit against Henry for breaching the duty?

(A) Frank.

(B) Deborah.

(C) Frank or Gordon.

(D) Deborah or Gordon.

(E) Frank, Deborah, or Gordon.

225. Judge Cardozo famously and enduringly defined the standard of behavior for trustees in *Meinhard v. Salmon*, 164 N.E. 545 (N.Y. 1928). What was his famous definition?

ANSWER:

226. Veronica is the settlor of an irrevocable trust for the benefit of Jamie. Yvonne is the sole trustee. The terms of the trust permit Yvonne "to sell trust property on the terms and conditions the trustee determines." Yvonne would like to purchase some of the trust property.

What is your legal advice to Yvonne?

(A) Yvonne may purchase the property as long as she acts in good faith and pays fair and reasonable consideration.

(B)   Since Yvonne has the power "to sell trust property on the terms and conditions the trustee determines," she may purchase the trust property on whatever terms and conditions she determines.

(C)   Yvonne may purchase the property as long as she does so with the consent of Veronica after full disclosure.

(D)   Yvonne may purchase the property as long as she does so with the consent of Jamie after full disclosure.

(E)   Yvonne may purchase the property as long as she does so with the consent of Jamie after full disclosure and as long as Yvonne acts in good faith and the terms and conditions are fair and reasonable.

227.   Compare and contrast "trustee duties" with "trustee powers."

ANSWER:

228.   Benny is the trustee of an irrevocable trust for Lana's benefit. By its own terms, the trust terminates one year from today. The only trust property is a rental house leased to a third party. When the trust terminates, the rental house will be distributed to Lana. The house is leased annually, and the lease will expire next month. Benny would like to extend the lease for another full year. This means the lease would not expire until after the trust terminates. What is the effect of Benny's extending the lease beyond the trust's term?

(A)   When the trust terminates and the house is distributed to Lana, the lease is binding on her and upon the lessee.

(B)   When the trust terminates and the house is distributed to Lana, the lease is not binding on Lana but remains binding upon the lessee.

(C)   When the trust terminates and the house is distributed to Lana, the lease binds neither Lana nor the lessee.

(D)   Since Benny does not have the power to extend the lease beyond the term of the trust, the lease is *void ab initio*.

229.   Merwan is the trustee of an irrevocable trust for the benefit of Faith. Under the terms of the trust, Merwan is *required* to make a $10,000 cash distribution directly to Faith next week. Faith has been engaging in a series of disturbing activities that have convinced Faith's friends and family that she suffers from a debilitating combination of serious mental illness and drug addiction. Her family is expecting to begin proceedings to have Faith declared incapacitated and to have a guardian appointed. However, they have not yet begun such proceedings, which means that at this time Faith has not been declared incapacitated by a court. Based on what he knows of the situation, Merwan believes that Faith is incapacitated. Faith's family pleads with Merwan not to make

the cash distribution directly to Faith because they are afraid she will use it to finance a drug binge, flee the state, and commit suicide. Faith's family has asked Merwan to pay some of Faith's outstanding medical and living expenses. These payments will be for Faith's benefit, but she will not receive the cash distributable to her under the terms of the trust instrument.

What legal advice would you give Merwan?

(A)   Merwan must follow the express terms of the trust instrument and pay Faith directly.

(B)   Merwan can pay Faith's outstanding living and medical expenses rather than make a cash distribution to her.

(C)   Merwan could deviate from the express terms of the trust instrument and make an indirect distribution for Faith's benefit rather than a direct distribution to her but only if a court determines her to be legally incapacitated prior to the time the distribution is required.

(D)   Merwan could deviate from the express terms of the trust instrument and make an indirect distribution for Faith's benefit rather than a direct distribution to her but only if a court proceeding to determine the issue of her legal capacity is commenced prior to the time the distribution is required.

230.   Aaron is the trustee of an irrevocable trust for the benefit of Maxey. Aaron has determined that it would be reasonable for his annual compensation for serving as trustee to be increased from 3% of the trust's net asset value to 4% of the trust's net asset value. He would like this increase to be effective at the beginning of next year.

What are Aaron's responsibilities for implementing this compensation increase?

(A)   Aaron must have Maxey's consent to increase his rate of compensation.

(B)   Aaron must have prior court approval of the increase in his rate of compensation.

(C)   Aaron must notify Maxey in advance of increasing his rate of compensation.

(D)   Aaron must notify Maxey and the court in advance of increasing his rate of compensation.

231.   With respect to the situation described in Question 8 above, as Aaron's attorney, what factors would you advise him to consider in determining whether his compensation is "reasonable?"

ANSWER:

232.   Sergio decided to create an irrevocable trust for the benefit of Blake. The trust property was to be several city blocks of low-income rental housing. Sergio discussed the trust with Francisco who is a full-time rental housing manager. Sergio wanted Francisco to

serve as trustee because of his housing management skills since Sergio knew how difficult the management would be. Francisco agreed to be trustee. Based on the rental management services market, the trust instrument expressly provided that Francisco would be entitled to 20% of the annual net receipts generated by the trust property as compensation for serving as trustee. When the trust was created, Sergio and Francisco contemplated that the net receipts from the rentals would be about $100,000 per year. However, six months after the trust was created, Francisco, as trustee, made the prudent decision to sell the trust property to a real estate developer who had surprised the market by deciding to redevelop a large area of the city. Whereas managing the rentals would have required 800 hours of Francisco's time each year, the negotiation of the sale required only 80 hours. Because of this sale, the net receipts generated from the trust for the year were $10,000,000.

With respect to Francisco's entitlement to $2,000,000 as his compensation for the year, which of the following is the best statement?

(A)   The terms of the trust instrument expressly provided the rate of compensation. Thus, Francisco is entitled to the $2,000,000.

(B)   The terms of the trust instrument expressly provided the rate of compensation, and the terms of the trust instrument override any statutory requirements unless a court determines Francisco acted in bad faith or was grossly negligent. Thus, Francisco is entitled to the $2,000,000 unless a court determines he acted in bad faith or was grossly negligent.

(C)   Francisco and Sergio have a valid contract as to the rate of compensation. There is no indication that Francisco acted improperly in negotiating the rate nor is there any indication that Sergio did not have complete information during the negotiations. Thus, Francisco is entitled to the $2,000,000.

(D)   Even though the trust instrument expressly provided the rate of compensation, the trustee is never entitled to unreasonably high compensation.

233.   Angela, Susan, and Mandi are co-trustees of an irrevocable trust for the benefit of Laura. The three co-trustees agree that it is prudent to sell a parcel of real estate owned by the trust. Angela and Susan believe it is prudent to sell the property to Jennifer, who will pay $100,000 down and make payments to the trustees pursuant to a 10 year, 8% fixed interest note. Mandi objects to this sale, insisting that the note should have an adjustable interest rate. Mandi has informed Angela and Susan that she does not believe the sale is prudent if the note has a fixed rate of interest but believes it is only prudent if the rate is adjustable. Jennifer has accepted Angela's and Susan's terms but rejected Mandi's terms because she does not want an adjustable rate note. Angela, Susan, and Mandi meet at the title company office to close the sale. Angela and Susan execute the documents to effect the sale with the fixed interest rate note. Jennifer demands that Mandi also sign the documents since she is a co-trustee. Angela and Susan insist Mandi sign.

Which of the following is the best statement?

(A) Angela and Susan do not have the authority to sell the trust property over Mandi's objection since the three co-trustees must agree.

(B) Mandi can only avoid liability for any breach committed by Angela and Susan by refusing to sign the documents.

(C) If Mandi signs the documents, she is not liable for any breach committed by Angela and Susan since she has informed them of her objections.

(D) If Mandi signs the document, she is not liable for any breach committed by Angela and Susan since she has informed them of her objections—unless the breach amounts to a serious breach.

234. Under the prudent investor rule, what are the investment expectations for a trustee?

(A) To invest only in those investments statutorily authorized as prudent.

(B) To prudently preserve the value of the trust and avoid speculative investments.

(C) To invest in low-risk investments with guaranteed returns.

(D) To maintain a diversified portfolio of investments, which may include very low risk investments and very high risk investments.

235. In addition to considering the purposes, terms, and distribution requirements of the trust, what other types of circumstances should a trustee consider prior to making any investment decision?

ANSWER:

236. In 1988, Todd made a $10,000 investment in a publicly-traded corporation. This investment is now worth $5,000,000. He created an irrevocable trust for his grand-daughter Nancy with only this $5,000,000 investment. Dale is the trustee. Todd believes that the investment in this corporation will increase in value, and indeed, all of Todd's other investments are in this corporation.

What are Dale's investor-related responsibilities with respect to this investment?

(A) He must diversify the trust, which means he must sell at least part of this investment and use the proceeds to purchase another investment. Regardless of how "good" a particular investment is, it is never prudent to fail to diversify the trust portfolio.

(B) Since the investment was the initial trust property received by Dale, he is under no obligation to diversify the trust's assets. However, if he does sell some or all of the investment, the proceeds must be invested in a diversified portfolio.

(C) If he determines the investment is prudent, he need not diversify the trust's assets.

(D) Since the investment was the initial trust property received by Dale, he is under no obligation to diversify the trust's assets as long as he determines the investment is prudent. However, if he does sell some or all of the investment, the proceeds must be invested in a diversified portfolio.

237. Todd creates an irrevocable trust for the benefit of his granddaughter, Sally. Dale is trustee. The trust is funded only with Todd's great-grandparent's home on Cape Cod. The purpose of the trust is to preserve this family home for Sally. It is the only asset in the trust though Todd had promised to make sufficient annual cash contributions to maintain the home.

What are Dale's investor-related responsibilities with respect to this investment?

(A) The home is trust property but not a trust "investment," thus the prudent investor rule does not apply.

(B) He must diversify the trust, which means he must sell at least part of this investment and use the proceeds to purchase another investment. Regardless of how "good" a particular investment is, it is never prudent to fail to diversify the trust portfolio.

(C) Since the investment was the initial trust property received by Dale, he is under no obligation to diversify the trust's assets. However, if he does sell some or all of the investment, the proceeds must be invested in a diversified portfolio.

(D) Given that the purpose of the trust is to preserve the home for the beneficiary, there is no duty to diversify the trust's investments.

238. Mariah is trustee of an irrevocable trust for Diego. Mariah has limited financial expertise and was appointed as trustee because she is Diego's closest living family member. Mariah is concerned about her limited financial expertise and believes it prudent to hire an outside investment manager. Mariah discusses her need for an investment manager with her attorney, her accountant, her insurance manager, and several friends and family members. Several of these people refer her to individual investment managers with whom they have established good relationships and for whom they vouch as to personal integrity and professional skill. Mariah meets with each of these managers, providing the trust-related information and discussing their credentials, experiences, and specialties. She selects three finalists and then interviews several of the finalists' existing clients, who are all very well pleased with the managers. She confirms that each of the manager's credentials are legitimate and that they each bear the credentials most commonly suggested to be important. She then hires one of the finalists. Her lawyer drafts an investment management agreement with the manager that establishes the scope and terms of the manager's duties. On a monthly basis, Mariah and her accountant each review the manager's activities before approving the monthly management fee. Unfortunately, in one single month the manager imprudently makes a series of high-risk derivative investments and loses 90% of the trust's investments' value.

Assuming the portfolio was imprudently managed, is Mariah liable for the manager's mismanagement?

(A) Yes. Trustees are not authorized to delegate important responsibilities such as investment management.

(B) No. Trustees are authorized to delegate responsibilities whenever it would be prudent for them to do so if they exercise reasonable care, skill, and caution in selecting the agent, establishing the terms of the delegation, and periodically reviewing the agent's performance. A trustee who takes these steps is not liable for the agent's acts.

(C) Yes. Although trustees are authorized to delegate whatever responsibilities they choose, they are responsible for the actions of their agents.

(D) Yes. Although trustees are authorized to delegate responsibilities whenever it would be prudent for them to do so if they exercise reasonable care, skill, and caution in selecting the agent, establishing the terms of the delegation, and periodically reviewing the agent's performance, they remain responsible for the actions of their agents.

239. Section 104 of the Uniform Principal and Income Act grants trustees the power to adjust between income and principal instead of applying allocation rules that would be inappropriate for the trust.

How does this power potentially reduce the tension between income and principal beneficiaries?

ANSWER:

240. Section 104 of the Uniform Principal and Income Act grants trustees the power to adjust between income and principal instead of applying allocation rules that would be inappropriate for the trust.

How is this integral to the prudent investor rule?

ANSWER:

241. Barbara is trustee of an irrevocable trust for the benefit of her granddaughter, Shannon. The trust instrument explicitly provides that "the trustee is wholly and completely authorized to refuse to provide to the beneficiary any information related to the administration of the trust." Shannon has requested Barbara keep her informed as to the material activities of the trust's administration.

What is Barbara's obligation to provide the information to Shannon?

(A) Barbara does not need to provide the information because the trust instrument authorized her to withhold it.

(B) Even though the trust instrument authorizes Barbara to withhold the information, she may exercise the power to withhold the information only if she determines that it is prudent and in Shannon's best interest.

(C) Regardless of what the trust instrument provides, Shannon is entitled to be kept reasonably informed as to the trust's administration.

(D) Since Barbara is authorized by the trust instrument to withhold the information, she may withhold the information as long as she does so in good faith.

242. Megan establishes an irrevocable trust for the benefit of her son, Edward. Megan's husband, Rich, is the trustee. Edward has always had a strained relationship with his parents, and Megan was very concerned that Edward would not be able to sue Rich, as trustee. Megan trusts Rich to serve as the best trustee he can under the circumstances, so the trust instrument provides that "no beneficiary is entitled to sue my husband, Rich, for any actual or alleged violation of any duty to the beneficiary."

What is the effect of this provision?

(A) The provision effectively relieves Rich from any liability for serving as trustee.

(B) The provision does not reduce Rich's liability since such liability is imposed by statute and cannot be altered by the trust instrument.

(C) The provision effectively relieves Rich of any liability for breaching the trust as long as the breach is not committed in bad faith or with reckless indifference

(D) The provision relieves Rich of any liability for breaching the trust as long as the breach is not committed in bad faith or with reckless indifference, but it does not relieve him of any liability for violating his fiduciary duties to manage the trust prudently.

243. On Christmas day, Isabella gives her husband a $250 watch.

      Is this a taxable gift for federal transfer tax purposes?

      (A) No. Inter-family gifts such as Christmas gifts are not gifts for federal tax purposes.

      (B) Yes. This is a gift. However, it qualifies for the marital deduction.

      (C) No. This is not a gift because it is under the annual exclusion amount.

244. Angel owns a car with a fair market value of $15,000. He sells it to his daughter, Samantha, for $2,000.

      Has Angel made a taxable gift?

      (A) No. A sale is not a taxable gift.

      (B) No. Angel has not made a gift unless the value of the car exceeds the annual exclusion amount.

      (C) Yes. Angel has made a taxable gift of $13,000.

      (D) Yes. Angel has made a taxable gift of $1,000.

245. Jessica is a used car dealer. She sells a used car to a customer, Rebecca. According to a national publication of car values, the car has a value of $25,000. However, she sold it to Rebecca for $20,000. Has Jessica made a gift to Rebecca for federal transfer tax purposes?

ANSWER:

246. Lorenzo creates a trust that is revocable during his lifetime but becomes irrevocable at his death. The trust provides that at Lorenzo's death his home is to be given to his daughter, Janice.

      Which of the following best describes whether Lorenzo made a gift for federal transfer tax purposes?

      (A) Lorenzo has not made a gift of his home to Janice. By retaining the power to revoke the trust, he has not parted with dominion and control over his home.

      (B) Lorenzo has made a gift of his home to Janice.

(C)   Lorenzo has made a gift of a future interest in his home to Janice.

(D)   Lorenzo has parted with dominion and control of his home, but he has not made a gift.

247.   Ramon creates a revocable trust to pay income to his son, Ernest, for Ernest's lifetime and then on Ramon's death to pay the principal to Ernest's son, Felipe. Tia is the trustee. In the current year, the trust has $5,000 income, which Tia distributes to Ernest.

Which of the following best describes the federal gift tax consequences of the described transactions?

(A)   Ramon made a gift of the trust corpus to Ernest when he created the trust.

(B)   Ramon made a gift of a life estate to Ernest when he created the trust.

(C)   Ramon made a gift of $5,000 whenever Tia distributed the income.

(D)   Ramon did not make a gift to Ernest because he has the power to revoke the trust.

248.   Refer to Question 247. Which is the best statement as to how the $5,000 income is taxed for federal *income* tax purposes?

(A)   The $5,000 income is taxable to Ramon because he retained the power to revoke the trust.

(B)   The $5,000 income is taxable to Ramon because he retained the power to revoke the trust. However, he will be entitled to a deduction since the $5,000 was distributed to Ernest.

(C)   The $5,000 income is taxable to Tia as trustee of the trust (but not personally), however she (*i.e.*, "the trust") will be entitled to a deduction for the $5,000 distribution to Ernest.

(D)   Ernest will be taxable on the $5,000 income as he received the $5,000 distribution.

249.   In the current year, Johana makes a $12,000 gift to Denise, a $12,000 gift to Greta, a $15,000 gift to Karli, and a $10,000 gift to Heidi.

By how much has Johana exceeded the total annual exclusion amount available to her this year?

(A) $1,000

(B) $3,000

(C) $37,000

(D) $49,000

250.   Ali is Sara's father. Sara is a 22-year-old law student. In the current year, her tuition is $17,000. Ali pays pays the law school for Sara's tuition. He also gives $10,000 to Sara to use towards her other expenses.

Which of the following statements is the best statement as to the characterization of these gifts?

(A) Ali has made $27,000 in taxable gifts.

(B) Ali has made $15,000 in taxable gifts: $12,000 of the $27,000 is excluded because of the annual exclusion.

(C) Ali has made $17,000 in taxable gifts. The $10,000 paid to Sara is a gift covered by the annual exclusion. However, the $17,000 paid to the law school is not a gift because it is paid to the school as part of the school's ordinary course of business, and thus, no part of it qualifies for the annual exclusion.

(D) Ali has not made any taxable gifts.

251. Clifford creates an irrevocable trust with Harold as trustee. Clifford's 25-year-old son, John, is the sole beneficiary. The terms of the trust direct that Harold will give John notice any time that Clifford makes a contribution to the trust and that John will have the right to withdraw the amount contributed to the trust for a reasonable period of time after receiving the notice (*e.g.*, 30 days). However, if John does not withdraw the amount contributed, the power will lapse and the contribution will be added to the trust principal. John will only be entitled to income from the trust until the trust terminates when he is 40; at that time, he will receive the remaining principal. Clifford's wife, Eve, agrees to split gifts with Clifford. This year, Clifford contributes $20,000 to the trust.

Assuming that the terms of the trust are respected, which of the following describes the gift tax consequences of the described transaction?

(A) The $20,000 contribution exceeds the available annual exclusion.

(B) The $20,000 contribution does not qualify for the annual exclusion because it is not a present interest.

(C) The $20,000 contribution qualifies for the annual exclusion because it is a present interest.

(D) The $20,000 contribution does not exceed the available annual exclusion, but the contribution does not qualify for the annual exclusion because it is not a present interest.

252. Four years before Omar died, Xavier gave a life estate in his vacation home to Omar and a remainder interest in the home to Omar's daughter, Selma. Now that Omar has died, is this life estate included in his gross estate?

(A) Yes. Even though the life estate is not part of Omar's probate estate, it is part of his gross estate, and thus, it must be included under Internal Revenue Code § 2033.

(B) Yes. Life estates are included in gross estates under Internal Revenue Code § 2036.

(C) No. A life estate created by another person is not included in the gross estate under Internal Revenue Code § 2036 or otherwise.

(D)   No, unless the gift of the life estate was taxable.

253.   Mark and Elaine are engaged to be married on October 12. On June 1, Mark deposits $50,000 in a joint and survivor account. Assume the account does not bear interest. The money in the account is payable to Mark or Elaine or the survivor of them.

Which of the following best describes the gift tax consequences of the described transaction as of June 1?

(A)   Mark has made a gift of $50,000.

(B)   Mark has made a gift of $25,000.

(C)   Mark has not made a gift because he has the right to withdraw the $50,000.

(D)   Mark has not made a gift because Elaine's right to withdraw deposits does not begin until Mark's death.

254.   Refer to Question 253. Assume that Elaine withdraws $10,000 on June 2 for her own personal use.

How would that change your answer?

ANSWER:

255.   Refer to Question 253. Assume that Mark deposited $50,000 on June 1, but Elaine also deposited $50,000 on June 1.

Which of the following is the best statement as to when Elaine has made a gift to Mark for federal gift tax purposes?

(A)   Since they deposited equal amounts, neither has made a gift.

(B)   Elaine made a gift of $50,000 to Mark on June 1.

(C)   Elaine will have made a gift to Mark on the date, if any, on which he makes a withdrawal.

(D)   Elaine will not have made a gift to Mark until the date, if any, on which he makes a withdrawal in excess of $50,000 for his own personal use.

256.   Refer to Question 255. However, assume Mark deposited $50,000 and Elaine deposited $25,000 on June 1. If Mark dies the day after the deposits, how much in the account is included in his gross estate?

(A) $25,000

(B) $37,500

(C) $50,000

(D) $75,000

257. Refer to Question 256. However, assume Mark and Elaine are married on June 1 when they each make the deposits. If Mark dies the day after the deposits, how much in the account is included in his gross estate for federal estate tax purposes?

(A) $25,000

(B) $37,500

(C) $50,000

(D) $75,000

258. Refer to Question 257.

Will there by any tax liability due on the amount included in Mark's gross estate?

ANSWER:

259. Hannah purchases a life insurance policy on her own life. Her husband is the sole beneficiary of the policy. He will be paid $500,000 when she dies. Hannah has the right to change the beneficiary.

Assuming she does not change the beneficiary, which of the following is the best statement of the estate tax consequences of the policy when she dies?

(A) Life insurance proceeds are tax free under Internal Revenue Code § 101.

(B) The $500,000 will be included in Hannah's estate as a result of Internal Revenue Code § 2042 and will generate tax liability assuming the taxable estate exceeds the applicable exclusion amount.

(C) Although the $500,000 will be included in Hannah's estate as a result of Internal Revenue Code § 2042, it will not generate a tax liability as the payment to the husband will qualify for the marital deduction of Internal Revenue Code § 2056.

(D) Although the $500,000 will be included in Hannah's estate as a result of Internal Revenue Code § 2042, it will not generate a tax liability since the $500,000 is less than the applicable exclusion amount.

260. Gabriela consults with her attorney, Jason. Jason recommends that Gabriela create a revocable trust to avoid probate when she dies. Gabriela follows all of Jason's recommendations, including completely transferring all of her assets to this "Living Trust." When Gabriela dies, all of the assets held in the Living Trust are to be paid to her alma mater, Stony Woods College.

Which of the following is the best statement of the expected estate tax consequences of the policy when Gabriela dies?

(A)   Since the assets in the Living Trust will not be subject to probate, they will not be included in her gross estate.

(B)   The assets in the Living Trust will be included in her gross estate under Internal Revenue Code § 2038 because she has the power to revoke the trust. However, the assets distributed to Stony Woods College should qualify for the charitable deduction under Internal Revenue Code § 2055 and will not generate tax liability so long as the amount of the deduction does not exceed the applicable exclusion amount.

(C)   The assets in the Living Trust will be included in her gross estate under Internal Revenue Code § 2038 because she has the power to revoke the trust. However, the assets distributed to Stony Woods College should qualify for the charitable deduction under Internal Revenue Code § 2055 and not generate any tax liability regardless of the applicable exclusion amount.

(D)   The assets in the Living Trust will be included in her gross estate under Internal Revenue Code § 2038 because she has the power to revoke the trust and will generate tax liability if the amount exceeds the applicable exclusion amount.

261. Natalie died. She was survived by two children, Evan and Madeline, and three grandchildren, Brian, Angelina, and Trevor. Natalie's gross estate for federal transfer tax purposes has been valued at $4,000,000. At the time of her death, she owed debts secured by real estate included in her gross estate of $400,000 and unsecured debts of $100,000 to third parties.

Which answer best describes the proper amount that can be deducted from Natalie's *gross* estate to determine the amount of the *taxable* estate for federal transfer tax purposes?

(A) $500,000

(B) $400,000

(C) $100,000

(D) $0

262. Refer to Question 261, but assume that the expenses of Natalie's last illness amounted to $40,000, Natalie's funeral expenses amounted to $20,000, and the expenses incurred in the administration of her estate are $10,000.

Which answer best describes the proper amount that can be deducted from the *gross* estate to determine the amount of *taxable* estate for federal transfer tax purposes?

(A) $70,000

(B) $60,000

(C) $50,000

(D) $40,000

263. Refer to Question 261, but assume that Natalie married Ahmad shortly before she died, and Natalie's will has been admitted to probate and devises property valued at $2,000,000 to Ahmad, property valued at $1,000,000 equally to Evan and Madeline, and property valued at $430,000 to Appaloosa River Valley Hospital.

Which answer best describes the additional amount that can be deducted from the *gross* estate to determine the amount of the *taxable* estate for federal transfer tax purposes?

(A) $430,000

(B) $1,430,000

(C) $2,430,000

(D) $3,430,000

264. Refer to Question 263, but assume the $2,000,000 was not devised outright to Ahmad, instead $1,000,000 was devised to a trustee in trust for Ahmad with directions for Yasmin as trustee to distribute to Ahmad such amounts of income and principal as Ahmad would need for his health, support, education, and maintenance. At Ahmad's death, Yasmin as the trustee is to deliver the remaining trust estate to Evan and Madeline. The other $1,000,000 was devised in trust to Yasmin as a trustee with directions to pay to Ahmad all of the trust income for the remainder of his lifetime, and at his death, the principal is to be delivered to Evan and Madeline.

Which answer describes the additional amount that can be properly deducted from the *gross* estate to determine the amount of the *taxable* estate for federal transfer tax purposes?

(A) $430,000

(B) $1,430,000

(C) $2,430,000

(D) $0

265. Refer to Question 264 and explain whether or not the trust estates of the described trusts would be included in Ahmad's gross estate at the time of his death, and if included, further explain who would be responsible for the payment of any resulting transfer taxes at Ahmad's death.

ANSWER:

266. When Nolan died, he devised $500,000 into a valid, enforceable testamentary trust. Nolan's wife, Dalia, was the trustee, and the terms of the trust directed Dalia to pay to herself all of the income. She was also granted the authority to distribute principal to herself as needed for her health, support, or maintenance. At Dalia's death, the trust

estate is to be distributed to Nolan's daughter from a prior marriage, Tyra. At Dalia's death, the trust estate had a fair market value of $10,000,000. Dalias's will devised all of her property to Avery, her daughter from a prior marriage.

What amount, if any will be added to Dalia's gross estate by reason of her interests in the described trust?

(A) $0

(B) $500,000

(C)   The value of Dalia's life estate in the trust estate.

(D) $10,000,000

PRACTICE FINAL EXAM: QUESTIONS

267. Adam died in 2003. Under his 2001 will, he devised the family farm to his only surviving child, Baird for life, remainder to Faye, who is Baird's only child. He devised the residue of his estate to his alma mater, Pennswood Academy. Faye died this week. She was survived by her husband, Henry, and their children, Lana and Mitch. She was also survived by Baird. Under Faye's 2004 will, she devised all of her property to Henry.

Which answer best describes who succeeds to the future interest in the family farm that Faye owned prior to her death?

(A) Baird.

(B) Pennswood Academy.

(C) Henry.

(D) Lana and Mitch.

268. Refer to Question 267. How would your answer differ if the family farm had been devised by Adam to Baird for life, remainder to Faye, if Faye survives Baird?

(A) My answer would not change.

(B) Pennswood Academy.

(C) Baird.

(D) Lana and Mitch.

269. Refer to Question 267. How would your answer differ if Faye had predeceased Adam?

ANSWER:

270. Refer to Question 267. How would your answer differ if the family farm had been devised to Kerry in trust with directions for Kerry to pay the income to Baird for life, and, at Baird's death, deliver the family farm to Faye?

(A) My answer would not change.

(B)   Pennswood Academy.

(C)   Baird.

(D)   Lana and Mitch.

271.   David and Chava are married. They make an appointment with an attorney, LaDonna, to discuss estate planning. LaDonna recommends a complex estate plan. Part of the plan involves David's creating an irrevocable trust for the benefit of Chava. David and Chava accept LaDonna's recommendations. The estate plan is implemented, and David and Chava pay LaDonna and have no further contact with her. LaDonna, David, and Chava have never communicated with one another as to the terms of LaDonna's representation. Six months later, David makes an appointment with LaDonna. He and Chava are now divorced and he wants legal advice regarding options to terminate the trust he created for Chava or to otherwise modify it so as to eliminate any meaningful benefit from the trust to Chava.

May LaDonna assist David?

(A)   Yes. She has no obligations to Chava as David will be her client.

(B)   Yes. Even though she may have some duties related to her prior representation of Chava, this representation is a discrete legal matter substantively independent of the prior representation.

(C)   No. Chava is an active client.

(D)   No. Chava is a former client.

272.   Art was a widower. Art died intestate. He had two children, Heath and Cody. Heath, however, predeceased his father, Art, leaving one child, Shay. Cody also predeceased his father, Art, leaving two children, Linda and Tessie. Linda survived her father, Cody, but she predeceased her grandfather, Art, leaving two children, Colleen and Martha. Thus, Art is survived by Shay (his grandson; Heath's son), Tessie (his granddaughter; Cody's daughter), Colleen (his great-granddaughter; Linda's daughter), and Martha (his great-granddaughter; Linda's daughter). Which of the following is the best statement?

(A)   Shay, Tessie, Colleen, and Martha would each take ¼; under a strict per stirpes approach, Shay would take ⅓; Tessie would take ⅓; Colleen would take ⅙; and Martha would take ⅙.

(B)   Shay would take ⅓; Tessie would take ⅓; Colleen would take ⅙; and Martha would take ⅙; under a strict per stirpes approach, Shay would take ½; Tessie takes ¼; Colleen takes ⅛; and Martha takes ⅛.

(C)   Shay would take ½; Tessie would take ¼; Colleen would take ⅛; and Martha would takes ⅛; under a strict per stirpes approach, Shay takes ⅓; Tessie would take ⅓; Colleen would take ⅙; and Martha would take ⅙.

(D)   Shay, Tessie, Colleen, and Martha would each take ¼; under a strict per stirpes approach, Shay would take ½; Tessie takes ¼; Colleen takes ⅛; and Martha takes ⅛.

273. Clarence had four children: Arthur, Florence, Samuel, and Edna. Their mother, his only wife, Minnie, died in 2002. On October 10, Arthur died of an intentional drug overdose. He had never been married and he had no children. Believing her father's parenting style had caused Arthur much of his misery, Edna stabbed her elderly father repeatedly after learning of Arthur's overdose. Clarence was rushed to the hospital, but he died on October 11. On their way to visit their father in the hospital, Florence and Samuel were involved in a car accident on October 11. Florence died immediately. Samuel did not die until October 12. Distraught, Edna committed suicide on October 18. Florence's husband was Dexter; they had one child, Grace. Samuel's wife was Vonda; they had one child, Louis. Edna's husband was Palmer; and they had one child, Nellie. Clarence died intestate. However, Edna has a will that left her entire estate to her husband, Palmer.

Which answer best describes the effect of Edna's crime on the distribution of Clarence's estate?

(A) The fact that Edna murdered Clarence disqualifies Edna as an heir, and the one-third of the estate to which Edna would have been entitled passes to Palmer.

(B) The fact that Edna murdered Clarence disqualifies Edna as an heir, and the one-third of the estate to which Edna would have been entitled passes to Nellie.

(C) The fact that Edna murdered Clarence disqualifies Edna as an heir, and the one-third of the estate that Edna would have been entitled passes to Grace and Louis.

(D) The only legal remedy of Grace and Louis is to impose a constructive trust on Palmer to avoid unjust enrichment on the part of Edna, Nellie, or Palmer.

274. On June 1, Helena meets with her lawyer, Maria. At Maria's office, Helena executes a will leaving her entire estate to the Highland County Hospital. Maria keeps the will in her safe at the office when Helena leaves. On July 1, Helena begins to think leaving her entire estate to the hospital might not be as preferable as leaving half to the hospital and half to the Rockingham Academy of Performing Arts. So she handwrites a note to her lawyer that reads "I've changed my mind. I don't want my June 1 will. That will is no good anymore. Void it for me. I'll come in next week and discuss my plans with you." She signed the note and mailed it on July 2. On July 3, she decided it would make more sense to e-mail Maria, and so she e-mailed her a note that read exactly as the handwritten note. Maria received the e-mail on July 3, and immediately wrote "VOID" across each page of the June 1 will and through Helena's signature. On July 4, Helena's July 2 handwritten note arrives, and Maria runs the June 1 will through the office shredder and places the July 2 handwritten note in the office safe. On July 5, Helena dies.

Which of the following is the best statement?

(A) The June 1 will was revoked on July 4 when Maria physically destroyed it pursuant to Helena's instructions.

(B) The June 1 will was revoked on July 3 when Maria wrote "VOID" on each page pursuant to Helena's instructions.

(C)   The June 1 will was revoked on July 3 when Maria was informed that the June 1 will no longer reflected Helena's testamentary intentions.

(D)   The June 1 will was revoked on July 2 when Helena handwrote the note to Maria that the will was "no good anymore."

275.   Manny is a well known chef. Recently, he was involved in flambé accident in his restaurant. His hands were badly burned. Though he is expected to recover fully, he has become very concerned about dying. He asked his lawyer, Pho, to draft a will for him. Pho drafted the will for him, and mailed it to him. When Manny opened the will in the back bedroom at this house, Shauna and Paco were visiting him. He asks them to witness his will execution, and they agree to sign as witnesses after he signs. Since he is unable to sign his name, he asks Shauna to sign his name for him, and she agrees. Shauna walks out of his house to her car in the front driveway to pick up her felt tip pen and a cooking magazine she had brought for Manny. While inside the car, she signed Manny's name to the will. She returns to Manny's bedroom and hands him the magazine and the will. Manny thanks her for signing the will, and then hands the will back to Shauna. Paco and Shauna sign the will as witnesses.

Does Shauna's signature on Manny's behalf count as his signature?

(A)   No. She did not sign Manny's name in his conscious presence even though she did sign at his direction.

(B)   No. She did not sign Manny's name in his line of sight even though she did sign at his direction.

(C)   Yes. She signed Manny's name in his conscious presence and at his direction.

(D)   Yes. She signed Manny's name at his direction. There is no requirement that she also do so in his conscious presence.

276.   Nima died survived by her two children, Choden and Dorjee. However, under the terms of her will, the residuary of her estate is to be distributed one-half to her friend, Tashi, and one-half to her niece, Pasang. Pasang survived Nima but died within 24 hours of her. She was survived by her daughter, Sonan. Under her will, she left her estate to her husband, Lobsang.

Which of the following best describes who is ultimately entitled to Nima's residuary estate?

(A)   Tashi receives 100%.

(B)   Tashi receives 50% and Sonan receives 50%.

(C)   Tashi receives 50% and Lobsang 50%.

(D)   Tashi receives 50%, Choden receives 25%, and Dorjee receives 25%.

277.   Fred has died testate. His will made a gift of "the family chicken farm to my son, Hal, if he is living at my death, but if he is not then living, to his children." Hal had two

daughters, Brinna and Golda. Golda had two sons, Samuel and Zach. Both Hal and Golda predeceased Fred. Under Hal's will, his estate was to be distributed to the Boyarin Academy of Theater. Under Golda's will, her estate was to be distributed to her husband, Allen. Brinna, Samuel, Zach, and Allen survived Fred by more than 120 hours.

How should Fred's family chicken farm ultimately be distributed?

(A) Since Hal died testate, the chicken farm should be distributed under his will to the Boyarin Academy of Theater.

(B) Brinna should receive a ½ interest in the chicken farm, but the remaining ½ interest to should be distributed under Golda's will to her husband, Allen.

(C) Brinna should receive the chicken farm.

(D) Brinna should receive a ½ interest in the chicken farm and Samuel and Zach should each receive a ¼ interest.

278. Adair died partially intestate. $100,000 is to be distributed under the intestacy statute. His will contained a provision that read "I wholly disinherit my brother, Blair." Blair died 94 hours after Adair died. Blair was survived by Blair's three children, Euna, Fergie, and Iona. Adair's sister, Lindsay, predeceased Adair, survived by her son, Cameron, and her widower, Don. Which of the following is the best statement as to the ultimate distribution of the $100,000?

(A) Blair takes $50,000; Don takes $50,000.

(B) Cameron takes $50,000; Euna, Fergie, and Iona each take $16,666.

(C) Cameron, Euna, Fergie, and Iona each take $25,000.

(D) Euna, Fergie, and Iona each take $33,333.

279. Ben has died testate. His probate estate was valued at $4,000. You represent the only creditor of Ben's estate. Your client's claim is valued at $12,000. You have discovered that Ben had a joint bank account with rights of survivorship in Ben's brother, Aviashai. The bank account has a balance of $16,000. In response to your inquiries, Aviashai has provided you records showing that he had contributed $10,000 to the account and that Ben only contributed $5,000, and that $1,000 interest has accrued. Aviashi has taken the position that, as a non-probate asset, the bank account is not subject to Ben's creditor's claims.

What is your analysis of your client's rights?

ANSWER:

280. Petros died testate. His will created a testamentary trust for the lifetime of his wife, Anna, with the remainder to their son, Theo, if he is then living, otherwise, to Theo's

then living descendants. Anna is living, though her will provides that her entire estate will be distributed to Theo. Theo is a lawyer very concerned about limiting his liability for malpractice claims. He decides to create a multi-generational trust for his descendants. His good friend Tae is his trustee. He then executes a deed conveying to Tae, as trustee, Theo's remainder interest in the trust established by Petros along with whatever property he ultimately receives from his mother's estate.

Assuming the trust terms do not prohibit the transfer of beneficial interests, which of the following best describes the effect of Theo's conveyance?

(A)   Theo has failed to create a trust.

(B)   Theo has created a trust funded with his contingent remainder interest in the trust created by his father and the right to whatever property, if any, he becomes entitled to receive from his mother's estate.

(C)   Theo has created a trust funded by his right to whatever property, if any, he becomes entitled to receive from his mother's estate.

(D)   Theo has created a trust funded with his contingent remainder interest in the trust created by his father.

281.   Javier has died. Under his will, his condo in Brooklyn Heights was devised to his grandchildren who reach age 21. He was survived by his only child, Carlos, and Carlos's only two children, Christina and Francisco, ages 8 and 9, respectively. The remainder of his estate was given to the Red Hook School for the Performing Arts.

Who owns the condo in Brooklyn Heights upon Javier's death?

(A)   The Red Hook School for the Performing Arts owns fee simple title subject to divestment if any child of Carlos's reaches age 21.

(A)   The Red Hook School for the Performing Arts owns fee simple title.

(C)   The Red Hook School for the Performing Arts owns fee simple title subject to divestment if Christina or Francisco reach age 21.

(D)   Carlos owns fee simple title.

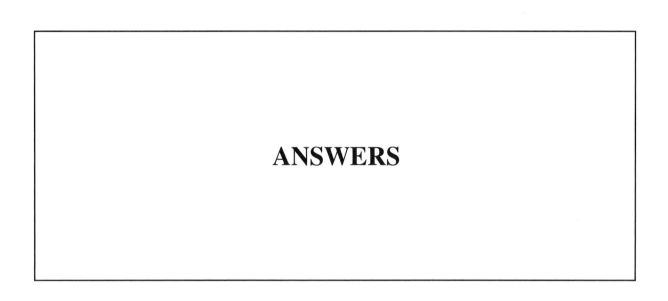

ANSWERS

1. **Answer (A) is incorrect.** Upon the client's death, the personal representative has the legal rights of the client, which includes the rights to any confidential information held by the deceased client's lawyer.

    Answer (B) is incorrect. Raul has no right to authorize the disclosure of the information held by the client's lawyer, even if he is the "object" of such information. Only the client and the client's personal representative have this right.

    Answer (C) is incorrect. Spouses have no greater rights than any other third party to any confidential information held by the deceased client's lawyer.

    Answer (D) is correct. In general, the lawyer's duty of confidentiality continues after the death of a client. Accordingly, a lawyer ordinarily should not disclose confidential information following a client's death. However, if consent is given by the client's personal representative, or if the deceased client had expressly or impliedly authorized disclosure, the lawyer who represented the deceased client may provide an interested party with information regarding a deceased client's estate plan and intentions. ACTEC Commentaries on the Model Rules of Professional Conduct Section 1.6 (4th ed. 2006) (hereinafter, "ACTEC Commentary _____"). In this situation, the client did not authorize the disclosure. Thus, consent by the bank would be required.

2. **Answer (A) is incorrect.** It is not necessary that clients expressly authorize disclosure of information since there are situations in which they do so by implication. As explained below, this is one of those situations.

    Answer (B) is correct. A lawyer is impliedly authorized to disclose otherwise confidential information to the courts, administrative agencies, and other individuals and organizations as the lawyer believes is reasonably required by the representation. This authority includes making arrangements, in case of the lawyer's death or disability, for another lawyer to review the files of his or her clients. It is assumed that reasonable clients would likely not object to, but rather approve of, efforts to ensure that their interests are safeguarded. ACTEC Commentary 1.6. Of course, if the client objects to such arrangements, the lawyer cannot claim this implied authorization.

    Answer (C) is incorrect. While a lawyer does have implied (even if not explicit) authorization to share confidential information with partners, associates, and employees to the extent reasonably necessary to the representation, as explained above, the lawyer also has implied authorization to make arrangements with lawyers who are not partners or associates in case of the lawyer's death or disability.

Answer (D) is incorrect. The authorization from the client is implied, so it is not necessary for it to be express. Further, there is no requirement that a lawyer seek court approval for the arrangement.

3. **Answer (A) is correct**. When a lawyer reasonably believes that a client is at risk of substantial harm unless action is taken and that a normal client-lawyer relationship cannot be maintained because the client lacks sufficient capacity to make decisions, the lawyer is entitled to take protective measures deemed necessary—and to disclose information to the extent necessary. These measures include seeking a court-appointed guardian or similar representative or consulting with family members, support groups, professional services, adult-protective agencies, or others who have the ability protect the client. ABA Model Rules of Professional Conduct 1.14(b) (hereinafter "Model Rule _____") and Comment 5 to Model Rule 1.14 (hereinafter, "ABA Comment _____"); ACTEC Commentary 1.6. In this situation, because Pam reasonably believes that Thelma is going to suffer substantial harm if no one intervenes, she may take the steps she believes necessary to protect Thelma from herself. She should not disclose any information except what is necessary to protect Thelma.

    Answer (B) is incorrect for the reasons explained above.

    Answer (C) is incorrect. A lawyer does not need pre-approval by a court to take the protective steps discussed above.

    Answer (D) is incorrect. The protective alternatives available to the lawyer are not limited to court actions. The lawyer may take less formal alternatives, such as contacting family members or adult-protective agencies.

4. **Answer (A) is incorrect.** A client may wish to have family members or other persons participate in discussions with the lawyer. When necessary to assist in the representation, the presence of such persons generally does not affect the applicability of the attorney-client evidentiary privilege. Nancy's participation was necessary for Jolene to understand Martha's directions, so the privilege should not be affected. ABA Comment 3 to Model Rule1.14. Thus, **Answer (C) is correct**.

    Martha's and Jolene's attorney-client relationship is independent of Nancy's and Jolene's. Nancy's participation in the discussions did not affect the formation of the relationship between Martha and Jolene, nor does a pre-existing relationship with Nancy and Jolene affect the applicability of the attorney-client privilege for information Martha provides. **Thus, Answers (B) and (D) are incorrect.**

5. **Answer (A) is correct**. Absent an agreement otherwise, when multiple parties consult with a lawyer on a matter, the presumption is that the lawyer represents the clients jointly rather than separately. ACTEC Commentary 1.6. The best practice, of course, is to detail the terms of representation in writing.

    Answer (B) is incorrect. The presumption is that the representation is joint.

Answer (C) is incorrect. Representation is either joint or separate, never both.

Answer (D) is incorrect. Forming the attorney-client relationship does not require discussing the details of the relationship. As Andy and Helen jointly sought legal assistance from Bea, unless there is an agreement otherwise, the presumption is that Bea represents them jointly.

6. "Joint representation" means I represent both of you, collectively. What one of you discusses with me may be disclosed to the other, if the discussion is legally relevant to the representation. I cannot withhold legally relevant information from either of you. I cannot give legal advice or take any actions without your mutual knowledge and consent. If a conflict arises between you or you have differences of opinion, all I can do is point out the "pros" and "cons" of the positions, opinions, and alternatives. If a conflict arises that makes it impossible for me to perform ethically with respect to each of you, it would be necessary for me to withdraw from being your lawyer. *Joint Spousal Engagement Letter* in ACTEC ENGAGEMENT LETTERS: A GUIDE FOR PRACTITIONERS (ACTEC Commentaries on the Model Rules of Professional Conduct, 3d. ed 1999).

7. **Answer (B) is correct.** In deciding how to respond to a private communication with one spouse when a lawyer represents the spouses jointly, the lawyer must consider the relevance and significance of the information. If the information is irrelevant to the legal representation, then it need not be communicated to the other. A disclosure of prior adultery may be considered irrelevant under the circumstances. Merely knowing one spouse's secret does not mean the attorney must inform the other spouse. The attorney's obligation is only with respect to relevant and significant information. Unless Helen's prior adultery seems likely to Bea to affect Andy's and Helen's joint estate planning, Bea need not disclose it. ACTEC Commentary 1.6. Thus, **Answers (A) and (D) are incorrect**.

Answer (C) is incorrect. One of the consequences of joint representation is that matters disclosed by one of the joint clients may be disclosed by the attorney to the other client. ACTEC Commentary 1.6.

8. **Answer (A) is incorrect.** One of the consequences of joint representation is that matters disclosed by one of the joint clients may be disclosed by the attorney to the other client. ACTEC Commentary 1.6.

Answer (B) is correct. Since the information is inherently relevant and significant, Bea should discuss the consequences with Andy. She should explain to him her ethical duties to both Andy and Helen, jointly. She may encourage Andy to tell Helen or to consent to Bea telling her. If Andy refuses, Bea likely will have to withdraw from representation. Nevertheless, before withdrawing, Bea should discuss the situation with Andy and use her professional judgment as how best to limit the negative consequences to both clients. Thus, **Answer (C) is incorrect**.

Answer (D) is incorrect. In deciding how to respond to a private communication with one spouse when a lawyer represents the spouses jointly, the lawyer must consider the relevance and significance of the information. ACTEC Commentary 1.6. Since the estate plan involves coordinating the non-probate and probate assets, the information about the beneficiaries of the retirement accounts is inherently relevant and significant even though Bea was not retained to review the designations.

9. **Answer (A) is correct.** The general rule is that the executor (or other fiduciary) is the lawyer's client. What duties, if any, owed by the lawyer to the beneficiaries of the estate vary among jurisdictions, but the fiduciary is the client. ACTEC Commentary 1.13.

   Answer (B) is incorrect. A minority of cases and ethics opinions have adopted the so-called entity approach under which the estate is characterized as the lawyer's client. Generally, however, an estate (unlike a corporation or partnership) is not considered an entity.

   Answers (C) and (D) are incorrect. While a lawyer may owe certain duties to those interested in an estate (beneficiaries or creditors), the general rule is that the executor (or other fiduciary) is the lawyer's client.

10. **Answer (B) is correct.** A lawyer may accept a gift from a client. Nevertheless, a substantial gift may be voidable by the client under the doctrine of undue influence, which treats client gifts as presumptively fraudulent. In no event, however, may a lawyer suggest a substantial gift, unless the lawyer and client are closely related. ABA Comment 6 to Model Rule 1.8. Thus, Manny may accept the gifts. **Answer (A) is correct.**

    Answers (C) and (D) are incorrect. In some jurisdictions, a substantial gift may be voidable under the doctrine of undue influence, which treats such gifts from clients as presumptively fraudulent. However, this prevents neither the giving nor the receiving of the gift, rather it puts the burden on the lawyer to show that there was no undue influence in the event the issue is raised.

11. No. If a substantial gift from a client to her attorney requires the preparation of a legal instrument, such as a will or conveyance, the client must have another lawyer's advice. ABA Comment 7 to Rule 1.8. A $50,000 gift is a substantial gift, of course. The sole exception to this rule is where the client is a relative of the donee, which does not apply here. ABA Comment 7 to Rule 1.8.

12. Lilly may offer to retain the will subject to Josh's later instructions. She should provide Josh with a letter or other writing confirming that she is holding the documents for safekeeping subject to his future instructions. The letter may, but need not, also indicate that the executor named in the will is not required to hire her as the lawyer to assist with administering the assets. Of course, the will should be properly identified and appropriately safeguarded while in Lilly's possession. ACTEC Commentary 1.8.

13. **Answer (A) is incorrect**. Generally, once the settlor creates a trust, he or she has no legal rights with respect to it. Thus, Henry is not the client since he has no legal rights involved in the administration of the trust.

    Answer (B) is correct. While a lawyer may owe certain duties to the beneficiaries of a trust in certain jurisdictions, the general rule is that the trustee is the lawyer's client. ACTEC Commentary 1.13. Thus, **Answers (C) and (D) are incorrect**. See above Question 9 regarding estates, as the principle is the same.

14. **Answer (B) is incorrect.** While Model Rule 1.8 does prohibit an attorney from drafting a will that would provide him a substantial gift, being appointed as a fiduciary is not a gift. Being paid as an executor is compensation for services.

    Answer (C) is correct. The Model Rules do not prohibit the drafting lawyer from being named as a fiduciary in a will. In some areas of the country, this is common practice; in other areas, it is not. Generally, it is best for the lawyer not to suggest being named and to provide written information to the client explaining his or her options and how executor's fees and other compensation are determined. The objective is to make it clear (and preserve as evidence) that the client understood the advantages and disadvantages and the costs and benefits before making a decision. It is neither required nor prohibited that the attorney charge for legal services in order to be named as executor. Thus, **Answers (A) and (D) are incorrect**. ACTEC Commentary 1.7.

15. No, unless Henrietta establishes that the clause was fair and that its existence and contents were adequately communicated to Barry. In determining whether the clause was fair, the court will consider: (1) the extent of the prior relationship between Henrietta and Barry; (2) whether Barry received independent advice; (3) Barry's sophistication with respect to business and fiduciary matters; (4) Henrietta's reasons for inserting the clause; and (5) the scope of the particular provision inserted. Comment to UTC § 1008(b).

16.   **Answer (B) is correct.** If the will had not disinherited Trevor, he would have taken one-half of the intestate estate (*i.e.*, 300 shares). However, the Uniform Probate Code authorizes a testator to disinherit an heir for purposes of intestate distribution (as well as, of course, testate distribution.) UPC § 2-101(b). (Note that not all states permit this type of disinheritance.) Trevor's share passes to his descendants as if he had *disclaimed* his intestate share. Thus, Alan takes half of Nolan's intestate estate. Cora, Lara, and Tyra split the other half equally. UPC §§ 2-103(3); 2-106; 2-1106(b)(3)(A). Importantly, if Trevor had actually predeceased Nolan (or had failed to survive Nolan by 120 hours) (*see* UPC § 2-104), then the disinheriting provision of the will would have no effect, and in that case, each of Alan, Cora, Lara, and Tyra would have taken equal ¼ shares under UPC §§ 2-103(3) and 2-106. Comments to UPC § 2-101. **Answers (A), (C), and (D) are incorrect** for the reasons explained.

17.   **Answer (A) is correct.** A legal decree of separation is *not* deemed to be a divorce under UPC § 2-802. Thus, Camila is Orlando's surviving spouse for purposes of UPC § 2-102. Because Orlando's only surviving descendant is also Camila's only surviving descendant, Camila is entitled to the entire intestate estate under UPC § 2-102(1)(ii).

      Answers (B) and (C) are incorrect. Gerald's mother is entitled to the entire intestate estate under UPC § 2-102(1)(ii) because she was his father's surviving spouse.

      Answer (D) is incorrect. Since Orlando has a surviving descendant as well as a surviving spouse, his parents are not entitled to any part of the estate. UPC § 2-102(1)(ii).

18.   Since Orlando is not survived by a descendant but is survived by his parents, Camila is only entitled to the first $200,000 plus ¾ of the remaining balance of the estate. UPC § 2-102(2).

19.   Since Orlando's only descendant, Gerald, is also Camila's descendant but she also has a descendant, Andrea, who is not Orlando's descendant, Camila takes the first $150,000 plus ½ of the remaining balance of the estate. UPC § 2-102(3).

20.   Camila takes the first $100,000 plus ½ of the remaining balance of the estate since Orlando has a descendant, Jen, who is not also Camila's descendant. UPC § 2-102(4).

21.   **Answer (D) is correct.** Angel was not survived by Madeline, and he had no descendants. Thus, his entire estate passes to his sole surviving parent, his mother, Rosa. UPC § 2-103(2). His brother, Joe, would take only if his mother, Rosa, had not survived, so **Answer (C) is incorrect**. UPC § 2-103(3).

Answers (A) and (B) are incorrect insofar as Madeline's parents, Ted and Claire, are not Angel's heirs in any event. UPC § 2-103.

22. Under UPC § 2-1106, because of her disclaimer, Rosa is treated as if she predeceased Angel. Thus, Joe takes the estate as if Angel had no surviving parent. UPC § 2-103(3).

23. Horacio does not take Angel's estate because great-grandparents do not inherit intestate estates under the Uniform Probate Code. Grandparents and descendants of grandparents are the most remote family members who may inherit an intestate estate. UPC § 2-103(4). Thus, Angel's estate passes to the state. UPC § 2-105. Note that Horacio, as Angel's next-of-kin, would inherit the estate in many jurisdictions.

24. **Answer (C) is correct**. Generally, an individual who fails to survive the decedent by 120 hours (*i.e.*, 5 days) is deemed to have predeceased the decedent. UPC § 2-104. However, this section is not applied whenever it would result in the estate passing to the state under UPC § 2-105. Since grandparents and descendants of grandparents are the most remote family members who may inherit an intestate estate, Tony's estate would pass to the state (rather than his great-grandfather, Luis) if Marla were deemed to have predeceased him. UPC §§ 2-103(4); 2-105. Thus, the general rule requiring survival for 120 hours does not apply on these facts, and Marla takes the estate. Chuck takes Marla's estate under UPC § 2-103. Since Marla's estate is augmented by Tony's, Chuck receives Tony's estate. **Answers (A), (B), and (D) are incorrect** for the reasons explained.

25. **Answer (B) is correct**. UPC § 2-106 adopts the system of representation called per capita at each generation, which always provides equal shares to those equally related. Eduardo and Serena, as grandchildren, each receive an equal ⅓, while Nina and Miranda, as great-grandchildren, each receive an equal ⅙. **Answer (A) is incorrect**.

Answer (C) is incorrect. Unlike the per capita at each generation system of representation of the UPC, the distribution of Answer (C) reflects "strict" or "English" per stirpes, which is an older system of representation used in some non-UPC jurisdictions.

Answer (D) is incorrect. Though Eduardo is the sole surviving child, the deceased child's share is distributed to her descendants.

26. No. On these facts, the result under a modern per stirpes system and the result under per capita at each generation system of the Uniform Probate Code is the same.

27. Eduardo takes ⅓; Serena takes ⅓; Nina takes ⅙; and Miranda takes ⅙. UPC § 2-106. Christopher's existence has no consequence because he left no descendants. Tina, too, is ignored because her mother, Serena, is still living.

28. **Answer (A) is correct**. UPC § 2-106 adopts the system of representation called per capita at each generation, which always provides equal shares to those equally related. Under UPC § 2-106(c), the sole surviving sibling (of four) takes ¼; the remaining ¾

is divided into 6 shares of ⅛ each with one share to each of the three surviving nieces and nephews (of six); the remaining ⅜ is distributed equally to the five grand-nieces and grand-nephews (all of whom survived). Jesse Dukeminier, Stanley M. Johanson, *et al.*, WILLS, TRUSTS AND ESTATES 79-80 (7th ed. 2005) (hereinafter, "Dukeminier _____"). Note that Elisa being Aaron's half-sister is of no consequence under the Uniform Probate Code. UPC § 2-107. However, some jurisdictions continue to discriminate against half-blooded relations (*e.g.*, providing them with one-half the share of a full-blooded relative.)

Answer (B) is incorrect. The distribution described in Answer (B) would result under both the strict/English per stirpes and the modern per stirpes systems of representation, which are each in effect in some jurisdictions. However, the Uniform Probate Code uses the per capita at each generation system.

Answer (C) is incorrect. Since the survivors belong to different generations of descendants of Aaron's parents, they do not take equally.

Answer (D) is incorrect. Though Booker is the sole surviving sibling, the deceased siblings' shares are distributed to their descendants who survive Aaron.

29. **Answer (D) is correct.** Delmar's sole surviving parent, Corine, takes the entire estate. UPC § 2-103(2). Under the Uniform Probate Code, the siblings (and, thus, the descendants of any predeceased siblings) would only take in the event that neither parent survived. Thus, **Answers (A), (B), and (C) are incorrect**.

30. The general rule is that for inheritance purposes an adopted individual becomes part of the adopting family and is no longer part of the natural family. However, there is an important exception when a child is adopted by his or her stepparent (the spouse of the custodial natural parent). Under this exception, Lennon is now part of Alan's family for inheritance purposes, but he also continues to be part of his mother's family. Lennon and his descendants also continue to have a right of inheritance from and through Baird, but Baird and his family do not have a right to inherit from or through Lennon. UPC § 2-114.

31. **Answer (A) is incorrect**. Beryl is not entitled to the entire estate. She takes the first $100,000 plus ½ of the remaining balance of the estate since Adam had descendants who were not Beryl's. UPC § 2-102(4).

Answer (D) is correct. The Uniform Probate Code does not provide a method for determining shares of a probate estate following an advancement. However, this question reflects the official Comments to UPC § 2-109 which use the common law hotchpot method. The first step is to add the value of the advancements back to the value of Adam's probate estate. This combined figure is called the "hotchpot estate." Adam's hotchpot estate is $250,000 (*i.e.*, 190,000 + $50,000 + $10,000). Beryl's intestate share of a $250,000 estate under UPC § 2-102(4) is $175,000 ($100,000 + ½ of $150,000). The remaining $75,000 is to be divided equally among Cassandra, Daphne, and Electra (*i.e.*, $25,000 each). This means that Cassandra has received an advancement (*i.e.*, $50,000) greater than the share to which she is entitled (*i.e.*, $25,000). Cassandra can retain the $50,000 advancement, but she is not entitled to any additional amount. For the second step, Cassandra's advancement is disregarded. Thus, the second step is to determine the revised hotchpot estate: $200,000 ($190,000 + $10,000). Beryl's intestate share is $150,000 ($100,000 + ½ of $100,000). The remaining $50,000 is divided equally between Daphne and Electra (*i.e.*, $25,000 each). From Adam's intestate estate, Daphne receives $15,000 (already having received $10,000 of her ultimate $25,000 share as an advancement), and Electra receives $25,000. The final division of Adam's probate estate is $150,000 to Beryl, $0 to Cassandra, $15,000 to Daphne, and $25,000 to Electra. Comments to UPC § 2-109. Thus, **Answers (B) and (C) are incorrect**.

32. **Answer (D) is correct**. According to general principles of conflict of laws, the substantive law of a decedent's domicile normally governs rights of succession to the decedent's personal property. UPC § 1-301 follows these principles. Because all of the described assets are personal property, the law of the state of Michiana will determine how the assets pass by intestate succession to Kenton's heirs, who are determined under the law of Michiana. UPC §§ 1-301, 1-302. William M. McGovern, Jr. And Sheldon F. Kurtz, WILLS, TRUSTS, AND ESTATES § 1.2 (3rd ed. 2004) (hereinafter, "McGovern _____").

    Answer (A) is incorrect. Even though the heirs may reside in different states and certain of Kenton's assets are located in different states, these facts do not trigger the application of any federal statutes to determine who owns what. The 14th Amendment does require that governing state law not violate the "due process" and "equal protection" clauses of the Constitution of the United States.

    Answer (B) is incorrect. While federal banking laws govern many of the practices of the bank, the succession of the checking account is a matter of state law. While (i) the state of Westphalia may have jurisdiction over the shares of stock due to the corporation being a Westphalian corporation and (ii) the state of Newberg has jurisdiction over the tangible personal property located in Newberg, the succession of those assets is a matter of the law of the state where Kenton was domiciled, Michiana.

    Answer (C) is incorrect. While (i) the state of Westphalia may have jurisdiction over the shares of stock due to the corporation being a Westphalian corporation and (ii) the state of Newberg has jurisdiction over the tangible personal property located in Newberg, the succession of those assets is still a matter of the law of Michiana.

33. **Answer (B) is correct**. UPC § 1-201 (38) defines the term "property" to include both real and personal property, and UPC §§ 1-301 and 1-302 appear to give the state of Michiana the authority to determine the rights of succession to the real property in the states of Westphalia and Newberg. However, conflict of laws principles provide that the substantive law of the decedent's domicile normally governs the rights of succession to the decedent's personal property, but the law of the situs of real property usually

governs the rights of succession to the real property. McGovern § 1.2. Note, however, that since all three states have adopted the UPC, there is no substantive difference as to which state's law applies though in practice significant differences may arise. Statutes in Westphalia and Newberg may require that a final order by a court in Michiana "be accepted as determinative of ownership" of real property in those states. UPC § 3-408.

Answer (A) is incorrect. Conflict of laws principles generally provide that the law of the decedent's domicile governs the succession to the decedent's personal property, but the law of the situs of real property governs the succession of the real property. A state statute may permit the probate of a will under certain circumstances even if the will was not executed in accordance with the formalities of the state's applicable wills act. UPC § 2-506.

Answers (C) and (D) are incorrect. Assuming that the "due process" and "equal protection" clauses of the 14th Amendment of the Constitution of the United States have not been violated, the laws of Michiana, Westphalia, and Newberg control the succession of real property located in those states.

34. Undue influence occurs if the wrongdoer exerted such influence over the testator that it overcame the testator's free will and caused the testator to make a will that the testator would not otherwise have made. Restatement of the Law, 3d, Property (Wills and Other Donative Transfers), § 8.3(b) (hereinafter, "Restatement of Wills _____".) Duress is similar but involves the wrongdoer threatening to perform or performing a wrongful act that coerces the testator into making a will that the testator would not otherwise have made. Restatement of Wills § 8.3(c). Fraud does not involve threats; it only requires that the wrongdoer knowingly or recklessly made false representations to the testator about a material fact that was intended to and did lead the testator to make a will that the testator would not otherwise have made. Restatement of Wills § 8.3(d). A will is invalid to the extent it is procured by any of the three. Restatement of Wills § 8.3(a).

35. **Answer (A) is incorrect.** UPC § 2-501 requires a person to be of "sound mind" when executing a will. The test for mental capacity under Restatement of Wills § 8.1 does not require the testator to have actual knowledge of the nature and extent of property.

 Answer (B) is incorrect. UPC § 2-501 requires a person to be of "sound mind" when executing a will. Since the test for mental capacity under Restatement of Wills § 8.1 does not require the testator to have actual knowledge of the nature and extent of property, a mistaken belief is irrelevant.

 Answer (C) is incorrect. The test for mental capacity does refer to the testator's knowledge in that it requires the testator to be capable of knowing and understanding in a general way the nature and extent of his or her property. UPC § 2-501; Restatement of Wills § 8.1.

 Answer (D) is correct. UPC § 2-501 requires a person to be of "sound mind" when executing a will. The test for mental capacity under Restatement of Wills § 8.1 requires the testator to be capable of knowing and understanding in a general way the nature and extent of his or her property, the natural objects of his or her bounty, and the disposition that he or she is making of that property, and the testator must also be capable of relating these elements to one another and forming an orderly desire regarding the disposition of the property. Thus, it is not necessary that Mitt actually know the specific value of his assets.

36. **Answer (A) is incorrect.** UPC § 2-501 requires a person to be of "sound mind" when executing a will. The test for mental capacity under Restatement of Wills § 8.1 does not require the testator to have actual knowledge as to the natural objects of his or her bounty.

Answer (B) is incorrect. UPC § 2-501 requires a person to be of "sound mind" when executing a will. Since the test for mental capacity under Restatement of Wills § 8.1 does not require the testator to have actual knowledge as to the natural objects of his or her bounty, Robert's mistaken belief is irrelevant.

Answer (C) is incorrect. The test for mental capacity does refer to the testator's family members in that it requires the testator to be capable of knowing the natural objects of his or her bounty. UPC § 2-501; Restatement of Wills § 8.1.

Answer (D) is correct. UPC § 2-501 requires a person to be of "sound mind" when executing a will. The test for mental capacity under Restatement of Wills § 8.1 requires the testator to be capable of knowing and understanding in a general way the nature and extent of his or her property, the natural objects of his or her bounty, and the disposition that he or she is making of that property, and the testator must also be capable of relating these elements to one another and forming an orderly desire regarding the disposition of the property. It is important that the definition relates to the capability to know, not actual knowledge. In *Williams v. Vollman*, 738 S.W.2d 849 (Ky.Ct. App.1987), an elderly testator was held competent to execute a will even though he was unaware of the deaths of his wife and daughter. The news had been kept from him for fear that it would weaken his resolve to live. Reporter's note 16 to Restatement of Wills § 8.1.

37.   The results would not differ. Restatement of Wills § 8.1(a) explicitly provides the same test for wills and for any revocable will substitute. A revocable will substitute is not only revocable but serves to pass property to others at death while not depriving the owner of the benefit of the property during life. Inter vivos revocable trusts are an example of such revocable will substitutes. Comment e to Restatement of Wills § 8.1; comment b to Restatement of the Law, 3rd, Trusts § 11 (hereinafter, "Restatement of Trusts _____".)

38.   Pursuant to UPC § 3-407, the contestants of a will have the burden of establishing lack of testamentary intent or capacity, undue influence, fraud, duress, mistake, or revocation.

39.   **Answer (A) is incorrect**. The fact that she had not been found by a court to be incapacitated is not determinative of testamentary capacity. Comment h to Restatement of Wills § 8.1.

Answer (B) is incorrect. "Totality of the circumstances" is not part of the test for determining testamentary capacity. The test for testamentary capacity under Restatement of Wills § 8.1 requires the testator to be capable of knowing and understanding in a general way the nature and extent of his or her property, the natural objects of his or her bounty, and the disposition that he or she is making of that property, and the testator must also be capable of relating these elements to one another and forming an orderly desire regarding the disposition of the property.

Answer (C) is correct. A person who is mentally incapacitated part of the time but who has lucid intervals during which he or she has testamentary capacity can make a valid will during such an interval. Comment m to Restatement of Wills § 8.1.

Answer (D) is incorrect. The legal test for testamentary capacity is not a medical standard. A physician's opinion of testamentary capacity is not necessary.

40. **Answer (B) is correct**. An adjudication of mental incapacity does not conclusively establish that the testator subsequently lacked testamentary capacity, but it does raise a rebuttable presumption to this effect, shifting the burden of proof to the proponent to show the testator possessed testamentary capacity. Comment h to Restatement of Wills § 8.1. Thus, **Answer (A) is incorrect**.

Answer (C) is incorrect. An adjudication of mental incapacity does have an effect on the application of the testamentary capacity. It raises a rebuttable presumption that the testator did not have capacity. Comment h to Restatement of Wills § 8.1.

Answer (D) is incorrect. In a significant deviation from many states' laws, UPC § 5-411 does permit a court to authorize a conservator to make a will for the incapacitated person. However, even though Lorraine may be able to petition the court to take such steps, she does not necessarily have the exclusive power to make a will for Harold who may still possess that ability.

41. **Answer (C) is correct**. An insane delusion is a belief that is so against all evidence and reason that it must be the product of derangement. Comment s to Restatement of Wills § 8.1. However, a person who suffers from an insane delusion is not necessarily deprived of the capacity to make a will. *Id.* Such a person's will would be invalid only to the extent that it was the product of the insane delusion. Comment s to Restatement of Wills § 8.1; McGovern § 7.1; Dukeminier 148. Serge's delusion about alien communications did not affect his will since he left his entire estate to his wife as was consistent with his prior estate plan. If, for example, Serge, as a result of his delusion, left his entire estate in trust for the benefit of aliens, the will would be invalid. Thus, **Answers (A) and (B) are incorrect**.

Answer (D) is incorrect. A person who is mentally incapacitated part of the time but who has lucid intervals during which he or she has testamentary capacity can make a valid will during such a lucid interval. Comment m to Restatement of Wills § 8.1. However, since the delusion does not appear to have had any effect on the disposition of Serge's property, the will is valid despite the delusion. Comment s to Restatement of Wills § 8.1. Thus, there is no need to argue that he wrote the will during a lucid interval in order to establish that it is valid (*i.e.*, even if he believed the aliens were sitting beside him when he wrote the will, that insane delusion had no effect on what he wrote as evidenced by the fact that he left his estate to his wife—rather than, say, the alien sitting next to him.)

42.   **Answer (A) is correct**. Louisa was in a confidential relationship with Marcus because she was his attorney. Given the suspicious circumstances, she has the burden of proof to come forward with evidence that Marcus was free from undue influence when he executed the will. Illustration 3, comment h to Restatement of Wills§ 8.3.

Answer **(B) is incorrect**. As the contestants of the will, the general rule is that the hospital would have the burden of establishing undue influence. However, as explained, since Louisa had a confidential relationship with Marcus, the suspicious circumstances shift the burden of proof to her. Illustration 3, comment h to Restatement of Wills§ 8.3.

Answer **(C) is incorrect**. The suspicious circumstance is Marcus's execution of the will because Louisa drafted the will and she was not a natural object of Marcus's bounty. Illustration 3, comment h to Restatement of Wills § 8.3.

Answer **(D) is incorrect** for the reasons explained.

43.   **Answer (A) is correct**. The general rule is that the contestant to a will has the burden to prove undue influence. UPC § 3-407. However, in many jurisdictions that burden may be shifted if the alleged wrongdoer was in a confidential relationship with the testator and there were suspicious circumstances. Theo was not Pearl's attorney; instead, he very wisely referred her to Donna. Thus **Answer (B) is incorrect**. However, since Rachel was Pearl's care giver, it could be concluded she was in a confidential relationship with Pearl. However, there are no suspicious circumstances surrounding the execution of the will. Theo's referring Pearl to Donna was appropriate in the circumstances and certainly does not establish a suspicious circumstance, nor is the disposition of Pearl's property in the will unnatural. Indeed, it is natural to disinherit a child who refused to help a parent when ill and in need and to prefer someone who did provide the needed care. Thus, **Answers (C) and (D) are incorrect**. Illustration 5, comment h to Restatement of Wills § 8.3.

44.   **Answer (A) is incorrect**. If a devise in a will was procured by undue influence, duress, or fraud, only that devise, not the entire will, is ordinarily invalid. Comment d to Restatement of Wills § 8.3.

Answer **(B) is incorrect**. Hal was not merely mistaken as to the contents of the will but had been fraudulently induced by Barry to sign it. Thus, the portion of the will procured by the fraud is invalid. Comments d and j to Restatement of Wills § 8.3.

Answer **(C) is correct**. A gift is procured by fraud if the wrongdoer knowingly or recklessly made a false representation to the donor about a material fact that was intended to and did lead the donor to make a donative transfer that the donor would not otherwise have made. Barry knowingly lied to Hal about the will intending to induce Hal's execution of it. Thus, Barry committed fraud. However, the fraud only extended to the bequest to Barry since the will was otherwise prepared as Barry described and Hal intended. The result is that the bequest to Barry is invalid, but the will otherwise remains as written. Illustration 8, Comment j to Restatement of Wills § 8.3.

Answer (D) is correct. Hal's failure to review the will does not invalidate it. As explained above, it is Barry's fraud that invalidated Hal's will to the extent it was not drafted as Hal intended.

45. UPC § 3-905 provides that a provision in a will purporting to penalize any interested person for contesting the will or instituting other proceedings relating to the estate is unenforceable if probable cause exists for instituting proceedings. There is probable cause for instituting a proceeding when there is evidence that would lead a reasonable person, properly informed and advised, to conclude that there is a substantial likelihood that the challenge would be successful. Comment c to Restatement of Wills § 8.5. Given the circumstances, a reasonable person would conclude that there was a substantial likelihood that the challenge would be successful, so the no-contest clause would not penalize Uma and Leo—even if they lost the case.

46. No. Since Nick does not receive any benefit under the will (*i.e.*, he is wholly disinherited), the no-contest clause provides no incentive for him not to contest the will. In order for a no-contest clause to discourage someone from contesting a will, the person must be receiving some benefit under the will that would be put at risk by the contest. In other words, the no-contest clause trap must be baited with a benefit in the will. Otherwise, the contestant has nothing to lose. Lawrence H. Averill, Jr. UNIFORM PROBATE CODE IN A NUTSHELL (5th ed. 2001) § 7[a][1] (hereinafter, "Averill _____".)

47.	**Answer (C) is correct.** UPC § 2-502(a)(2) requires that the will be signed by the testator or in the testator's name by some other individual in the testator's conscious presence and at the testator's direction (*i.e.*, **Answer (D) is incorrect**). Requiring "conscious presence" means that Jo need only be within the range of one of Mario's physical senses, such as hearing. She need not be in his physical presence or within his line of sight (*i.e.*, **Answers (A) and (B) are incorrect**). As they spoke with one another about the telephone call while she was in the kitchen, she was in his conscious presence. While the UPC has eliminated any requirement that the witnesses sign *as witnesses* in either the testator's or one another's presence, it is necessary that any proxy who signs on behalf of the testator do so in the testator's conscious presence. For a discussion contrasting the conscious presence requirement and the line of sign requirement more generally, *see* Andersen § 7[B][2][d]. Virtually all states permit someone to sign on behalf of the testator. Some states may impose additional requirements. For example, New York requires that the proxy also sign his own name. N.Y. Est. Powers & Trust Law § 3-2.1(a)(1). As a practical matter, this is undoubtedly wise even when not legally required.

48.	**Answer (B) is correct.** UPC § 2-502(a)(3) requires the witnesses to observe either the signing of the will or the testator's acknowledgment of that signature or acknowledgment of the will. Since an acknowledgment of the will suffices, there is no requirement that a witness actually see the will being signed (*i.e.*, **Answer (A) is incorrect**) or that the testator acknowledge both the signature and the will (*i.e.*, **Answer (D) is incorrect**). The issue is whether or not Mario acknowledged the will to Keith and Jo. The UPC's language does not require *verbal* acknowledgment, and the notes to the UPC state that an acknowledgment need not be expressly stated but can be inferred from the testator's conduct. Mario asked Keith and Jo to witness the will. They knew Mario had asked Jo to sign the will for him, and Mario saw the signature Jo had made for him. Mario indicated his approval; thus, it can be inferred that Mario had acknowledged the will to Keith and Jo (*i.e.*, **Answer (C) is incorrect**). Not all jurisdictions permit acknowledgment by non-verbal implication: Oregon, for example, requires that the witnesses must see the testator sign the will or hear the testator acknowledge the will. Or. Rev. Stat. § 112.235; Comment f and statues relevant to comment f, Restatement of Wills § 3.1.

49.	**Answer (A) is correct.** UPC § 2-502(a)(3) requires that the will be signed by at least two individuals, each of whom signed *within a reasonable time after* witnessing either the signing of the will or the testator's acknowledgment. While the ideal will execution ceremony involves near simultaneous signatures by the testator and the witnesses, this process is not legally required. Indeed, as explained below, the UPC does not even require the witnesses to sign in the testator's presence. Jo and Keith signed the following morning which is arguably within a reasonable time period. As explicitly noted in the UPC notes, the UPC does not require signing before the testator's death (*i.e.*, **Answer (C) is incorrect**). At least one court has affirmed that "reasonable time" may include a time after death. *See, e.g.*, *In re Estate of Jung*, 210 Ariz. 202, 109 P.3d 97, 102 (Ariz. App.2005). The issue of witnesses signing after a testator's death can arise in any state that does not require the witnesses to sign in the testator's presence. In some of those states (including states with the UPC or variations of it on this point), courts have concluded that the witnesses must sign before the testator's death because the will becomes effective at death—and if the will is not valid at death, it cannot become so afterwards. *See, e.g.*, *Estate of Saueressig*, 28 Cal. 4th 1045, 1056, 44 CR3d 672, 680 (Calif. 2006); *In re Estate of Flicker*, 215 Neb. 495, 339 N.W.2d 914 (Neb. 1983); *Matter of Estate of Royal*, 826 P.2d 1236, 1238-1239 (Colo.1992); *Matter of Estate of Mikeska*, 140 Mich.App. 116, 362 N.W.2d 906, 910-911 (Mich. 1985); *Rogers v. Rogers*, 71 Or.App. 133, 691 P.2d 114, 115 (Or. 1984).

Answer (B) is incorrect. The UPC does not require witnesses to sign in the testator's presence. The only presence requirement in the UPC is the "conscious presence" requirement described in UPC § 2-502(a)(2) when someone signs on behalf of the testator. Some non-UPC statutes require the witnesses to sign the will in the testator's presence (*see, e.g.,* Tex. Prob. Code Ann. § 59). Some impose additional requirements for presence: requiring the testator to sign (or acknowledge) in the presence of witnesses (*see, e.g.,* R.I. Gen. Laws § 33-5-5*)* or that witnesses sign in the presence of each other (*see, e.g.*, Iowa Code Ann. § 633.279). Depending upon the jurisdiction, "presence" may mean the less restrictive "conscious presence" test (*see* the answer above) or the more restrictive "line-of-vision" test (*i.e.*, must be able to see if chooses to look). Comment p and statutes relevant to comment f, Restatement of Wills § 3.1.

Answer (D) is incorrect. The UPC does not contain a specifically prescribed time limit for the witnesses to sign but rather a "reasonable time" requirement. N.Y. Est. Powers & Trust Law § 3-2.1(a)(4) is an example of a statute that does have a specifically prescribed time period: it requires the witnesses to sign within 30 days.

50. **Answer (B) is correct.** UPC § 2-504(c) provides that a signature affixed to a self-proving affidavit attached to a will is considered a signature affixed to the will if necessary to prove the will's due execution. Since the signatures on the affidavit are necessary to prove the will's due execution, each signature will be considered as affixed to the will (*i.e.*, **Answer (A) is incorrect**). This provision in the UPC was intended for this type of situation since some courts had refused to consider the affidavit's signatures as part of the will. Most courts in states with self-proving affidavits have, however, followed the UPC approach. Comment r Restatement of Wills § 3.1. In some of those states, though the will is deemed signed as a consequence of the affidavit's signature, the will is not considered self-proved. *See, e.g.*, Tex. Prob. Code Ann. § 59(b). That is, the signatures are counted once, but not twice, which means there remains a significant disincentive to signing only the affidavit.

Answer (C) is incorrect. Consistent with the historical Anglo-America norm, the UPC does not require wills to be notarized. Self-providing affidavits, however, must be notarized. *See* UPC § 2-504.

Answer (D) is incorrect. Usually, the fact that the witnesses' signatures precede the testator's is not problematic so long as the testator and the witnesses sign in a single, continuous transaction. Comment m, Restatement of Wills § 3.1. This occurred with Jorge, Wendy, and Chayah sitting together at Jorge's dining table. However, some courts have imposed a strict requirement that the testator sign first. *See, e.g., Wheat v. Wheat*, 156 Conn. 575, 244 A.2d 359 (Conn. 1968).

51. No state requires either an attestation clause or a self-proving affidavit. However, attestation clauses are customarily used in all states, and self-proving affidavits are typically used in those states that permit them. An attestation clause reciting what the witnesses observed and did is located below the testator's signature and above the witnesses' signatures. Though never required, it is useful because it raises a *rebuttable* presumption of the truth of the recital. Comment q to Restatement of Wills § 3.1. A self-proving affidavit is a separate instrument from a will. When it is used, it is usually affixed to the will. Its precise legal effect varies among those states that permit them, but its purpose is to eliminate the need for having the witnesses testify upon the filing of the will to prove its authenticity. In some jurisdictions a self-proved will *conclusively* establishes that all formalities have been met. Comment r to Restatement of Wills § 3.1. When there is a self-proving affidavit, the UPC *conclusively* presumes that all the signature requirements have been met and creates a *rebuttable* presumption that all of the other requirements have been met. Comment r to Restatement of Wills § 3.1. Remember: the witnesses' signature on a will—with or without an attestation clause—need not be notarized, but the signatures on a self-proving affidavit must be notarized. (Review the answer above, regarding when signatures on a self-proving affidavit may be counted as if on the will; *see, e.g.*, Dukeminier p. 211 regarding when a notary may be counted as a second witness (some states, yes; some states, no)).

52. **Answer (E) is correct.** Luz's gift makes her an interested witness; however, Nina's appointment does not (even though she is entitled to a fee for serving as executor, she has to earn it—it is not a gift). The UPC § 2-505 provides that "the signing of a will by an interested witness does not invalidate the will or any provision of it." Thus, the gift to Luz did not disqualify her from serving as a witness. Several states have similar rules, such as Florida Stat.Ann. § 732.504 and New Jersey Stat.Ann. §§ 3B:3-7, 8. Statutory note b to Restatement of Wills § 3.1.

Answer (A) is incorrect. Only under the original common law rule would the will be void because Luz was an interested witness. Modern statutes change the result in various ways (see above and below).

Answer (B) is incorrect. In many states an interested witness takes no more than what the witness would have taken if the testator had died intestate. For example, *see* Ill.

Comp. Stat. ch. 110 1/2, ¶ 4-6, Indiana Ann. Code § 29-1-5-2(b)(c) and New York Est. Powers & Trusts Law § 3-3.2. Similar statutes provide that the gift is preserved so long as there is one or more other disinterested witnesses who can corroborate the will's execution, such as Texas Probate Code Ann. §§ 61, 62 and Washington Rev. Code Ann. § 11.12.160. Statutory note c to Restatement of Wills § 3.1.

Answers (C) and (D) are incorrect. As explained above, Nina is not an interested witness, and Luz's interest in the will does not affect the will's validity under UPC § 2-505. However, in some states, the will would be valid, but the gift to Luz would be voided. For example, Louisiana Civil Code Ann. arts. 1591-1593 and Rhode Island Gen. Laws § 33-6-1, 3. Statutory note d to Restatement of Wills § 3.1.

53. **Answer (B) is the correct answer.** UPC § 2-502(b) provides that a will is as valid as a holographic will, whether or not witnessed, if the signature and material portions of the document are in the testator's handwriting. Thus **Answer (A) is incorrect** because witnesses are not required for a holographic will, and **Answer (C) is incorrect** because there is no requirement that it be dated. A minority of states follow the UPC approach to unattested holographic wills (*i.e.*, not requiring the entire will to be in the testator's handwriting but only material portions). For example, Mich. Comp. Laws Ann. § 700.2502(2), (3) and Cal. Prob. Code §§ 6111, 6111.5. Statutory note 1(a), (b) to Restatement of Wills § 3.2.

Answer (D) is incorrect. However, almost half of the states have no statutory holographic will provision. Statutory note 2 to Restatement of Wills § 3.2.

Answer (E) is incorrect. However, many states that permit unattested holographic wills require that the entire document and signature be in the testator's handwriting. Since this will includes both handwritten and pre-printed portions, it will not be valid. While some states are more liberal with respect to non-handwritten language in the will (*i.e.*, the courts will merely ignore such language; this is the surplusage approach), the pre-printed language in this will is necessary to the will. If the pre-printed language were ignored, the document consists of nothing but names and dates. Tex. Prob. Code Ann. § 60, for example, is one of many statutes that requires the will to be entirely in the testator's handwriting. Some states have additional requirements, such as being dated (*e.g.*, Okla. Stat. Ann. tit. 84, § 54). Other states have their own variations, such as only permitting members of the armed forces to use unattested holographic wills (*e.g.*, N.Y. Est. Powers & Trusts Law § 3-2.2). Statutory note 1(c) to Restatement of Wills § 3.2.

54. **Answer (E) is correct.** UPC § 2-502 requires only that a duly attested will be "in writing." It does not require it to be written in English. It does not require that the type of writing be identical throughout the will. Thus, part of the will may be handwritten while part of it is printed by computer, or part of it may be in one language while the remainder is in another. The will includes all of the writing at the time of the testator's signature; therefore, the will as changed to include the Urdu handwriting is a valid attested will. Therefore, **Answers (A) and (D) are incorrect**. No state requires a will

be written in English, though one written in another language raises practical problems, such as accurate interpretation and, possibly, questions of testamentary intention and undue influence.

Answer (B) is incorrect. UPC § 2-502 requires that the will be signed by at least two individuals, each of whom signed within a reasonable time after he or she witnessed either the signing of the will or the testator's acknowledgment of that signature or acknowledgment of the will. In this situation, the two witnesses witnessed the signing of the will, and thus, they met the requirements. There is no requirement that witnesses know the instrument being signed is a will, and therefore, there is no requirement that they be able to testify as to the testator's testamentary intentions. Even in those states that have a publication requirement ensuring that the witnesses know the instrument is a will, there is no requirement that the witnesses know the terms of the will.

Answer (C) is incorrect. In most jurisdictions that permit holographic wills, a testator may validly make a handwritten alteration of a previously executed attested will so long as the alteration and signature are entirely in the testator's handwriting (and any other requirements, such as dating, are fulfilled). Comment g to Restatement of Wills § 3.2. Asma's will, however, was not a *previously* executed will when she made the handwritten alterations (*i.e.*, it was not an executed will until *after* the handwritten alterations had been made). Thus, the alterations do not constitute a holographic codicil.

55. **Answer (A) is incorrect**. UPC § 2-502(b) provides that a will is valid as a holographic will, whether or not witnessed, if the signature and material portions of the document are in the testator's handwriting. There are no requirements that the handwriting be on any particular material, such as paper. Purported holographic wills have been written on tractor fenders, bedroom walls, and furniture. In the case of the tractor fender, the entire fender was admitted to probate and stored with the case files. Dukeminer 239-240.

Answer (D) is correct. Although all of the writing was in the testator's handwriting, there was no signature. UPC § 2-502(b) requires not only that material portions of the document be in the testator's handwriting but also that it actually be signed by the testator in his handwriting. There is no requirement that it be dated. Thus, **Answers (B) and (C) are incorrect**.

Answer (E) is incorrect. Witnesses are not required under UPC § 2-502(b) so long as the if testator's signature and material portions of the document are in the testator's handwriting.

56. **Answer (D) is correct**. If the proponent of the document establishes by clear and convincing evidence that the decedent intended the document to constitute the decedent's will, UPC § 2-503 provides that a document is treated as if it had been executed in compliance with UPC § 2-502. Given the circumstances, it is clear that Jo intended for the document to be her will—even though she did not complete signing it and the witnesses did not sign it.

Answer (A) is incorrect because UPC § 2-503's specific purpose is to "save" wills that do not meet the requirements of UPC § 2-502 so long as there is clear and convincing evidence that the defective execution did not result from irresolution or from circumstances suggesting duress or trickery. Comments to UPC § 2-503. Very few states have adopted laws similar to this section. For example: Colo. Rev. Stat. § 15-11-503 (with significant deviations); Haw. Rev. Stat. Ann. § 560:2-503; Mich. Comp. Laws Ann. § 700.2503; Mont. Code Ann. § 72-2-523; S.D. Codified Laws § 29A-2-503; and Utah Code Ann. § 72-2-503. Statutory note 1 to Restatement of Wills § 3.3.

Answer (B) is incorrect. UPC § 2-503 does not require "substantial compliance" with UPC § 2-502 in order to "save" a defectively executed will. It only requires clear and convincing evidence that the decedent intended the document to be her will, which is a much more liberal standard. For a comparison of the two standards, *see* Dukeminer 233-235 and Anderson 56-62.

Answer (C) is incorrect because the only portion of the will in Jo's handwriting is her partial signature.

57. **Answer (D) is correct**. UPC § 2-507 provides that a will can be revoked by executing a subsequent will that expressly revokes the previous will. Since the handwritten note conforms to the requirements for a holographic will under UPC § 2-502, the handwritten note is a subsequent will. The terms of the subsequent will expressly revoke the previous will (*i.e.*, "Yesterday's will is void."). A valid holographic will (such as the note) revokes a valid formal attested will (such as the Monday will.) The subsequent will does not have to include new testamentary provisions. UPC § 1-201(55). **Answers (C) and (E) are incorrect**.

Answers (A) and (B) are each incorrect because the Monday will was revoked before the lawyer received the handwritten note. UPC § 2-507(b) provides for revocation by "revocatory act," such as writing "void" on the will, whether or not the cancelling words touch the words of the will. However, if another person take revocatory action on behalf of the testator, it must be in the testator's conscious presence. For a discussion of the necessity of the revocatory words touching the words of the will and similar requirements in some states, *see* reporter's note 6 to Restatement of Wills § 4.1.

58. **Answer (A) is incorrect.** Dependant relative revocation applies to make an otherwise valid revocation ineffective. In this case, there has not been an otherwise valid revocation. Also note that although the UPC takes no official position on the judicial doctrine, there is likely to be little room for the doctrine in those jurisdictions that have adopted both UPC § 2-503 and UPC § 2-509. Comment to UPC § 2-507.

Answer (C) is correct. The lawyer did not take the actions in the testator's conscious presence. If another person takes revocatory action on behalf of the testator, it must be in the testator's conscious presence.

Answer (B) is incorrect. The printed note does not qualify as a holographic will, so it cannot revoke the will. Revocation by subsequent will cannot be effective unless the subsequent will is valid. The subsequent will does not have to include new testamentary provisions. UPC § 1-201(55). **Answers (C) and (E) are incorrect**.

59. **Answer (B) is correct**. Since the 2005 will does not explicitly revoke the 2000 will, the question is whether the 2005 will was intended to replace rather than supplement the 2000 will. UPC § 2-507(d) provides that the testator is presumed to have intended a subsequent will to supplement rather than replace a previous will if the subsequent will does not make a complete disposition of the testator's estate. The comment to the section explains that this presumption is made when the subsequent will does not have a residuary gift (or otherwise fails to dispose of the entire estate). So long as this presumption is not rebutted by clear and convincing evidence, the subsequent will revokes the previous will only to the extent the subsequent will is inconsistent with the previous will. Thus, in this situation, as there is no other evidence, each will is fully operative on the testator's death to the extent they are not inconsistent. Since it is not inconsistent to give both Anna and Maria their cash gifts, both gifts are made. Franklin, however, rather than Julio, receives the household effects because the 2005 will's gift to Franklin revoked the 2000 gift to Julio. Pradeep's residuary gift stands since nothing in the 2005 will is inconsistent with it.

    Answers (A), (C), (D), and (E) are incorrect. Inconsistent will provisions are not blended together.

60. Since Seth intended to revoke the 2005 will when he tore-up the will, the presumption is that those parts of the 2000 will revoked by the 2005 will are revived. UPC § 2-509(b) provides that, if a subsequent will that partly revoked a previous will is thereafter revoked by a revocatory act, a revoked part of the previous will is revived unless it is evident from the circumstances of the revocation of the subsequent will or from the testator's contemporary or subsequent declarations that the testator did not intend the revoked part to take effect as originally executed. Thus, as there is no evidence that Seth did not intend to revive those part of the 2000 will, those parts were revived by his revocation of the 2005 will. Comment to UPC § 2-509(b).

61. UPC § 2-507(c) provides that the testator is presumed to have intended a subsequent will to replace a previous will if the subsequent will makes a complete disposition of the testator's estate. The comment to the section explains this presumption is made when the subsequent will makes a residuary gift (or otherwise disposes of the entire estate). So long as this presumption is not rebutted by clear and convincing evidence, the subsequent will replaces the previous will. Thus, in this situation, as there is no other evidence, the 2005 will entirely replaces the 2000 will. **Answer (C) is correct. Answers (A), (B), and (D) are incorrect** since no part of the 2000 will is valid.

62. **Answer (D) is correct**. *See* above Question 59 regarding the 2005 will wholly revoking the 2000 will on these facts. UPC § 2-509(a) provides that, if a subsequent will that

wholly revoked a previous will is thereafter revoked by a revocatory act, the previous will remains revoked unless it is revived. The previous will is revived if it is evident from the circumstances of the revocation of the subsequent will or from the testator's contemporary or subsequent declarations that the testator intended the previous will to take effect as executed. Thus, if no contrary evidence is introduced, or if the evidence is inconclusive, the 2000 will remains revoked by the 2005 will. **Answers (A), (B), and (C) are incorrect** for the reasons explained. Comment to UPC § 2-509(b).

63. **Answer (B) is correct**. UPC § 2-509(c) provides that, if a subsequent will that revoked a previous will in whole or in part is thereafter revoked *by another later will* (rather than a revocatory act), the previous will remains revoked in whole or in part, unless its revoked part is revived. The previous will or its revoked part is revived only to the extent it appears *from the terms of the later will* that the testator intended the previous will to take effect. Evidence of the testator's intention to revoke the initial will is limited to the text of the final will; no evidence extrinsic to the final will is permitted. This is a different rule than when the second will (on these facts) is revoked by a *revocatory act*. The result in this situation is that neither the 2000 will nor the 2005 will controls the distribution of the probate estate, which will be distributed under the intestacy statute. **Answers (A), (C), and (D)** are incorrect for the reasons explained.

64. **Answer (A) is incorrect**. It does not acknowledge the doctrine of integration, which means that all papers present at the time of the execution and intended to be part of the will are part of the will. Thus, the envelope and the papers inside it can be integrated into a single will. Restatement of Wills § 3.5.

     Answer (B) is incorrect. Due execution does not require the testator's signature or the signature of the witnesses to appear on a page containing provisions of the will. Comment e to Restatement of Wills § 3.5.

     Answer (C) is incorrect. Since the pages inside the envelope and the envelope are integrated into the will, the will was validly executed and attested. There is no "error."

     Answer (D) is correct. Under the doctrine of integration, a will can consist of sheets of paper containing dispositive or other provisions that are inside an envelope on the outside of which are the signature of one or more of the testator and the witnesses. Comment e to Restatement of Wills § 3.5. The physical connection provided by sealing the envelope supports an inference that the sheets inside and the envelope were present at the time of execution and were intended by the testator to be part of the will. Comment e to Restatement of Wills § 3.5.

65. **Answer (A) is incorrect**. If the letter met the requirements for being a valid will, it would be a codicil to the will. However, this is not the only way in which the letter may affect the disposition of the estate. For example, a document not meeting the requirements of a valid will may be incorporated by reference into a valid will.

Answer (B) is incorrect. UPC § 2-510 provides that any writing in existence when a will is executed may be incorporated by reference if the language of the will manifests the intent to incorporate and descries the writing sufficiently to permit its identification. However, under the doctrine of republication by codicil, a will is treated as re-executed (*i.e.*, re-published) as of the date of the last validly executed codicil unless the effect would be inconsistent with the testator's intention. Restatement of Wills § 3.4. Thus, any writing in existence on the date of the codicil may be incorporated by reference if the intention and identification are clear as they are on these facts. **Thus, (D) is correct**.

Answer (C) is incorrect. As explained above, extrinsic documents may be incorporated by reference. However, this answer refers to UPC § 2-513 which allows separate writings to dispose of items of tangible personal property other than money regardless of whether or not the writings were in existence when the will was executed. Both § 2-510 and § 2-513 give testamentary effect to writings that do not qualify as validly executed wills. The latter section is more liberal but only applies to gifts of tangible personal property other than money; the former section applies to gifts of any type of property but is more restrictive because the document must be in existence when the will was executed.

66. **Answer (A) is correct.** UPC § 2-512 provides that a will may dispose of property by reference to acts and events that have significance apart from their effect upon dispositions made by the will, whether they occur before or after the execution of the will. While the taping of the names to the household effects are acts referenced in the testator's will, the sole significance (*i.e.*, purpose) of the acts is to direct the disposition of the property with the tape on it. Thus, the acts do not qualify under UPC § 2-512.

Answer (B) is incorrect since the actions do have significant independence as required under UPC § 2-512.

Answer (C) is incorrect because the actions permitted under UPC § 2-512 are not required to occur before or at the will's execution but may occur later.

Answer (D) is incorrect because UPC § 2-513 requires the writings to describe the property and be signed by the testator. If each piece of tape named the beneficiary, described the property, and was signed, each might qualify under UPC § 2-513. Also, note that if each were wholly in the testator's handwriting, each might also qualify as a holographic codicil.

67. **(A), (B), and (C) are true**. Dukeminer 288-294; McGovern § 4.9.

(D) is not true. In terms of the laws of wills, joint and mutual wills are inherently revocable and do not have unique revocation requirements. However, any will—joint, mutual or otherwise—that is executed pursuant to a binding contract may not be revoked without potential contractual consequences. Contracts not to revoke a will are simply contracts; they do not involve the laws of wills. Under UPC § 2-514, the execution of a joint or mutual will does not create a presumption of a contract not to revoke the will or wills. Dukeminer 288-294; McGovern § 4.9.

68. **Answer (B) is correct**. There is an ambiguity because the description of the tract does not fit any tract actually owned when Zane executed his will. The preponderance of the evidence as to Zane's intention should determine how the will is interpreted. His ownership of a similarly described tract that was not devised to anyone else and his building the house on that tract show by a preponderance of the evidence that Zane intended to give the tract he did own to Fred. Illustration 2, Restatement of Wills § 11.2.

In some jurisdictions, extrinsic evidence may only be considered by a court if the ambiguity is *latent* (*i.e.*, the problem is not with the text but with its application, such as a mis-described beneficiary or asset) rather than *patent* (*i.e.*, the text of the will itself lacks clear meaning). Reporter's note 2 to Restatement of Wills § 11.2.

Answer (C) is incorrect. Zane's intention need only be proven by a preponderance of the evidence. Restatement of Wills § 11.2.

Answers (A) and (D) are incorrect for the reasons explained.

69. **Answer (D) is correct**. When the ambiguity is with respect to the description of property and there is no evidence or rule of construction that would assist in resolving the ambiguity, the solution of last resort is to construe the document to refer to the property having the lowest value. Since Dawn intended to give Julia one of the three bracelets, at the very least, we know she intended to devise a bracelet of at least the lowest value. Illustration 4 and comment k to Restatement of Wills § 11.2. Thus, **Answers (B) and (C) are incorrect**. Note that some state courts disfavor the use of extrinsic evidence more than the Restatement position. Reporter's note 2 to Restatement of Wills § 11.2.

Answer (A) is incorrect. Even when there is no resolution of an ambiguity, the gift in an ambiguous provision need not always fail. The will should be construed to carry out the donor's intention to make a gift whenever it can be. Comment k to Restatement of Wills § 11.2.

70. Since the ambiguity is in the description of the donee, a solution of last resort would be to construe the document to refer to all the persons to whom the description applies. It is clear from the will that Dawn intended to devise the property to one of her cousins named Julia. Thus, as a solution of last resort, the provision may be construed to refer to both cousins named Julia, and each would take half of the $250 bracelet as tenants in common. Illustration 9 and comment k to Restatement of Wills § 11.2.

71. **Answer (A) is correct**. Although the text of the devise is not ambiguous on its face, the extrinsic evidence reveals that the language did not precisely fit any person when

the will was executed. Thus, extrinsic evidence of Abel's intention may be considered in resolving the ambiguity. The testimony of the drafting attorney is exactly the sort of extrinsic evidence that is probative of Abel's intention. Illustration 6 and comment j to Restatement of Wills § 11.2. Note that some state courts disfavor the use of extrinsic evidence more than the Restatement position. Reporter's note 2 to Restatement of Wills § 11.2.

Answers (B), (C), and (D) are each incorrect because extrinsic evidence should be used to determine Abel's intention especially since the drafting attorney has offered to provide such evidence.

72.   The use of two provisions to make pecuniary gifts to the same person creates an ambiguous situation since it is reasonable to infer that Bud would have used a single provision to make a pecuniary gift to each person. Thus, extrinsic evidence, if available, should be introduced to determine Bud's intention. This evidence may show Bud intended to make a gift of $5,000 or $25,000 (or, presumably less likely, $30,000) to Wayne. It may also be used to show if Bud intended to make one gift to Wayne and another gift to someone else. Illustration 11, comments k and o to Restatement of Wills § 11.2. Reporter's note 2 to Restatement of Wills § 11.2.

73.   **Answers (A) and (B) are incorrect**. There is no evidence whatsoever that Hersh intended to give half of $10,000 to each woman or that he intended to give $10,000 to each woman. Thus, neither Answer (A) nor Answer (B) resolves the ambiguity. Both answers are inconsistent with what is known about Hersh's intention: he intended to give $10,000 to one Anna.

Answer (C) is correct. If there is not a preponderance of the evidence to manifest Hersh's actual intention, then there is a constructional preference for the result that favors the family member. This constructional preference is to attribute to Hersh what is considered to be a common intention of testators. This attribution is necessary because which Anna Hersh actually intended to benefit is unknown (or at least not known by a preponderance of the evidence). Comment j to Restatement of Wills § 11.3. Thus, **Answer (D) is incorrect**.

74.   **Answer (A) is incorrect**. There is no evidence whatsoever that Hersh wanted to give half of $10,000 to each of two women. What is known about Hersh's intention is that he intended to give $10,000 to one Anna.

Answer (B) is incorrect. No distinction is made between whole bloods and half bloods. Comment j to Restatement of Wills § 11.3.

Answer (C) is incorrect. No distinction is made between adopted and biological family members. Comment j to Restatement of Wills § 11.3.

Answer (D) is correct. Anna Casto is a closer family member than Anna Thurber, thus the construction that benefits Anna Casto is to be preferred. Comment j to Restatement of Wills § 11.3.

75. **Answer (B) is incorrect**. This provision is not ambiguous because it can be implemented as written with certainty. However, even though the terms are possibly correct expressions of Gerald's intention, there is extrinsic evidence suggesting that they may not be. This is not an issue of resolving an ambiguity but of reforming a mistake. Comment a to Restatement § 12.1.

     Answer (C) is incorrect because it misstates the standard of proof. Restatement § 12.1.

     Answer (D) is correct. Although at variance with many state courts, the Restatement position authorizes the reformation of wills to reflect mistaken expressions of intention. The standard for reformation is clear and convincing evidence, which is higher than the standard of proof for resolving ambiguities (which is preponderance of the evidence, Restatement § 11.1) Comment i to Restatement § 12.1. Thus, **Answer (A) is incorrect**. Note that UPC § 2-601 does not require reformation but does allow for the judicial adoption of a general reformation doctrine for wills. Comment to UPC § 2-601.

76. No. The issue is whether the will as executed reflected Gerald's intention at the time of execution. Gerald's later-formed intentions require additional testamentary action, such as executing a codicil. Reformation is not available to correct a failure to prepare and execute a will, nor is it available to give effect to the testator's post-execution change of mind or any other changes of circumstances. Comment h to Restatement § 12.1.

77. **Answer (A) is correct**. UPC § 2-604(b) abandons the "no-residue-of-a-residue rule." The UPC provides that, if the residue is devised to two or more persons and if one share fails to pass for any reason (*e.g.*, death of a beneficiary), the failed share passes to the other residuary devisees in proportion to the interest of each in the remaining part of the residue. Thus, Nick receives his 50% and Marie's. **Answer (C) is incorrect**.

     Answer (B) is incorrect. The "no-residue-of-a-residue rule" would have this result, and the intestate heirs would succeed to Marie's failed gift. Although this rule remains in effect in some states, it is revoked in the Uniform Probate Code.

     Answer (D) is incorrect. The Uniform Probate Code requires Marie to survive Harlan by 120 hours. If she survived for the 120 hours but died before the residuary estate was distributed, her estate would have received 50% of the residue, but she died within 24 hours.

78. Yes. Under the "anti-lapse" statute of the Uniform Probate Code, since Marie is a descendant of Harlan's grandparents, the gift to her failed because she failed to survive Harlan by 120 hours. However, a substitute gift is made to Wanda as Marie's surviving descendant. UPC § 2-603(b)(1).

79. No. The substitute gift would still be made to Wanda even though the will conditioned the gift to Marie upon her survival. This result under the current Uniform Probate Code is inconsistent with the result under the prior Uniform Probate Code and most state laws which except from the anti-lapse statute gifts expressly conditioned upon survival.

UPC § 2-603(b)(3). This aspect of the current Uniform Probate Code has been criticized a great deal. Dukeminier 395-397.

80. **Answer (D) is correct**. Example 6 to UPC § 2-603 explains that, in a situation such as this, half of the gift goes to the surviving child and the other half goes to the surviving grandchildren who were the children of the deceased child. Because the alternative devise to Alfonso's children is a class gift and because one of the class members, Jessica, failed to survive Jose by 120 hours and left descendants who survived Jose by 120 hours, subsection (b)(2) applies and substitutes Luis and Nick for Jessica. Thus, **Answers (A), (B), and (C) are incorrect**.

81. **Answer (D) is correct**. In a significant departure from the laws of many states, the Uniform Probate Code § 2-606 adopts an intent theory for ademption of specific gifts. The code presumes that a gift should adeem if the property specifically gifted in a will is not owned when the testator dies. However, the code allows the beneficiary the opportunity to prove that ademption was not intended by the testator. Example 3 to Uniform Probate Code § 2-606 makes clear that deliberately giving away such property is good evidence that the testator intended the gift to adeem; however, Isabel is entitled to produce evidence to the contrary, but she has the burden of proof.

   Answers (A) and (B) are incorrect. Isabel would only be entitled to the cash value if she met her burden of proof showing that Tina did not intend the gift to adeem even though she deliberately gave it away. UPC § 2-606(a)(6).

   Answer (C) is incorrect. Uniform Probate Code § 2-606 abandons the identity theory of ademption.

82. Yes. Since Tina did not deliberately give the painting away after executing her will, Isabel could likely establish that Tina did not intend the gift to adeem, which would entitle Isabel to a cash bequest instead. Example 2 to Uniform Probate Code § 2-606. Remember, however, that Uniform Probate Code § 2-606's intention theory is a significant departure from the laws of many states.

83. **Answer (C) is correct.** Following the traditional approach, the Uniform Probate Code includes all stock from stock splits in the gift. However, the Uniform Probate Code also includes all stock dividends too, which is not the traditional approach. Under UPC § 2-605, Monica is entitled to all 440 shares. Thus, **Answers (A) and (B) are incorrect**.

84. **Answer (A) is correct**. Unlike stock dividends, cash dividends paid on the stock during the testator's life are not included in the gift made to the beneficiary. This is both the traditional approach and the approach of UPC § 2-605. **Answers (B), (C), and (D) are incorrect**.

85. For a marriage lasting 15 years or longer, the elective-share percentage is 50%. Thus, Diane's elective-share amount is 50% of $600,000 (*i.e.*, Aaron's $300,000 probate estate + Aaron's $100,000 nonprobate transfer + Diane's $200,000 assets). All of Dynai's

assets count first toward satisfying the elective-share amount. Aaron's probate estate and nonprobate transfers to others are liable for the unsatisfied balance of $100,000. Illustration 1 to Restatement of Wills § 9.2. (Note that UPC § 2-202 has only been adopted in a few states. Also, note that in a community property state a spouse's testamentary power of disposition is typically limited to the spouse's half of the community probate property because the surviving spouse retains half of the community property. McGovern § 3.8.)

86. **Answer (C) is the correct answer**. Since all of the described assets comprise Christopher's probate estate, Emily is entitled to an amount equal to the value of her elective share percentage of the augmented estate less the value of Emily's property included in the augmented estate, and Ava will inherit the balance. *See* UPC §§ 2-202 – 2-210. (In a community property state, a spouse's testamentary power of disposition is typically limited to the spouse's half of the community probate property because the surviving spouse retains half of the community property. *See* McGovern § 3.8.)

    Answer (A) is incorrect. UPC §§ 2-209 – 2-210 prevent Ava from succeeding to Christopher's entire probate estate notwithstanding the terms of Christopher's will unless the value of Emily's property included in the augmented estate exceeds the percentage share amount. If Christopher and Emily lived in a non-community property state that has not adopted the augmented estate concept followed in the Uniform Probate Code or adopted an elective share system, Answer (A) would be correct.

    Answers (B) and (D) are incorrect. Madison, as Christopher's heir, is entitled to an intestate share of his probate estate only if he died intestate. Since there is a valid will, Madison does not receive anything.

87. **Answer (D) is correct**. Matthew will receive an intestate share of Haskell's probate estate since Matthew was omitted from the will. UPC § 2-302(a)(1). In almost every state that has not enacted the Uniform Probate Code, statutes grant marital and non-marital "omitted" or "pretermitted" children certain rights in their parents' estates under some circumstances; the details vary from state to state. McGovern § 3.5.

    Answer (A) is incorrect. Matthew is an "omitted child" and entitled to the share Matthew would have received had Haskell died intestate.

    Answer (B) is incorrect. The birth of the children after the execution of the will did not revoke the will.

    Answer (C) is incorrect. Since Candace is the surviving parent of Aiken and Jenna, they are not entitled to an interest in Haskell's estate.

88.   Common will substitutes include certain revocable inter vivos trusts, life insurance policies, pension and profit-sharing plans, and multiple-party accounts with banks and other financial intermediaries, if their written terms direct, in effect, that the assets be paid to the designated person. Will substitutes also include payable-or transfer-on-death arrangements, joint ownership with right of survivorship, and annuities with death benefits. Comment a to Restatement of Wills § 7.1.

89.   **Answer (D) is correct.** Abe's trust instrument need not be executed in compliance with the statutory formalities precisely because the trust is not a will. A will transfers ownership of probate property *at death*. However, the property subject to Abe's trust is not probate property at death because it is then treated as no longer owned by Abe but rather by the trustee and the beneficiary. An inter vivos trust (unlike a will) is a means to *presently* transfer ownership during the settlor's lifetime. Abe transferred legal title to Naomi and a nonpossessory future equitable interest to Helena when the trust *was created,* not when Abe died. The fact that Helena's interest was subject to Abe's power to revoke or amend the trust, or is subject to a condition of surviving Abe and may be subject to other conditions, does not transform the trust into a will (*i.e.*, the trust instrument need not comply with the statutory formalities for wills). Comments a and b to Restatement of Wills § 7.1. **Answers (A), (B), and (C) are incorrect** for the reasons explained.

90.   No. Abe's declaration of trust effected a present transfer of an equitable nonpossessory future interest to Helena in just the same way it would have had he entered into an agreement of trust with a third party. That is, whether or not the settlor serves as trustee does not affect whether or not the trust must comply with the statutory formalities for wills in order for beneficial interests to pass as a result of the settlor's death. Comment b to Restatement of Wills § 7.1.

91.   **Answers (A), (C), and (D) are incorrect.** Since it is the present assignment of a contract right, a life insurance beneficiary designation need not comply with the statutory formalities required for a will. There is no distinction between initial beneficiary designations and subsequent designations. When the insured dies, the proceeds are paid to the current beneficiary pursuant to the terms of the policy. Comment c to Restatement of Wills § 7.1.

      Answer (B) is correct. The proper execution of a life insurance beneficiary designation form creates a contract right in the designated beneficiary to collect the proceeds of the policy on the insured's death. Although the life-insurance contract pays out at death, the beneficiary designation immediately confers a contract right on the beneficiary subject to the terms of the policy, which usually reserve to the owner the right to change the beneficiary and that the beneficiary survives the insured. Since it confers a contract right, life insurance beneficiary designations need not comply with the statutory formalities required for a will. The proceeds pass to the beneficiary outside of probate pursuant to the terms of the policy. Thus, as Helena held the right to collect the proceeds when Abe died, she, rather than Naomi or an intestate heir, is entitled to the proceeds. Comment c to Restatement of Wills § 7.1.

92. No. The terms of the policy are what control payments. The most recent beneficiary designation executed in compliance with the terms of the policy conferred the contractual right to receive the proceeds to Helena so long she survived Abe and Abe had not filed the requisite forms with the insurance company to change beneficiaries. Abe's will does not override the terms of the life insurance policy. If Helena were a beneficiary under the will, she may be put to an equitable election to deliver the proceeds as directed in the will in exchange for the devise to her in the will. Note that in certain jurisdictions wills can determine the beneficiary of some nonprobate assets, but that is exceptional. For example, *see* Wash. Rev. Code §§ 11.11.003-11.11.901. For discussion, *see* Dukeminier 332-333. These so-called "super wills" provide a single document for determining ownership in an effort to reduce (presumed unintentional) inconsistencies between nonprobate and probate dispositions. The Uniform Probate Code expressly prohibits the use of wills to change rights of survivorship or pay-on-death designations in bank accounts. UPC § 6-213(b). Although the Uniform Probate Code takes no explicit position on the use of wills to change beneficiary designations on other nonprobate assets, the general rule in most jurisdictions is that wills are ineffective to do so. However, concern to ameliorate situations in which testators were confused or uneducated has led to some inconsistencies in the law and may provide policy rationales for more "super will"-type legislation. Roger W. Andersen, Understanding Trusts and Estates § 2 (3rd ed. 2003) (hereinafter "Andersen _____".)

93. **Answer (A) is incorrect**. Nathan's interest in the farm was not conditioned on his surviving Mina. Survivorship language was not used. Mina reserved only a life estate, and so she had no interest in the farm at her death that would pass through probate.

Answer (B) is incorrect. While revocable deeds are legally permissible, this was not a revocable deed. Mina made a completed and irrevocable gift to Nathan. She could not revoke it by her will or otherwise. Andersen § 17.

Answer (C) is correct. The deed made a present and irrevocable gift of a nonpossessory future interest to Nathan. As a lifetime gift, the deed was not a will and did not need to comply with the statutory formalities for a will. It removed the farm from Mina's probate estate, and since it was an irrevocable gift, she had no authority to revoke it and give the farm to Dawson under her will. Since no survivorship language was used, at Nathan's death his remainder interest passed to Rebecca pursuant to his will. This question is based on *Henkle v. Henkle*, 600 N.E.2d 791 (Ohio App. 1991) though the same result would be reached elsewhere. Andersen § 17. **Answer (D) is incorrect** for the reasons explained above.

94. Each of the following issues, factors, and considerations must be explored with Anthony because there is no "one size fits all" analysis.

Costs and Transfers. While it is true that probate court costs and executors' commissions will be avoided, the total costs for a living trust might be higher. If the beneficiaries receive the assets free-of-trust at Anthony's death, the assets will still have to be transferred to the beneficiaries when Anthony dies, but the use of a living trust will also require the assets to be transferred to the trustee while Anthony is alive. Also, transfers to the trust while Anthony is alive may entail other costs (such as the legal costs of preparing deeds or stock transfer fees). Since they tend to be more complicated than wills, the legal fees for preparing living trusts are often greater than the fees for a comparable will. Whether or not avoiding probate reduces costs depends on each client's situation and varies from state to state. For example, if Anthony owns real estate in another state, avoiding ancillary probate with a living trust may save considerable expenses. *See* Dukeminier 318-319.

Timing and Flexibility. The trustee who succeeds Anthony when Anthony dies will not need to seek court authorization to administer the trust estate. The trust continues with its investments, and usually, a trustee has considerably more flexibility in managing a trust than an executor has with managing an estate. Avoiding the delays of probate or the restrictions on an executor may be important, especially if Anthony owns a closely-held business for example. Since he is a professional, it would be important to understand how his obstetrics practice is organized and operated. *See* Dukeminier 318.

Creditors' Rights. In probate, there often is a shortened statute of limitations that applies to creditors that is usually without an analog for living trusts. Thus, probate may be useful to cut-off the rights of some creditors. This may be very important for Anthony. As an obstetrician exposed to malpractice claims, the shortening of the limitations period through probate could be very valuable and may be lost by avoiding probate. *See* Dukeminier 318.

Privacy. One clear advantage that living trusts have over wills is that probate is a public process, but trust administration typically is not. The terms of the will, the names and addresses of the executor and beneficiaries, as well as information on assets and creditors are all likely to become public information if Anthony's estate passes through probate. Avoiding this publicity may be important to Anthony for personal, business, or strategic reasons (*e.g.*, reducing the likelihood of a disgruntled non-beneficiary "fishing" for a legal challenge to the disposition). *See* Dukeminier 318-319.

Avoiding Will Contests. Living trusts may help defend against will contests. The reduced publicity may be one factor. Another factor is that, if Anthony funds and manages the trust as trustee for some while before his death, it will be more difficult (as a practical matter) for anyone to prove he did not know the terms of the trust or had executed the trust instrument while mentally incapacitated or under undue influence. *See* Dukeminier 320.

The Law of Wills. By not using a will, the law of wills may or may not apply to solve unanticipated problems. That is, depending upon the jurisdictions involved, the laws of wills relating to divorce, adoption, lapse, ademption, *etc.* may or may not apply to a revocable trust. The result is that often these rules of construction are applied inconsistently to nonprobate transfers, such that there is considerable lack of certainty, which may result in litigation. Even very careful drafting of the revocable trust may not solve unanticipated problems that might (or might not) be solved by these doctrines. *See* Dukeminier 320.

Estate Tax Issues. Despite what Anthony may have read in those anti-probate books, the assets of the living trust will be fully included in his gross estate for federal tax purposes even though not part of any probate estate. *See* Dukeminier 321.

Pour Over Will. Even when the intention is to fully fund a living trust, it is not unusual for one or more assets to fail to be transferred to the trust, such as an asset acquired after the living trust is executed. Thus, there is a need for "pour over" wills that "pour over" into the trust any assets not in the trust when the settler dies. Anthony will need to execute a pour over will, and to the extent any assets pass pursuant to the will into the trust, probate will be necessary. *See* Dukeminier 310.

Miscellaneous Specific Issues. In some jurisdictions, the costs and expenses of probate may be controlled by statute and may be high enough that avoiding probate is almost always a good idea. Depending on jurisdictions, there may be restrictions on wills that do not apply to living trusts (e.g., pretermitted child statutes or reduced complications for trustees of inter vivos trusts compared to testamentary trusts). There may also be concerns that a person who is not a resident of Anthony's state would not be allowed to serve as executor of his estate but can serve as trustee of his living trust. *See* Dukeminier 319-320.

95.   **Answer (A) is incorrect**. UPC § 2-511(a) expressly provides that a will may validly devise property to the trustee of a trust regardless of the existence of the corpus of the trust.

Answers (B) and (C) are incorrect. UPC § 2-511(a) expressly provides that a will may validly devise property to the trustee of a trust even if the trust is amended after the execution of the will. Note that this is a different rule than the general rule under UPC § 2-510 for incorporating a writing into a will by reference, which requires the writing to be in existence when the will is executed.

Answer (D) is correct. UPC § 2-511(a) expressly provides that a will may validly devise property to the trustee of a trust regardless of the existence of the corpus of the trust and even if the trust is amended after the execution of the will.

96.   **Answer (B) is correct**. While divorce commonly revokes benefits under a will for a former spouse, UPC § 2-804 enlarges this revocation to benefits conferred on spouses in revocable inter vivos trusts, life insurance, pension plans (to the extent permitted

under federal law), pay-on-death transfers and other nonprobate transfers. Further, it also revokes benefits for the former spouse's relatives (regardless of age) who are not the decedent's heirs. UPC § 2-804(a)(5), -(b)(1). The property that would otherwise pass to the relatives of the former spouse is instead distributed as if all of the relatives disclaimed. UPC § 2-804(d). Thus, for life insurance policies, the proceeds will be paid to the alternative beneficiary if one is named. In this case, the Park Slope Hospital will be entitled to the proceeds. **Answers (A), (C) and D are incorrect** for the reasons explained.

97.   **Answer (C) is correct.** A provision in a promissory note directing payments to someone other than the payee in the event of the payee's death is a valid nonprobate transfer at death under UPC § 6-101. It does not need to comply with the statutory formalities for wills nor does it have to be probated. Also the personal representative does not have any power or duty with respect to the note. Comment to UPC § 6-101. Thus, Nan has no power over it as executor. Jen has the sole right to be paid as a result of the terms of the note. **Answers (A) and (B)** are incorrect for the reasons explained.

98.   **Answers (A) is incorrect** because the antilapse provisions of UPC § 2-706 apply to give Ava her father's share of the proceeds.

        Answer (B) is correct. UPC § 2-706 applies to many nonprobate transfers antilapse provisions that parallel those that apply to wills under UPC § 2-603. Thus, given their family relationship, Ava is entitled to receive Gary's full share of the proceeds just as she would be entitled to receive his full share of a gift under Frieda's will. Comment to UPC § 2-706. Note that the antilapse provisions in some states do not apply to nonprobate transfers.

        Answer (C) is incorrect. The antilapse provision entitles Ava to the full share her father would have received. UPC §§ 2-706, 2-603.

        Answer (D) is incorrect. Although no alternative beneficiary was designated, none was needed since Coyt and Ava survived Frieda. However, if the terms of the policy provided an alternative beneficiary to take in the event that both children did not survive Frieda, the terms of the policy would have prevailed over the antilapse provisions of UPC § 2-706. Comment to UPC § 2-706.

99.   **Answer (A) is correct.** Although the antilapse provisions of UPC § 2-706 apply to life insurance beneficiary designations and many other types of nonprobate transfers, the provisions do not apply to interests held in joint tenancy with rights of survivorship or to parties of multi-party joint accounts held with rights of survivorship. UPC § 2-706. Thus, **Answer (B) is incorrect.**

        Answer (C) is incorrect. Joint accounts with rights of survivorship are nonprobate assets that pass outside the probate system.

        Answer (D) is incorrect for the reasons explained.

100. **Answer (A) is incorrect**. Divorce has significant effects on nonprobate transfers. UPC § 2-804 revokes benefits conferred on former spouses in revocable inter vivos trusts, life insurance, pension plans, pay-on-death transfers, and certain other nonprobate transfers.

Answer (B) is correct. Even though UPC § 2-804 revokes benefits conferred on former spouses in pension plans, David's pension plan was an ERISA plan. The U.S. Supreme Court has held that ERISA pre-empts state statutes such as UPC § 2-804. *Egelhoff v. Egelhoff*, 532 U.S. 151 (2001). Thus, his ex-wife Harriet rather than his seven year old daughter, Candace, is entitled to the pension plan despite the divorce—and despite the property settlement that specifically awarded the entire pension plan to David and other assets to Harriet. The facts of the question are based on those in *Egelhoff*. Though the decision has been criticized and lower courts have not been as quick to find federal pre-emption when ERISA is involved, this is a recent U.S. Supreme Court case. For discussion, *see* Dukeminier 340-341. Two morals are clear. The first is that the best practice is always to change nonprobate beneficiary designations immediately after a divorce. The second is that even in state-oriented laws, such as probate, federal pre-emption is always a potential issue. Note that, despite the pre-emption issue, the divorced spouse may be determined to have effectively waived his or her interest as part of the divorce proceeding with the waiver effective under federal common law. At least one state supreme court has so ruled. *Keen v. Weaver*, 121 SW.3d 721 (Tex. 2003). **Answer (C) is incorrect** for the reasons explained.

Answer (D) is incorrect. Resulting trusts may arise when express trusts fail, but here there was no intention to create a trust. Restatement of Trusts §§ 7.

101. **Answer (B) is correct**. The Uniform Probate Code provides that a multi-party account (*i.e.*, a "joint account") is presumed to belong to the parties in proportion to their net contributions, which is the contributions of the parties plus their pro rata share of interest and dividends appropriately reduced by withdrawals. This presumption can be overcome by clear and convincing evidence that one of the parties intended to make a gift to the other. UPC §§ 6-211, 6-206(b), comment to UPC § 6-211. **Answers (A), (C), and (D)** are incorrect for the reasons explained.

102. Unless there is a specified nonsurvivorship arrangement in the terms of the account, on the death of Ron, Tae, as the surviving party, owns the account. UPC § 6-212(a).

103. Yes. As his surviving spouse, Lori would own the amount Ron owed immediately before death: $533.33. UPC §§ 6-211, 6-212(a).

104. Yes. Tae and Lori would each own whatever they owned before Ron's death plus an equal share of what it was Ron owned. Thus, Tae would own $1,066.66 plus $266.66 and Lori would own $0 plus $266.66.

105. Unless there is a specified nonsurvivorship arrangement in the terms of the account, Lori as the surviving party owns the account even though she never contributed to the account. UPC § 6-212(a).

106.   Yes. However, no more than what Ron owned at the time of his death is liable: $533.33. UPC § 6-102.

107.   Before Lila's death, Penny has no right to the account. UPC § 6-211(c). However, after Lila's death, she is entitled to whatever remains in the account. UPC § 6-212(a).

108.   **Answers (A) and (B) are incorrect**. A joint tenant in real estate cannot devise his share by will. The joint tenants have rights of survivorship. When Sal died, his interest in the real estate ceased, and therefore, he had no more interest in the real estate that might have been devised by his will. If Sal wanted to convey the property pursuant to his will, he would have had to sever the joint tenancy during life, converting it into a tenancy in common. However, he has no power to sever the joint tenancy at his death with his will. Dukeminier 344-345; Averill § 18.

    Answer (D) is correct. As Sal's joint tenant, Tad succeeded to complete ownership of the real estate when Sal died. Furthermore, in most states, Sal's creditors will not be able to seize the interest he owned in the real estate during his life because his interest ceased at his death. The general rule is that a creditor must seize a joint tenant's interest during the tenant's lifetime. Thus, Tad is now the sole owner of the real estate, free and clear of any of Sal's creditor's claims. Dukeminier 345; Averill § 18. **Answer (C) is incorrect** for the reasons explained.

109. **Answer (C) is correct.** As her executor, Richard will have the duty to administer the assets comprising her probate estate. Having only a life estate in the family farm, Darla has no interest in the farm that survives her death to pass as part of her probate estate and subject to probate administration. Unless there is a specified nonsurvivorship arrangement in the terms of the account, on Darla's death, Carla, as the surviving party, owns the account they shared. UPC § 6-212(a). This means no part of the account becomes part of the probate estate. Similarly, Stephen is entitled to whatever remains in the other savings account as a result of the "POD" designation. UPC § 6-211(c). Thus, Darla's probate estate consists only of the securities account, the home, and her car, furnishings, and various other items of tangible personal property. Restatement of Wills § 7.1; Dukeminier 30; Averill § 2.

      Answers (A), (B), and (D) are incorrect for the reasons explained.

110. **Answer (E) is correct**. Life insurance proceeds paid to the designated beneficiary are not part of the probate estate. The same is true for real property held in a joint tenancy and interests in trusts, including "qualified terminable interest property" (QTIP) trusts. Restatement of Wills § 7.1; Dukeminier 30, 904-905; Averill §§ 2, 62[B].

      Answers (A), (B), (C), and (D) are incorrect for the reasons explained.

111. Since Darla personally retained the life estate in the family farm when she conveyed the remainder to Carla, the family farm is included in Darla's gross estate for federal tax purposes under IRC § 2036. Both savings accounts are included in her gross estate except for any portion of the multi-party account contributed by Carla. IRC § 2044. Similar rules apply for determining the value of the joint tenancy in the home includible in her gross estate. The life insurance policy is includible in her gross estate under IRC § 2042. Assuming the QTIP election was properly made, the QTIP trust, too, will be included in Darla's gross estate for federal tax purposes. IRC § 2056(b)(7). Thus, it is very important to remember that the laws determining what is included in the probate estate are independent of the laws determining what is included in the gross estate for federal tax purposes. Dukeminier 872-877, 904-905; Averill § 62.

112. **Answer (A) is correct.** Even if no notice of any type is given, UPC § 3-803(a)(1) bars any claim by creditors made after one year of the decedent's death.

      Answers (B) and (C) are incorrect. Providing notice by publication or mail shortens the period, but neither is required for the one-year limit. UPC § 3-803(a)(2).

      Answer (D) is incorrect for the reasons explained.

113.   **Answer (A) is incorrect.** Notice by publication in a newspaper requires a four-month claim period. UPC §§ 3-801, 3-803(a)(2).

      Answer (B) is incorrect. While mailing the notice to known creditors will limit those creditors claim period to 60 days, it does not reduce the one-year claim period of other creditors. UPC §§ 3-801, 3-803(a)(2).

      Answer (C) is incorrect. As explained below, those creditors receiving notice by mail will be limited to 60 days rather than entitled to the full four months. UPC §§ 3-801, 3-803(a)(2), Comment to 3-803

      Answer (D) is correct. Simultaneously mailing notice to known creditors and publishing notice for all other creditors is the most efficient means of barring as many creditors' claims as quickly as possible. Those receiving notice by mail will be limited to the 60-day period, and all others will be limited to the four-month period. By mailing the notice on the first date of the publication notice, the known creditors' claim period will end after the first 60 days of the four-month period. UPC §§ 3-801, 3-803(a)(2), Comment to 3-803.

114.   **Answer (D) is correct.** The multi-party account is only subject to the claims of Darla's creditors if the probate estate is insufficient to satisfy the debts. It is necessary for the creditor to make a written demand on the executor, and it is also necessary for the executor to initiate proceedings to collect on the account within one year of the death. UPC § 6-215.

      Answers (A), (B), and (C) are incorrect for the reasons explained.

115.   Generally, no probate proceeding under the Uniform Probate Code, whether formal or informal, may be initiated more than three years from the date of death. UPC § 3-108. Unless an exception applies, after this three-year period expires, Darla will be conclusively presumed to have died intestate.

116.   Unless a specific exception applies, Joe must file his petition within the latter of (i) three years from his mother's death or (ii) within twelve months of Richard's instituting the informal probate. UPC §§ 3-108, 3-401.

117.   **Answer (A) is correct.** Since there is an ongoing informal administration, Richard's powers are extensive. They include the power to make extraordinary repairs is provided by UPC § 3-715(7). The power to borrow money is provided by UPC § 3-715(16). The power to hold securities in the name of a nominee is provided by UPC § 3-715(14). The power to set his own reasonable compensation for serving as executor is provided by UPC § 3-715(18).

      Answers (B), (C), and (D) are incorrect for the reasons explained.

118   As executor, Richard must exercise his powers consistently with his fiduciary duties, which include the duty to observe the standard of care applicable to trustees and to

settle and distribute the estate expeditiously, efficiently and consistently with the best interests of the estate. UPC § 3-703.

119   Richard's principal responsibilities will be (1) to inventory and collect Darla's assets; (2) to manage the assets during the probate administration; (3) to receive and pay the claims of any creditors including taxes; (4) to clear any titles; and (5) to distribute the remaining assets to Stephen, who is entitled to receive them under Darla's will. Dukeminier 31.

120.   (1) Fully funded revocable inter vivos trusts are used to avoid the probate system.

(2) Testamentary marital trusts are commonly used to qualify gifts to spouses for the marital estate tax deduction while controlling the identity of the remainder beneficiaries.

(3) Trusts are often used to provide for the management of property for minors and incapacitated persons so that guardianship proceedings are not necessary.

(4) The use of trusts to hold property for beneficiaries can provide tax and creditor-protection benefits that outright gifts cannot. Dukeminier 488; Averill § 11.

121.   **Answer (D) is correct**. A valid, enforceable express trust has been created. UTC § 401 and 402 codify the generally accepted principles for the creation of an express trust. Restatement of Trusts § 22.

Answers (A), (B), and (C) are incorrect. Constructive trusts and resulting trusts are remedies to prevent unjust enrichment. These remedies are often used when express trusts have not been created. That is, when a settlor's apparent intentions cannot be carried out for one reason or another, courts may use constructive trusts or resulting trusts to prevent the "trustee" from being unjustly enriched. Restatement of Trusts §§ 7, 8, 21, 24.

122   **Answer (D) is correct**. A self-declaration of trust for personal property does not require a delivery of the property, because the settlor retains legal title. When Bo declared himself trustee of his personal property, an express trust was established. Comment e to Restatement of Trusts § 10. Note it is the better practice to have the settlor "re-title" the property in the settlor's name "as trustee."

Answers (A), (B), and (C) are incorrect because Bo validly established an express trust by his declaration, and no transfer of the property into his name as trustee was necessary.

123.   Yes. If the settlor is not the trustee, the property must be transferred to the trustee. The rule that no transfer is necessary only applies when the settlor is the sole initial trustee. Comment e to Restatement of Trusts § 10.

124   **Answer (D) is correct**. If a settlor's intention to create a trust is clear even though he or she fails to name a trustee, then the appropriate court will appoint a trustee. Restatement of Trusts § 31.

Answers (A) and (B) are incorrect. A valid trust was created.

Answer (C) is incorrect. There is no rule under which beneficiaries are necessarily entitled to serve as trustees. The court will appoint a successor trustee in its discretion. As a practical matter, it is likely that a court would appoint the executor of Dusan's estate.

125   **Answer (A) is correct**. A valid express trust has been created. Huan's intention is clearly manifest with the deed and the letter. Restatement of Trusts § 13; UTC § 402(a)(2).

Answer (B) is incorrect. The deed need not identify Lim as trustee.

Answer (C) is incorrect. Lim need not execute a written instrument.

Answer (D) is incorrect. The settlor's intention must be clear. However, no specific terms such as "trust" or "trustee" are required to create a trust. Of course, the use of the terms "trust" and "trustee" are likely to make the settlor's intention indisputable.

126.   **Answer (B) is correct**. A trust is created of Doug's equitable contingent remainder interest in the trust previously created by his father, but not of his expectancy in the estate of his mother. A person who expects to receive property in the future by the will of a living person or by intestate succession has no presently existing interest of which to make a declaration of trust or a transfer to another in trust. Such an expectancy is not a contingent future interest but a mere hope or expectation however well founded or likely to materialize. By all traditional and current concepts of property, expectancies are not property interests. Comment a, illustration 1 to Restatement of Trusts § 41. **Answers (A), (C), and (D) are incorrect** for the reasons explained.

127   **Answer (B) is correct.** A trust may be created, and once it is created, it may continue for the benefit of a person not in existence or not ascertainable at the time of the creation if the beneficiary and his or her interests will be ascertainable. Thus, a child who has not been born or conceived at the time of the creation of a trust can be a beneficiary of the trust. Comment c to Restatement of Trusts § 44. If Wallace dies without children, Nancy will hold the farm for his successors in interest. Illustration 1 to Restatement of Trusts § 44. Note that this disposition does not create a problem under the rule against perpetuities since the child's interest will vest, if it ever does, within 21 years of Wallace's death. Thus, **Answers (A), (C), and (D) are incorrect**.

128.   **Answer (A) is correct**. If the only proof of the oral trust is Ohan's testimony of what Armen told Ohan about the conveyance, it is likely that Idra will retain the fee simple title. Ohan's testimony is inadmissible hearsay. Accordingly, there is no admissible evidence of the oral agreement.

Answers (B), (C), and (D) are incorrect. Even if Ohan can produce other evidence of the oral agreement between Armen and Idra, the statute of frauds requires a written document in order to create an enforceable express trusts of real property. If it can be proven that Idra procured the transfer by fraud, duress, or undue influence or that Armen and Idra were in a confidential relationship at the time of the transfer a constructive trust in favor of Ohan would be the appropriate remedy. Restatement of Trusts § 24.

129. **Answer (C) is correct**. The statute of frauds requires a writing for the inter vivos creation of enforceable express trusts of interests in real property. Restatement of Trusts § 22. Since there is no writing evidencing the trust, Idra may retain the farm, notwithstanding her acknowledgment of the oral agreement unless Ohan can prove that Idra procured the transfer by fraud, duress, or undue influence or that Armen and Idra were in a confidential relationship at the time of the transfer. Comments h-j to Restatement of Trusts § 24.

Answers (A), (B), and (D) are incorrect. Assuming there is no other evidence of Idra's intent at the time of conveyance or of a special relationship existing between Armen and Idra at the time of the conveyance, a constructive trust is not appropriate. The prevailing view is a constructive trust can be imposed on a grantee of a deed only if the transfer was by fraud, duress, or undue influence or the transferor and transferee were in a confidential relationship at the time of the transfer. McGovern § 6.4. There are, however, cases suggesting the use of a constructive trust simply to prevent the unjust enrichment of a grantee who orally agrees but later refuses to hold in trust. Comments h-j to Restatement of Trusts § 24.

130. **Answer (C) is correct.** Because of the pre-existing confidential relationship that existed between Armen and Idra, and Idra's acknowledgment of their agreement, a court is likely to impose a constructive trust on Idra in favor of Ohan, to avoid unjust enrichment by Idra. Restatement of Trusts § 24.

Answers (A) and (B) are incorrect for the reasons explained.

Answers (D) is incorrect. The only proof of the oral trust is hearsay and inadmissable.

131. **Answer (A) is correct**. The testimony of June and Hector is likely to be the evidence needed to prove the creation of the oral express trust and its terms. Most states do not require a writing to create an inter vivos transfer in trust of personal property. Restatement of Trusts § 20. However, UTC § 407 does require "clear and convincing evidence" of the creation of the oral express trust and its terms. Note that some states may require only a "preponderance of the evidence."

Answer (B) is incorrect. Assuming Ohan has "clear and convincing" evidence of the oral agreement. Ohan can simply bring an action to enforce the express trust.

Answer (C) is incorrect. Armen's attempt to create the express trust did not fail for lack of a beneficiary or for failure of the trust's purpose.

Answer (D) is incorrect. Sufficient evidence is available to prevent Idra from retaining the boat for Idra's own use.

132.   **Answer (D) is correct**. Because the oral trust agreement does not satisfy the statute of frauds, Ohan cannot enforce the express trust. Restatement of Trusts § 24. The terms of the deed and the testimony of June and Hector confirm that Armen did not intend Idra to take the farm for Idra's own use, thereby leading to the imposition of a resulting trust in favor of Elma as Armen's successor in interest. Restatement of Trusts §§ 7, 8, 21, 24.

        Answer (A) is incorrect. In order to satisfy the requirements of the statute of frauds, the writing must not only manifest trust intention but also identify the trust property, the beneficiaries, and the purposes of the trust.

        Answer (B) is incorrect. In most states, Elma as Armen's successor in interest has standing to require Idra to return the property. Restatement of Trusts § 24. Note that some states may allow Ohan to impose the constructive trust to avoid Idra's unjust enrichment. Comment g to Restatement of Trusts § 24.

        Answer (C) is incorrect. Equity will not allow Idra to retain the property.

133.   **Answer (C) is correct**. The trust is "passive," and Ohan can demand the transfer of the property to himself. If the statute of uses or a similar "merger" statute is applicable, Idra's legal title merges with Ohan's equitable title, and Ohan owns fee simple title. Restatement of Trusts § 6.

        Answers (A), (B), and (D) are incorrect for the reasons given.

134.   **Answer (A) is correct**. A valid, enforceable express trust exists. Since an express trust exists, the farm is not the subject to the personal obligations of Idra. Restatement of Trusts § 42. UTC § 507 codifies the generally accepted principle.

        Answer (B) is incorrect. Because a valid, enforceable express trust has been established, the trust property is not subject to the personal obligations of Idra.

        Answers (C) and (D) are incorrect. Since an express trust exists, the farm is not the subject to the personal obligations of Idra. If Idra allows the creditor to attach the farm, she will breach her fiduciary duties to Ohan.

135.   **Answer (D) is correct.** Steven retained a reversionary interest in the properties when the trust was created because the remainder interest was not assigned to Tabitha because she was already dead. Harvey inherited Steven's reversionary interest when Steven died and has standing to seek the imposition of a resulting trust since the trust now lacks a beneficiary. See Restatement of Trusts §§ 7, 8.

        Answer (C) is incorrect. A resulting trust is the traditional remedy when a settler attempts to create an express trust but fails.

        Answers (A) and (B) are incorrect. Since Tabitha was not alive when the trust was created, Tabitha did not own an interest that Danny acquired pursuant to UPC § 2-707 or that Andy inherited in a non-UPC state.

136. **Answer (A) is correct**. An express trust is created in a will only if the testator manifests the intent to impose on the devisee legally enforceable duties to manage the property for another. However, only such manifestations of intent which are admissible as proof in a judicial proceeding may be considered. Restatement of Trusts § 13. The Uniform Trust Code has codified these generally acceptable common law principles. See UTC § 402 and commentary. Accordingly, without further admissible evidence of Bao's intent, the language in Bao's will is likely to be found to be "precatory" rather than "mandatory."

> **Answer (B) is incorrect**. Either Chan has fee simple title or an express trust was created for the benefit of Jin.

> **Answer (C) is incorrect**. An express trust was created for the benefit of Jin or Chan owns the stock beneficially.

> **Answer (D) is incorrect**. The use of the words "with the request" generally is considered to be "precatory" rather than "mandatory."

137. **Answer (A) is correct**. It is evident that Bao did not intend Chan to acquire the home for his personal use and benefit. All of the elements of an express trust are present. Restatement of Trusts §§ 13, 17. The Uniform Trust Code has codified these generally accepted common law principles. See UTC §§ 401, 402.

> **Answer (B) is incorrect**. An express trust has been created. Jin will seek to enforce the terms of the express trust.

> **Answer (C) is incorrect.** All of the elements of an express trust are present.

> **Answer (D) is incorrect**. Chan inherited only the legal title; Jin inherited an equitable interest in the vacation home.

138. **Answer (A) is correct**. Because Jin died before Bao, an express trust was not created. Restatement of Trusts § 17. The devise to Chan fails, and Bao's executor should deliver the stock to Bao's residuary beneficiary, the school. Restatement of Trusts § 8. The Uniform Probate Code has codified this generally accepted common law principle. See UPC § 2-604.

> **Answer (B) is incorrect**. Bao's attempt to create an express trust for the benefit of Jin failed because Jin died before the trust was created. Jin's heirs did not acquire any interest in the vacation home.

> **Answer (C) is incorrect**. The executor should not deliver the stock to Chan. If Chan already has the stock, the charity may need to seek the imposition of a resulting trust to acquire the vacation home as Bao's successor in interest.

> **Answer (D) is incorrect**. It is evident that Bao did not intend Chan to acquire the vacation home for his personal use and benefit.

139. The court should appoint a successor trustee to manage the family farm until Jiri attains age 21. An express trust can be created by the settlor's declaration that the settlor holds identifiable property for another. Restatement of Trusts § 10. The Uniform Trust Code has codified this generally accepted common law principle. UTC § 401. The fact that Karmil's declaration of trust was oral is problematic. However, the Uniform Trust Code has adopted the view that, absent a statute to the contrary, an express trust does not need to be evidenced by a trust instrument, if the creation of the oral trust and its terms can be established by clear and convincing evidence. UTC § 407. Assuming that Ayce's and Nona's testimony will be accepted by the court as "clear and convincing" evidence of the creation of the express trust, an express trust was created. The result will differ in a state where the statute of frauds requires a signed writing in order for trusts of real property to be enforceable. The statute of frauds in many jurisdictions requires oral declarations of trust to be in writing. In those states, Dana, as Karmil's heir, would likely retain the family farm. Restatement of Trusts § 22. However, a possible exception exists that may permit Jiri to seek a constructive trust on Dana to prevent Dana's unjust enrichment. See comment j to Restatement of Trusts § 24.

140. **Answer (A) is correct**. An express trust can be created by the settlor's declaration that the settlor hold identifiable property for another. Restatement of Trusts § 10. The Uniform Trust Code has codified this generally accepted common law principle. *See* UTC § 401. The fact that Karmil's declaration was oral is problematic. However, the Uniform Trust Code has adopted the view that, absent a statute to the contrary, an express trust does not need to be evidenced by a trust instrument if its creation and terms can be established by clear and convincing evidence. UTC § 407. The result will differ in a state where the statute of frauds requires a signed writing for declarations of trusts of personal property. Restatement of Trusts § 22.

    Answer (B) is incorrect. Assuming that the friends' testimony will be accepted by the court as "clear and convincing" evidence of the creation of the trust, an express trust was created. The statute of frauds in many jurisdictions requires oral declarations of trust to be in writing. In those states, Dana, as Karmil's heir, would likely retain the painting.

    Answer (C) is incorrect. The traditional view is that a constructive trust is an appropriate remedy when a transferee committed a fraud, exerted undue influence, or breached a confidential relationship. Neither Karmil nor Dana committed any of those acts. However, a possible exception exists that may permit Jiri to seek a constructive trust on Dana to prevent Dana's unjust enrichment. See comment j to Restatement of Trusts § 24.

    Answer (D) is incorrect. It is not the role of a personal representative to manage the settlor's inter vivos trust.

141. **Answer (C) is correct**. An express trust can be created by the settlor's declaration that the settlor was holding identifiable property for the benefit of another. Restatement of

Trusts § 10. The Uniform Trust Code has codified this generally accepted common law principle. See UTC § 401. The same result is likely to happen in a non-UTC state since the writing requirement of an applicable statute of frauds is satisfied. Restatement of Trusts § 23.

Answer (A) is incorrect. If Dana has possession and refuses to cooperate when Jiri seeks to enforce the express trust, the court may need to impose a constructive trust.

Answer (B) is incorrect. All of the elements of a valid, enforceable express trust are present.

Answer (D) is incorrect. It is not the role of a personal representative to manage the settlor's inter vivos trust.

142.   **Answer (A) is correct.** Assuming the Uniform Trust Code was in effect at the time the express trust was created, the settlor may revoke the trust unless the terms of the trust provide the trust is irrevocable. UTC § 602(a). The Uniform Trust Code has reversed the generally accepted common law rule that trusts are presumed to be irrevocable. See Restatement of Trusts § 63. Presumably, a court would likely find that Karmil's conveyance to Phan was clear and convincing evidence of Karmil's intent to revoke the trust. The result is likely to be different in a state where inter vivos trusts are not presumed revocable. See Restatement of Trusts § 63.

   Answers (B) and (C) are incorrect. Karmil retained the power to revoke the trust. See UTC § 602. In a state that has not adopted the Uniform Trust Code approach or if the trust was created before the state adopted that approach, Jiri can file suit for breach of fiduciary duty by Karmil. If Jiri is successful, the court may impose a constructive trust on Phan since Phan was not a good faith purchaser.

   Answer (D) is incorrect. While a court may impose a constructive trust on a third party who participates in a trustee's breach of trust, the third party is generally not personally liable to the beneficiary if the third party is not aware of the trust. UTC § 1012.

143.   **Answer (D) is correct.** It appears as if a valid enforceable express trust was created during Andrew's lifetime even though title remained in Andrew's name until Andrew died. UTC §§ 401, 402. At Andrew's death, the family farm is a nonprobate asset, and Keith's equitable remainder interest became possessory. Restatement of Trusts § 10.

   Answers (A) and (B) are incorrect. An express inter vivos trust does not need to be executed with testamentary formalities. See UTC § 402. The family farm passes pursuant to the terms of the trust, not by the will or by intestate succession.

   Answer (C) is incorrect. Since Andrew did not change the title to the family farm when the trust was created, the family farm still appears to be a probate asset, and Keith will need to take steps to establish the existence of the trust and his ownership under the trust.

144. **Answer (D) is correct**. The fact that there was no transfer of title before Andrew's death and that Andrew retained the power to revoke the trust do not affect the trust's validity. UTC §§ 401, 402. *See* Restatement of Trusts § 10. Since Andrew did not revoke the apparently valid, enforceable express trust prior to his death, the terms of the trust control the disposition of the family farm. Since the trust was created by Andrew's declaration of trust, at his death the family farm is a nonprobate asset, and Keith's equitable remainder interest became possessory.

Answers (A) and (B) are incorrect. An express trust does not need to be executed with testamentary formalities. *See* UTC § 402.

Answer (C) is incorrect. Since Andrew did not change the title to the family farm when the trust was created, the family farm still appears to be a probate asset, and Keith will need to take steps to establish the existence of the trust and his ownership under the trust.

145. **Answer (B) is correct**. At common law, conditions of survivorship were not implied with respect to future interests. *See* comment to UPC § 2-707. The Uniform Probate Code reverses this presumption and requires a future interest owner in a trust to survive until the interest becomes possessory. UPC § 2-707. Because Keith died before Andrew without a descendant surviving Andrew, Keith's contingent remainder failed, and Andrew's reversionary interest in the family farm passed to Billy, as Andrew's sole heir under the intestate succession statute. UPC § 2-707(d); UPC § 2-103(1). The result may differ in a state that has not adopted the UPC approach. Restatement of Trusts § 55.

Answer (A) is incorrect. Pursuant to UPC § 2-707(d), the interest does not pass under Andrew's will but rather under the intestate succession statute. Under UPC § 2-103(1), Billy is Andrew's sole heir.

Answers (C) and (D) are incorrect. UPC § 2-707 required Keith to survive Andrew. In states that have not adopted the UPC approach, Keith's vested remainder is likely to have passed to Ivan and Wanda. Bogert, Trusts (6th ed. 1987) § 38 (hereinafter, "Bogert _____"). Note that, in those states, a successor trustee may need to be appointed in to order to have the property conveyed to Ivan and Wanda as Keith's successors in interest.

146. Since the stocks and the home are probate assets, the executor of Doug's estate will have to use them to satisfy Doug's debts. According to UPC § 3-902, shares of distributees abate without any preference between real or personal property. The stocks and real property should be abated proportionately. Note that in states that have not adopted the Uniform Probate Code approach typically provide that personal property should be abated prior to real property within the same classification of devises. Atkinson § 136. Accordingly, in a non-UPC state, the stock may need to be sold to pay the debts, and the real property will pass to Angelica assuming the state allows testamentary

additions to inter vivos trusts. Most states have statutes similar to UPC § 2-511, which allow probate assets to "pour over" into the trust. If testamentary additions to inter vivos trusts are not allowed, Bobby and Carlie would succeed to the estate remaining after all debts are paid. McGovern § 6.2.

147. **Answer (B) is correct.** Ramona is entitled to an elective share amount equal to the sum of the decedent's net probate estate augmented by the $100,000 in the revocable trust. UPC §§ 2-203, 2-205. Note that the answer may differ in a state that has not adopted the UPC approach. Restatement of Trusts § 25. For example, in a community property state, the surviving spouse will likely be entitled to half of the community probate assets and to be compensated for half of what the decedent contributed to the trust. *See* McGovern §§ 3.7, 3.8.

    Answer (A) is incorrect. The trust is valid.

    Answers (C) and (D) are incorrect. The augmented estate consists of the net probate estate and certain nonprobate dispositions.

148. **Answer (C) is correct.** If the creation and funding of the trust were to defraud Haskell's creditors, the creditors can pursue their claims against the trust estate pursuant to state law on fraudulent transfers. The transfer may also constitute a voidable preference in bankruptcy. *See* comment to UTC § 505. If Haskell was not insolvent because of the creation of the trust, the trust estate is not reachable to satisfy Haskell's debts. UTC § 505 adopts this generally accepted principle. Bogert § 48.

    Answers (A) and (B) are incorrect. If the creation and funding were to defraud the creditors, they can still reach the trust estate.

    Answer (D) is incorrect. The trust assets are not reachable by the creditors unless the creation and funding of the trust were to defraud the creditors.

149. **Answer (D) is correct.** During the lifetime of the settlor, the trust estate of a revocable trust is subject to claims of the settlor's creditors. *See* UTC § 505 (a) (1). The result is likely to be the same in a state that has not adopted the Uniform Trust Code. *See* Restatement of Trusts § 25.

    Answers (A), (B), and (C) are incorrect for the reasons given.

150. **Answer (B) is correct.** Following the settlor's death, the trust estate of a revocable trust continues to be subject to claims of the settlor's creditors. UTC § 505(a)(3) adopts this widely accepted principle. *See* Restatement of Trusts § 25. The result may differ in some non-UTC states. *See* Bogert, Trusts § 148.

    Answers (A), (C), and (D) are incorrect for the reasons given.

151. **Answer (A) is correct.** Assuming the terms of the trust, including its irrevocability, can be established by clear and convincing evidence, the fact that the express trust was

created pursuant to an oral agreement should not be determinative of the issue. UTC § 407. If the transfer to Candace was to defraud Haskell's creditors, the creditors can pursue their claims against the property transferred. If not, the property is not reachable to satisfy Haskell's debts. UTC § 505. The same result is likely to occur in a non-UTC state. Bogert § 48.

Answers (B), (C), and (D) are incorrect for the reasons given.

152.   **Answer (D) is correct.** The trust property is not subject to the personal obligations of the trustee. UTC § 507 has codified this generally accepted principle. *See* Restatement of Trusts § 42.

       Answers (A), (B), and (C) are incorrect. Trust property is not subject to the trustee's personal debts.

153.   As long as the creation of the oral trust and its terms can be established, the trust property cannot be reached by the trustee's personal creditors. Restatement of Trusts § 42. Since the trust is oral, the UTC requires "clear and convincing evidence" of the terms of the trust. *See* UTC § 407. The lack of a writing does not affect the validity of the trust as to the real property, and the trustee can properly perform notwithstanding the statute of frauds. Restatement of Trusts § 24. Note that in a state that has not adopted the UTC approach, the existence of the trust may need to be proven by only a "preponderance of the evidence." Restatement of Trusts § 20.

154.   **Answer (B) is correct.** Absent a "spendthrift" or "forfeiture" provision in the trust agreement, the court may authorize a creditor to reach a beneficiary's interest in the trust by attachment of either present or future distributions. UTC § 501 has codified this generally accepted common law principle. *See* Restatement of Trusts § 56.

       Answer (A) is incorrect. Aiken's interest is limited to the income the trust generates during Aiken's lifetime.

       Answer (C) is incorrect. It doesn't matter whether the debt is tortious or contractual in nature. **Answer (D) is incorrect.** To the extent a beneficiary's interest is not subject to a "spendthrift" or "forfeiture" provision, it is generally available to satisfy the beneficiary's creditors.

155.   **Answer (D) is correct.** Whether or not the trust agreement contains a "spendthrift" or "forfeiture" provision, a creditor of a beneficiary generally does not have standing to compel a trustee to make a discretionary distribution from the trust to the creditor or the beneficiary. UTC § 504. However, the creditor may be able to attach the beneficiary's interest, and although the interest is not subject to execution sale, the trustee may be held personally liable to the creditor for any amount paid by the trustee to the beneficiary if the trustee has been served with notice of the attachment. Comment c to Restatement of Trusts § 60.

Answer (A) is incorrect. Aiken's interest is effectively limited to whatever income, if any, is distributed to Aiken in Candace's discretion. The Restatement takes the position that the creditor is entitled to "judicial protection from abuse of discretion by the trustee." However, it also acknowledges that the trustee's refusal to make a distribution under these circumstances may not be an abuse of discretion. Comment e to Restatement of Trusts § 60.

Answer (B) is incorrect. Aiken does not have a mandatory right to the income.

Answer (C) is incorrect. Generally, the only creditor that may be excepted from the general rule is a child, spouse, or former spouse of the beneficiary with a judgment or order against Aiken for support. UTC § 504(c)(2).

156. **Answer (D) is correct.** Whether or not the trust agreement contains a "spendthrift" or "forfeiture" provision, a creditor of a beneficiary cannot compel a discretionary distribution from the trust even if the trustee has failed to comply with a standard of distribution. *See* UTC § 504. However, the creditor may be able to attach the beneficiary's interest, and although the interest is not subject to execution sale, the trustee may be held personally liable to the creditor for any amount paid by the trustee to the beneficiary if the trustee has been served with notice of the attachment. The Restatement limits the portion to which a creditor is entitled of the excess of the beneficiary's actual needs as set by the court. *See* comment c to Restatement of Trusts § 60. The result may differ in a state that has not adopted the UTC or the Restatement approach since Aiken's interest in the trust estate is limited to whatever income is necessary for Aiken's health, education, maintenance, or support, and when Aiken dies, Jenna is entitled to the income not properly distributed to Aiken. The Restatement takes the position that the creditor is entitled to "judicial protection from abuse of discretion by the trustee." However, it also acknowledges that the trustee's refusal to make a distribution under these circumstances may not be an abuse of discretion. Comment e to Restatement of Trusts § 60.

Answers (A), (B), and (C) are incorrect. The only creditor that may be excepted from the general rule is a child, spouse, or former spouse of a beneficiary with a judgment or order against Aiken for support. UTC § 504(c)(2).

157. **Answer (A) is correct.** A creditor of a beneficiary cannot compel a discretionary distribution from a trust even if the trustee has failed to comply with a standard of distribution. UTC § 504. The result may differ in a state that has not adopted the Uniform Trust Code approach. Here, Aiken's interest is limited to whatever income is distributed to Aiken pursuant to the described standard of distribution, and the hospital rendered medical services and should be able to garnish Aiken's interest in the trust. *See* Alan Newman, The Rights of Creditors of Beneficiaries Under the Uniform Trust Code: An Examination of the Compromise, 69 Tenn. L. Rev. 771 (2002).

Answers (B), (C), and (D) are incorrect for the reasons given. While UTC § 504 appears to prohibit the creditor from compelling a distribution, states that have not adopted the Uniform Trust Code approach may allow the hospital to collect from the trustee out of the trust's income if the trust agreement does not contain a "spendthrift" or "forfeiture" provision. *See* Restatement (Second) of Trusts §§ 154, 155, 157 (1959) (Restatement of Trusts (2nd) _____).

158.   **Answer (B) is correct**. Absent a "spendthrift" or "forfeiture" provision in the trust agreement, the court may authorize a creditor to attach a beneficiary's future interest in the trust estate. The Uniform Trust Code codifies this generally accepted common law principle. *See* UTC § 501. The court may even order a sale of the beneficiary's future interest. Restatement of Trusts § 56. However, the value of Jenna's remainder interest is diminished because it is contingent on Jenna surviving Haskell. UPC § 2-707.

   Answer (A) is in correct. The creditor cannot divest Aiken's interest in the trust.

   Answer (C) is incorrect. While a creditor, in theory, may force a judicial sale of a beneficiary's interest, such a sale cannot adversely affect the interests of other beneficiaries.

   Answer (D) is incorrect. Only Jenna's future interest can be attached.

159.   In most jurisdictions, a settlor has the power to include as part of the terms of the trust a provision that prevents a creditor from reaching a beneficiary's interest in the trust or a distribution by the trustee before its actual receipt by the beneficiary. This so called "spendthrift" provision is generally valid in most states as long as it prohibits both voluntary and involuntary transfers of beneficial interests. *See* Restatement of Trusts § 58. These generally accepted principles have been codified in UTC § 502. Accordingly, the creditor cannot attach the beneficiaries' interests in the trust, and the creditors must wait until there are actual distributions to the beneficiaries. If it is valid under state law, the spendthrift provision will be effective in bankruptcy. *See* comment a to Restatement of Trusts § 58. A few states do not recognize the effectiveness of "spendthrift" provisions. McGovern § 13.1.

160.   **Answer (C) is correct**. Even in jurisdictions that do not accept the effectiveness of "spendthrift" provisions, a settlor can generally place a "condition subsequent" on a beneficiary's interest that causes the beneficiary's interest to terminate or change if there is an attempted involuntary or voluntary alienation. Restatement of Trusts § 57.

   Answer (A) is incorrect. Aiken's interest is not affected by the termination of Jenna's interest.

   Answer (B) is incorrect. Aiken's interest is not enhanced by the termination of Jenna's interest.

   Answer (D) is incorrect. Most jurisdictions accept the effectiveness of these so called "forfeiture" provisions.

161. A spendthrift trust is one with a provision that prevents the transfer of a trust beneficiary's interest to another, whether the attempted assignment is by gift, sale, or exchange, or as security for a new or existing debt. Comment c to Restatement of Trusts § 58. Spendthrift provisions are very commonly used, and when applicable, prevent a beneficiary from devising his or her interest in a trust. Thus, much of the academic analysis of future interests assumes the trust has no spendthrift provisions, though in practice, most irrevocable trusts do.

162. The general common law rule is that, if the interest of a deceased beneficiary does not terminate or fail by reason of the beneficiary's death, the interest passes by will or intestate succession. Restatement of Trusts § 55. However, this rule has limited application in practice for two reasons. First, spendthrift provisions prevent the interest from devolving. Second, the interests of trust beneficiaries are usually intentionally designed (through careful drafting) not to survive the beneficiary's death. For example, the beneficiary's interest may explicitly terminate at the end of the beneficiary's life; this is a life estate. With respect to a future interest, the beneficiary's interest may be subjected to an expressed requirement of survival (*i.e.*, by the terms of the trust) or an implied survival requirement (*e.g.*, a statutory implication, such as found in UPC § 2-707). Comment a to Restatement of Trusts § 55.

163. At common law, with the first grant, Alondra's future interest in the first conveyance would pass to her devisees, if she leaves a will, or to her heirs, if she dies intestate. This is because there is no implied condition of survivorship on the future interest. However, with the second grant, the future interest has been made contingent on Alondra's surviving until the time of possession (*i.e.*, being alive at Damian's death). Thus, Alondra could not transfer the remainder to another person (either by will or through intestacy), if she dies before Damian. Dukeminier, 636. A beneficiary's interest that is subjected to an expressed requirement of survival to some certain time (*e.g.*, Alondra's outliving Damian) is not transferable prior to that time. Comment a to Restatement of Trusts § 55. However, the Uniform Probate Code has changed the common law and imposed its own conditions of survivorship. Thus, Alondra cannot transfer the remainder interest in either grant. UPC § 2-707.

164. **Answer (D) is correct**. At common law, Alice and Sam inherited fractional remainder interests in the trust estate. When Alice died, her vested one-half remainder interest passed pursuant to her will to her husband, Ted, since conditions of survivorship are not implied with respect to future interests. Restatement of Trusts § 55. Note that as a practical matters trusts are usually drafted with express limits or conditions that avoid inclusion of beneficial interests in a deceased beneficiary's estate. Comment a to Restatement of Trusts § 55. Consequently, this rule rarely applies with well drafted trusts. However, UPC § 2-707 converts Alice's one-half remainder interest into one contingent on her survival of Cindi, and since Alice did not survive Cindi, Alice's interest would revert to Joe. Averill § 11.05. Sam takes his one-half interest.

    Answers (A) is incorrect because the gift of the remainder interest was not a class gift.

    Answers (B) is incorrect for the reasons explained.

    Answer (C) is incorrect. It describes the common law result.

165. **Answer (A) is incorrect**. The gift of the remainder was a "fractional" gift to Alice and Sam, not a class gift.

    Answer (B) is incorrect. Alice was survived by Michael, so her interest does not revert to Joe.

    Answer (D) is correct. At common law, Alice's interest passed to Ted. *See* comment to UPC § 2-707 and Restatement of Trusts § 55. However, UPC § 2-707 convert's Alice's remainder interest into one contingent on Alice surviving Cindi, and since Alice did not survive Cindi, Michael would be substituted for Alice. **Answer (C) is incorrect** for the reasons explained.

166.   By requiring the trust estate to be distributed "to Donna's children," Joe created a class gift of the remainder interest. The class "opened" when the trust was created and "closed" at Cindi's death. Restatement of Property, Second, Donative Transfers § 26 (hereinafter, "Restatement of Donative Transfers _____"). At common law, Alice and Sam owned vested remainder interests subject to partial divestment when the trust was created, and Nancy acquired the same interest when Nancy was born. Restatement of Donative Transfers § 26.2. When Alice died, her interest passed pursuant to her will to Ted. However, UPC § 2-707 converts the remainder interests into ones contingent on surviving Cindi. Since Alice did not have any children, Sam and Nancy succeed to the trust estate. Thus, Ted, Sam, and Nancy succeed to the trust estate. Restatement of Donative Transfers § 27.3.

167.   **Answer (C) is correct.** If the child in embryo is born alive, the child becomes a "member of the class" and will acquire an interest in the trust estate, thereby partially divesting the other remainder beneficiaries. *See* Restatement of Donative Transfers § 26.2.

     Answers (A), (B), and (D) are incorrect for the reasons given.

168.   **Answer (B) is correct.** At common law, Joe created remainder interests contingent on the remainder beneficiaries surviving Cindi. In addition, Joe created alternative future interests in the survivor or survivors of the remainder beneficiaries. Restatement of Donative Transfers §§ 250, 277. The result is the same under UPC § 2-707 since the trust agreement created an alternative future interest. *See* UPC § 2-707(b)(4).

     Answer (A) is incorrect because there was no class gift to Donna's children (which would have included Nancy) but rather fractional gifts to Alice and Sam.

     Answer (C) is incorrect. Alice's interest was expressly conditioned on surviving Cindi, which means she had no interest at her death to pass to Ted.

     Answer (D) is incorrect. Joe expressly provided for alternative future interests in the event Alice or Sam died before Cindi. That is, he did not retain the interest for himself.

169.   **Answer (D) is correct.** At common law, Alice and her devisee, Ted, are excluded. Restatement of Donative Transfers § 27.3. If the child in embryo is born alive, the child will be a member of the class of beneficiaries. Restatement, Second, Donative Transfers § 26.2. The result is the same under UPC § 2-707.

     Answer (A) is incorrect. The child will be entitled to an interest if born alive.

     Answer (B) is incorrect. Alice's interest was expressly contingent on Alice surviving her grandmother Cindi, and the child in embryo may be entitled to an interest.

     Answer (C) is incorrect. The child will be entitled to an interest if born alive.

170. **Answer (A) is correct**. The class of remainder beneficiaries "closed" when Cindi died because Sam and Nancy were entitled to possession at that time. Any child conceived by Donna after that point in time is not a beneficiary. Restatement of Donative Transfers § 26.2. Note that the result is likely to be the same in a state that has adopted UPC § 2-707.

   Answers (B), (C), and (D) are incorrect because the class has already closed (*i.e.*, no new members to the class can be added after Cindi's death).

171. **Answer (C) is correct.** Savannah's remainder interest passes to Diego according to her will because there was no condition of survivorship in Luis's will. Conditions of survivorship are not implied with respect to future interests. Restatement of Property § 165.

   Answer (A) is incorrect. The remainder interest had been devised to Savannah when Luis died and then passed to Diego when Savannah died.

   Answer (B) is incorrect. Olivia only inherited a life estate.

   Answer (D) is incorrect. Savannah's vested remainder interest was devised to Diego by Savannah's will.

172. **Answer (C) is correct**. The remainder interest devised to Savannah was contingent on Savannah surviving her mother, Olivia. Because Savannah predeceased Olivia, Savannah's remainder interest ceased to exist, and Barclay University's alternative contingent remainder became a vested remainder. Restatement of Property §§ 157, 239.

   Answer (A) is incorrect. Savannah's interest was contingent on Savannah surviving Olivia.

   Answer (B) is incorrect. Olivia inherited a life estate.

   Answer (D) is incorrect. Savannah's interest was contingent on Savannah surviving Olivia.

173. Andrea and Julian would inherit the remainder interest. At common law, the gift to Savannah would have lapsed, and the remainder interest would have been devised to Barclay University. *See* comment to UPC § 2-603. However, most states have enacted "anti-lapse" statutes which create a substitute gift for the deceased devisee's descendants who survive the testator. UPC § 2-603 is a typical "anti-lapse" statute. At Savannah's death, Savannah did not own an interest in the family farm that she could devise to Diego under her will.

174. **Answer (A) is incorrect**. At common law, Savannah's equitable vested remainder would have been devised to Diego under Savannah's will. *See* Restatement of Trusts § 55. However, UPC § 2-707 converts Savannah's interest into a remainder contingent on Savannah surviving Olivia and creates a substituted gift for her children.

Answer (B) is incorrect. Olivia only inherited a life estate.

Answers (C) is incorrect because of the effect of UPC § 2-707.

Answer (D) is correct because Savannah's interest was contingent on her surviving Olivia and her children are the substitute takers. UPC § 2-707.

175. **Answer (D) is correct.** The generally accepted common law rule does not require Martin to reach age 21 prior to Sofia's death. Accordingly, the church's contingent interest became possessory at Sofia's death pending the determination of whether or not Martin attains age 21. Restatement of Property §§ 156, 240.

   Answers (A), (B), and (C) are incorrect for the reasons given.

176. **Answer (C) is correct.** Lily inherited a vested remainder subject to divestment if Lily died without any children surviving her. Lily was survived by her son, Victor; therefore, her vested remainder was not divested, so Lily's interest was devised to Jordan under Lily's will. Restatement of Property § 165.

   Answers (A) and (B) are incorrect. The remainder interest was devised to Jordan under Lily's will.

   Answer (D) is incorrect. The remainder interest was devised to Jordan under Lily's will. Note that the anti-lapse statute is not applicable.

177. **Answer (B) is correct.** Ana's will provides that Lily's vested remainder is divested if Lily is not survived by children. Under UPC § 2-702 Victor would have had to survive Lily by 120 hours. Thus, Lily's vested remainder was divested.

   Answer (A) is incorrect. Lily's interest has been divested.

   Answer (C) is incorrect. Bergman College will take possession when Natalia dies.

   Answer (D) is incorrect. Since there is no evidence that Victor survived Lily, Lily's interest terminated. The anti-lapse statute does not apply to "save" it for Victor.

178. **Answer (D) is correct.** At Maya's death, Eduardo inherited from Maya a vested remainder subject to divestment if Jade is not survived by any children. When Eduardo died, Eduardo devised that interest to Olivia. Olivia now owns the interest that will be divested if neither Mario or Gabriel (nor any other child of Jade) survives Jade. Restatement of Property §§ 157, 165.

   Answer (A) is incorrect. Eduardo's interest was not divested. Olivia inherited his interest and became a member of the class of remainder beneficiaries.

   Answer (B) is incorrect. Olivia inherited Eduardo's interest, and Gabriel became a member of the class of remainder beneficiaries.

Answer (C) is incorrect. Olivia's interest will be divested if Jade is not survived by any of her children.

179 **Answer (B) is correct**. The remainder interests of Mario, Eduardo, and Gabriel were contingent on each of them surviving Jade. When Eduardo died, his interest terminated. Restatement of Property § 157.

Answer (A) is incorrect. Eduardo's contingent interest terminated when he predeceased Jade.

Answer (C) is incorrect. Gabriel became a member of the class of contingent remainder beneficiaries when he was born.

Answer (D) is incorrect. The anti-lapse statute is not applicable.

180. Naomi and Aaron acquired fee simple title. A devise does not have to designate the beneficiary by name. The identity of the grandchildren is a fact of independent significance. Since the disposition of the ranch was a present or immediate class gift, the class closed at Axel's death. Children *conceived* after his death are not members of the "class" of beneficiaries, whether born during or following formal administration of his estate. Restatement of Donative Transfers § 26.1.

181. **Answer (B) is correct**. If the child in embryo is born alive, the class of beneficiaries closes, and that child acquires fee simple title. *See* comment c to Restatement of Donative Transfers § 26.1.

Answer (A) is incorrect. The child must be born alive before the child can acquire title to the property.

Answer (C) is incorrect. If the child in embryo is born alive, the class closes and any other children Sadie may have in the future are excluded.

Answer (D) is incorrect. If Sadie has a child who is born alive, the Boyarin Academy will be divested.

182. Because there were no members of the class of beneficiaries alive or "in embryo" at Axel's death, the class remains "open" until it biologically closes at Sadie's death. The Boyarin Academy acquires title subject to divestment upon the birth or adoption of Sadie's first child. The birth or adoption of any other children Sadie may have will partially divest any previous child or children. Restatement of Donative Transfers § 26.1.

183. No interest is good unless it must vest, if at all, not later than twenty-one years after some life in being at the creation of the interest. John C. Gray, THE RULE AGAINST PERPETUITIES § 201, at 191 (4th ed. 1942).

184. The two basic purposes of the rule against perpetuities are to keep property marketable for productive development in accordance with market demands and to limit "dead hand" control over the property, which prevents current owners from using the property to respond to their present needs. Dukeminier, 674.

185. Because of the unfairness or arbitrariness of applying the rule against perpetuities in many cases, two types of reforms have been suggested. One suggestion is the "wait and see" approach which would not consider the logical possibilities when judging the validity of interests but rather only the actual events that take place with respect to the interests. This "wait and see" approach is literally to wait until after the death of the relevant parties and then see whether or not there is a vesting. The second suggested reform of the rule is for courts to modify the terms of any trust that violates the rule so as to carry out the settlor's intention within the perpetuities period as best the court can. This is known as the "reformation" or "cy pres" reform of the rule. Dukeminier, 697-699; Andersen § 53.

186. The Uniform Probate Code combines approaches to ameliorating the consequences of the rule. The general rule is a "wait and see" approach that adopts a 90 year period. UPC § 2-901(a). If, at that time, an interest has still not vested or has failed, the court is authorized to reform the disposition in the manner that most closely approximates the transferor's manifested plan of distribution and is within the 90 years allowed. UPC § 2-903(1). Note that, in certain situations, the statute also allows earlier reformation. UPC § 2-903(2). Dukeminier, 700-702; Andersen § 53.

187. **Answer (C) is correct**. The executory interest is valid. Because Evan is dead and cannot have any more children, the class has "closed." If either Maria or Brian is alive on the one-hundredth anniversary of Natalie's death, that event will occur during each child's own lifetime, and the rule against perpetuities is not violated. UPC § 2-901. *See* Restatement of Donative Transfers, Chapter 1.

   Answer (A) is incorrect. The rule against perpetuities was not violated.

   Answer (B) is incorrect. If either Maria or Brian is alive on the one-hundredth anniversary of Natalie's death, the charity is divested.

   Answer (D) is incorrect. The class of beneficiaries is limited to Evan's children, Maria and Brian.

188.   John Brown Academy owns fee simple title subject to an executory limitation. Restatement of Property § 158. At common law, the grandchildren's executory interests would have violated the rule against perpetuities and have been invalid. At the time of Aiden's death, the possibility existed that the first child of Oscar to reach age 25 would not do so until after the expiration of the period of the "Rule." Restatement, Second, Donative Transfers, Chapter 1. However, under UPC § 2-901(a)(2), it is likely that the executory interest will vest, if it ever does, within 90 years of Aiden's death. If not, the interest can be reformed pursuant to UPC § 2-903. Some states that have not adopted the Uniform Probate Code approach have modified the common law rule in other ways that may validate the grandchildren's interests.

189.   **Answer (B) is correct**. Trevor had satisfied the condition of the devise prior to Aiden's death and acquired fee simple title at Aiden's death. Restatement of Property § 156.

        Answer (A) is incorrect. Because Trevor reached age twenty-five prior to Aiden's death, the John Brown Academy never acquired an interest in the farm.

        Answers (C) and (D) are incorrect. The devise was not a class gift. Since Trevor reached age 25 prior to Aiden's death and Trevor survived Aiden, no other child of Oscar acquires an interest in the farm.

190.   **Answer (C) is correct**. This does not violate the rule against perpetuities. All of Oscar's children will attain age twenty-one, if they ever do, within twenty-one years of his death. UPC § 2-901. *See* Restatement of Donative Transfers, Chapter 1. When the first child attains that age, John Brown Academy is divested and that child owns the fee simple title subject to partial divestment if any of Oscar's other children reach age twenty-one. Restatement of Property § 239.

        Answer (A) is incorrect. The grandchildren's executory interests are valid.

        Answer (B) is incorrect. The class of beneficiaries includes any grandchild who reaches the age of twenty-one.

        Answer (D) is incorrect. Aiden did not die intestate.

191.   **Answer (C) is correct**. There is not a perpetuities problem. Since Oscar died before Aiden, the class of potential beneficiaries was limited to Angelina, Trevor, and the child in embryo, and all three will attain age twenty-five, if they ever do, within their own lifetimes. Restatement of Donative Transfers, Chapter 1.

        Answer (A) is incorrect. The executory interests of the grandchildren are valid.

        Answer (B) is incorrect. The child in embryo is a life in being for perpetuities purposes if born alive.

        Answer (D) is incorrect. John Brown Academy will be divested as soon as the first child attains age twenty-five.

192.   Rockingham Valley State Hospital owns fee simple title subject to an executory limitation. Restatement of Property § 158. At common law, the executory interest conveyed to the grandchild would have violated the rule against perpetuities. Because the disposition is an inter vivos transfer by deed, at the time of the conveyance, there existed the possibility that Kaden could have another child who would be the parent of the first grandchild to reach age twenty-one and that grandchild may not reach age twenty-one until after the perpetuities period. However, under UPC § 2-901 (A)(2), it is likely that a grandchild will reach age twenty-one within 90 years of the original conveyance. If not, the interest can be reformed pursuant to UPC § 2-903. Some states that have not adopted the Uniform Probate Code approach have modified the common law rule in other ways that may validate the conveyance.

193.   **Answer (B) is correct.** The class of remainder beneficiaries includes any other children Nolan may have, but it does not violate the common law rule against perpetuities because all of the grandchildren's remainder interests will vest, if they do vest, by the time of Nolan's death or nine months thereafter. Restatement of Donative Transfers § 26.2.

       Answer (A) is incorrect. The remainder interest is devised to a class of beneficiaries that stays "open" until Nolan's death. Nolan is presumed to be capable of having more children. If Nolan has another child, that child acquires a vested interest and partially divests the other grandchildren. Of course, Nolan could also adopt more children.

       Answer (C) is incorrect. The specific devise is valid.

       Answer (D) is incorrect. The remainder interest does not violate the common law rule against perpetuities.

194.   Nolan has a life estate, and Dalia owns the remainder interest. However, Dalia's interest is subject to partial divestment if Nolan has more children. Restatement of Donative Transfers § 26.2. At common law, the remainder interest would have violated the rule against perpetuities because after the conveyance Alan could have had more children whose lifetimes could extend beyond the perpetuities period, and their children would have been included within the class of remainder beneficiaries. Consequently, the contingent remainder interests of the unborn grandchildren may not vest in time. Restatement of Donative Transfers, Chapter 1. In addition, even though Dalia's interest was vested at the time the trust was created, her interest would fail under the "all or nothing rule," which states that, if the interest of any potential class members might vest too remotely, the entire class gift is invalid. *Leake v. Robinson*, 2 Mer. 363, 35 Eng. Rep. 979 (Ch. 1817). However, under UPC § 2-901(a)(2), it is likely they will vest within 90 years of the conveyance. If not, the remainder interest could be reformed pursuant to UPC § 2-903. Some states that have not adopted the Uniform Probate Code approach have modified the common law in other ways that may validate the grandchildren's remainder interest.

195.   At common law, the remainder interests devised to Yasmin's grandchildren would have violated the rule against perpetuities. At the time of Fatima's death, there existed the

possibility that Yasmin could have more children who could then have more children who would be included in the class of remainder beneficiaries. Consequently, the remainder interests of those grandchildren of Yasmin may not vest until the death of one of Yasmin's after-born children after the perpetuities period. The "all or nothing" rule would have invalidated even the vested interests of the other grandchildren. Restatement of Donative Transfers, Chapter 1. However, under UPC § 2-901(a)(2), it is likely that the contingent interests will vest, if they ever do, within 90 years of Fatima's death. If not, the remainder interests of the grandchildren can be reformed under UPC § 2-903. Some states that have not adopted the Uniform Probate Code have modified the common law rule in other ways that may validate the grandchildren's interests.

196. At common law, the remainder interest of Hugo's children would have violated the rule against perpetuities. The identity of Hugo's widow will not be known until his death, and it is possible that she was not a "life in being" when Orlando died. Consequently, her remaining lifetime may extend beyond the perpetuities period, and the children's interest would remain contingent until then. The interest of any children born after Orlando's death would have violated the rule, and the "all or nothing" rule would have caused the interests of even Lara, Tyra, and Gerland to be invalid. Restatement of Donative Transfers, Chapter 1. However, under UPC § 2-901(a)(2), it is likely that the contingent interests will vest, if they ever do, within 90 years of Orlando's death. If not, the remainder interests of the grandchildren can be reformed under UPC § 2-903. Some states that have not adopted the Uniform Probate Code have modified the common law rule in other ways that may validate the grandchildren's interests.

197. Alaska, Arizona, Colorado, Delaware, Florida, Idaho, Illinois, Maine, Maryland, Missouri, Nebraska, New Jersey, Ohio, Rhode Island, South Dakota, Virginia, and Wisconsin have each taken some steps towards repealing the application of the rule against perpetuities to at least some private trusts. Some states have explicitly repealed the rule (*e.g.*, Alaska, Delaware, and South Dakota). Some states have not repealed the rule but rather made it optional by allowing settlors to opt-out of its application (*e.g.*, Colorado, Illinois, and Maine). Other states have instead established very lengthy perpetuities periods (*e.g.*, 360 years in Florida, and 1,000 years in Utah and Wyoming). Dukeminier, 719; Andersen, § 53[c].

198. The primary tax motivation is to take advantage of the federal generation-skipping transfer tax exemption. The exempt amount can be transferred to a perpetual trust. No estate tax or generation-skipping transfer tax will ever be due, and the trust can be used to benefit the beneficiaries forever. However, despite the potential tax savings, there are significant practical issues since it is impossible to adequately plan for how circumstances will change during the term of a perpetual trust. First, the number of beneficiaries will multiply. It will be impossible to know the number and needs of beneficiaries indefinitely. Secondly, the administrative costs compared to the multiplied number of beneficiaries may become unduly burdensome; such costs will increase as the number of beneficiaries increase, but each beneficiary's interest will decrease as

the number of beneficiaries increase. Thirdly, the trustees who serve in the future will have had no personal relationship with the settlor, and the settlor will have little control over who becomes trustee (*e.g.*, corporate trustees merge or are acquired and individual trustees die). Fourth, changes in the law are unpredictable, including changes in the tax law. For example, some future legal change may impose considerable taxes on perpetual trusts or may re-impose limits on trust duration. *See, e.g.*, Jesse Dukeminier and James E. Krier, *The Rise of the Perpetual Trust*, 50 U.C.L.A. L. Rev. 1303, 1338-1339 (2003).

199.   **Answer (C) is correct.** Mark owns the equitable life estate and is the donee of a power of appointment, and the New London Academy owns an equitable remainder interest that is subject to divestment if Mark validly exercises the power of appointment in a will. It will not be known until Mark dies whether the power is exercised and the charity is divested. Restatement of Donative Transfers (2nd) § 15.2. Kaspar and Uma are not beneficiaries. UTC § 103(2).

   Answer (A) is incorrect. Mark only owns an equitable life estate and is the donee of a testamentary non-general power of appointment.

   Answers (B) and (D) are incorrect. Mark's exercise of the power will not be effective until Mark's death. Until the power is exercised, the objects of the power have mere expectancies and, thus, are not beneficiaries.

200.   **Answer (B) is correct.** Mark was the donee of a non-general testamentary power of appointment. Since such a power is presumed to be "exclusive," Mark can appoint to any one or more of the objects of the power or permissible appointees. When the will is admitted to probate, the New London Academy is divested. *See* Restatement of Donative Transfers (2nd) § 21.1. Note that statutes in a few states provide that a power may be deemed non-exclusive.

   Answer (A) is incorrect. The New London Academy's remainder interest has been divested.

   Answer (C) is incorrect. Since the power was "exclusive," Mark was not required to include Erica. In addition, Mark was exercising a power of appointment and not devising his own property. Consequently, the typical "pretermitted" or "omitted" child statute, like UPC § 2-302, is not applicable.

   Answer (D) is incorrect. Neither Tina nor Erica acquired an interest in the trust estate.

201.   In order for the New London Academy's remainder interest to be divested, Mark, as the donee of the power, must validly exercise the power. A testamentary power can only be exercised in a document which is formally sufficient to be admitted to probate. Comment b to Restatement of Donative Transfers (2nd) § 18.2. Thus, the charity was not divested. UPC § 2-503 (or a similar statute in a non-UPC state) may provide the opportunity to probate the defective will if there is clear and convincing evidence that Mark intended the document to be Mark's will. If relief is not available under UPC § 2-503, Kyle and Uma could argue that the appointment is still effective according to Restatement of Donative Transfers (2nd) § 18.3.

202.   Armen should distribute the trust estate to the New London Academy. It is widely accepted that a general disposition of a testator's property in a will does not, as a general rule, exercise a non-general power of appointment. *See* Restatement of Donative Transfers (2nd) § 17.3. The Uniform Probate Code has codified this principle. *See* UPC § 2-608.

203.   **Answer (A) is correct**. Mark failed to exercise the power. Consequently, the New London Academy was not divested. Restatement of Donative Transfers (2nd) § 18.2.

       Answers (B), (C), and (D) are incorrect. Mark was not under any legal obligation to exercise the power. The permissible appointees have no standing to complain about Mark's inaction.

204.   **Answer (B) is correct**. Although Myra did not expressly exercise the general testamentary power in her will, a court is likely to find that the power was in fact exercised. It is generally accepted that a general power can be impliedly exercised if the donee's intent is clearly expressed and/or the disposition would otherwise be ineffective. *See also* Restatement of Donative Transfers (2nd) § 17.4.

       Answer (A) is incorrect. A court is likely to find that the power was impliedly exercised by Myra.

       Answers (C) and (D) are incorrect. The value of Myra's augmented estate in order to determine Peter's elective share amount does not include property over which Myra had a testamentary general power of appointment. *See* UPC § 2-205(1)(I). Note that the result may differ in an non-UPC state.

205.   **Answer (C) is correct**. Because Tammy's will contained a "gift over" in the event the power was not exercised, the Highland County Clinic's remainder interest was not divested. UPC § 2-608. Myra did not expressly or impliedly exercise the testamentary general power of appointment. *See* Restatement, Second, Donative Trusts § 17.3. The result may differ in a state that has not adopted the Uniform Probate Code. Some states have created a presumption by statute or case law that Myra did exercise the power.

       Answers (A) and (B) are incorrect. Myra did not have a legal obligation to exercise the power and did not manifest an intention to exercise the power.

       Answer (D) is incorrect. Because Myra did not hold an inter vivos general power, the trust estate is not included in Myra's augmented estate for Peter's elective share determination. *See* UPC § 2-205(1)(I). The result may differ in a non-UPC state.

206.   The home passes to Diego subject to Peter's marital share. UPC § 2-205(1)(I) appears to exclude the appointive property from the augmented estate. However, Myra's use of a "blending clause" to exercise the general testamentary power may have the effect of "capturing" the home for Myra's probate estate. *See* Restatement of Donative Transfers (2nd) § 22.1. If case law adopts the "doctrine of capture," the home may be

included in Myra's augmented estate in order to compute Peter's elective share amount, if any. The result may differ in a non-UPC state.

207.   **Answer (A) is correct.** Myra appears to have exercised the power in favor of an object of the power who predeceased Myra. However, due to the "blending clause" and the "doctrine of capture," the antilapse provisions of UPC § 2-603 create a substitute gift in favor of Alec even though Alec was not an object of the power. *See* Restatement of Donative Transfers (2nd) § 22.1. The result may differ in states that have not enacted the Uniform Probate Code.

   Answer (B) is incorrect. Diego died before Myra and could not devise the home to Launa.

   Answer (C) is incorrect. Peter did not acquire any interest in the home.

   Answer (D) is incorrect. The charity has been divested.

208.   **Answer (A) is correct.** Myra attempted to exercise the power in favor of an object of the power who had predeceased her. However, the antilapse provisions of UPC § 2-603(b)(5) create a substitute gift in favor of Alec whether or not Alec was an object of the power. The result may differ in states that have not enacted the Uniform Probate Code. *See* Restatement, Second, Donative Trusts § 18.6.

   Answer (B) is incorrect. Diego died before Myra and could not devise the home to Launa.

   Answer (C) is incorrect. Peter did not acquire any interest in the home.

   Answer (D) is incorrect. The charity has been divested.

209.   To the extent the probate estate is insufficient to satisfy Myra's debts, the home can be subjected to the payment of claims against Myra's estate since Myra's power was a testamentary general power of appointment. The home passed to Diego but subject to possibly being reached by Myra's executor to pay Myra's debts. *See* Restatement of Donative Transfers (2nd) § 13.4. If Myra's executor does not pursue the home, Myra's creditors can presumably pursue the home under the rules relating to fraudulent transfers if Myra's probate estate cannot satisfy the debts.

210.   **Answer (D) is correct.** It is generally accepted that during the settlor's lifetime the settlor's creditors may reach the maximum amount that can be distributed to or for the benefit of the settlor even if the initial creation and funding of the trust were not fraudulent transfers. Restatement of Donative Transfers (2nd) § 13.3; Restatement of Trusts § 60. The Uniform Trust Code has codified these principles. *See* UTC § 505(a)(2).

   Answers (A), (B), and (C) are incorrect. A settlor who is also a beneficiary cannot use a trust as a shield against the settlor's creditors.

211.   Whether or not the terms of the trust contain a "spendthrift provision," the entire trust estate, under modern practice, may to be available to Harley's creditors if: (i) someone other than Harley created the trust and granted a presently exercisable general power of appointment or (ii) Harley is the settlor/beneficiary of the express trust. UTC § 505 supports this conclusion. Even if Harley was not the settlor, his power to appoint to himself (even if limited by an ascertainable standard) allows the creditors to reach the maximum amount available to him. This result is "unaffected by a purported spendthrift restraint." *See* comment g, Restatement of Trusts § 60. The results may differ in a states that have not adopted the Restatement approach if someone other than Harley was the settlor.

212. **Answer (A) and Answer (B) are incorrect.** UTC § 405 describes the promotion of health as one of several alternative charitable purposes. It is not necessary, for example, that a charitable trust relieve the burdens of poverty if it qualifies by serving one of the other enumerated purposes. Since a hospital promotes health, a trust for the benefit of a hospital is charitable. Comments (a)(1) and J to Restatement of Trusts § 28.

    Answer (D) is incorrect. There is no requirement that employees of charities volunteer their services. Compensation to employees is a legitimate expense of operating any charity and is different than a distribution of profits to shareholders, which is prohibited. Comment J to Restatement of Trusts § 28.

    Answer (C) is correct. Since the hospital is a nonprofit corporation, it is not run to provide profit for shareholders. Thus, the fact that it charges fees for its services does not make it noncharitable. A charitable trust can be established for such a hospital. Comments (a)(1) and J to Restatement of Trusts § 28.

213. **Answer (C) is incorrect.** UTC § 405(b) authorizes a court to choose a charitable purpose or beneficiaries for a charitable trust that fails to specify such. However, court action under UTC § 405(b) is not necessary when the trustee has been given this power. Comment to UTC § 405.

    Answer (D) is correct. Giving the power to a trustee of a charitable trust to select appropriate purposes or recipients is a long-established technique and does not affect the charitable nature of the trust. It does not require court approval or any other specific formality. Comment to UTC § 405. Thus, **Answers (A) and (B) are incorrect.**

214. **Answer (A) is correct.** UTC § 405(c) is a substantial deviation from the general rule that settlors do not have standing to enforce trusts. It provides settlors of charitable trusts with such standing. Although the church is a charity, distributions that benefit non-charitable beneficiaries are a breach of trust.

    Answer (B) is incorrect. It states the general rule but misses the exception provided for settlors of charitable trusts by UTC § 405(c).

    Answer (C) is incorrect. Settlors of charitable trusts have this right as a result of statutory authorization. UTC § 405(c). Query if it would be contrary to public policy to enlarge or restrict this power.

    Answer (D) is incorrect. UTC § 405(c) gives standing to the settlor of a charitable trust. However, this does not preclude the right of the state attorney general to bring suits to enforce charitable trusts since generally each state charges the attorney general with the responsibility to oversee charities. Comment to UTC § 405.

215.   **Answer (A) is incorrect.** State law determination of the charitable nature of a trust is independent from the Internal Revenue Code requirements for either income tax exemption (IRC § 501) or deductibility of contributions (*e.g.*, IRC § 170 and § 2055). Thus, not all charitable trusts are exempt from income tax and entitled to receive deductible contributions.

Answer (B) is incorrect. IRC § 501(c) provides many alternative grounds for income tax exemption for a charitable trust, but not all of them entitle the trust to receive deductible contributions under IRC § 170 and § 2055.

Answer (C) is correct. A charitable trust that meets the criteria of IRC § 501(c)(3) will be both exempt from income tax and entitled to receive deductible contributions under IRC § 170 and § 2055. However, a charitable trust that fails to meet the criteria of IRC § 501(c)(3) may meet the criteria of IRC § 501(c)(4), which would mean it was exempt from income tax but not entitled to receive deductible contributions.

Answer D is incorrect for the reasons explained above.

216.   **Answers (A) and (B) are incorrect.** UTC § 405 describes several alternative charitable purposes. Unless the museum provides a benefit to the community, the trust will not qualify as charitable. The statute does not require that a trust forego charges or fees in order to qualify as charitable.

Answer (C) is correct. Unless it is proven that the artwork has objective artistic merit or there is some other public interest in the museum, the trust fails as a charitable trust since it does not promote a benefit to the community. While the display of some private collections are undeniably charitable (*e.g.*, The Menil Collection in Houston), not everyone who wants to preserve his or her eccentric collection of personally-created or personally-selected objects can establish a charitable trust to do so. Comment h and illustration 5 to comment on clause (f) of Restatement of Trusts § 28

Answer (D) is incorrect. While the state attorney general has the primary responsibility for the oversight of charitable trusts, it is not necessary to secure consent or recognition from the attorney general in order to establish a charitable trust.

217.   How the residuary estate should be distributed if the trust fails to be either a charitable trust or a private express trust depends upon the trustees' choice. If the trustees volunteer to serve as trustees of an honorary trust, the residuary estate will be held on the terms of the trust but not for longer than 21 years. However, unless the trustees volunteer to so serve, the residuary estate will pass to Harvey's heirs. UTC § 409.

218.   **Answer (C) is correct.** Trusts for the education of the settlor's relatives are not charitable. While scholarships always provide specific benefits to specific individuals

(rather than a general benefit to the public) and scholarship criteria may be applied to choose those individuals, trusts for the benefit of specific individuals (especially the settlor or members of the settlor's family) will fail to be charitable. When the group of potential beneficiaries is so narrowly defined, the trust is essentially a private express trust rather than a charitable trust. Comments a(1) and h to Restatement of Trusts § 28. Even though UTC § 405 provides that the advancement of education is a charitable purpose, no trust serves a charitable purpose if it is more for private than public benefit. Educating the settlor's family members is a private rather than charitable purpose even if the family members are in financial need or meet other reasonable scholarship criteria. Thus, **Answers (A), (B), and (D) are incorrect.**

219. **Answer (A) is incorrect.** UTC § 405 provides that advancement of religion is a charitable purpose. The common law recognition of the charitable nature of advancing religion can be traced historically until least 1639. Thus, *Answer (D) is incorrect.* However, while the context of this trust is a church, nothing in the terms of the trust are calculated to advance religion. Instead, the purpose of the trust is to financially enrich the children. *See Shenandoah Valley National Bank v. Taylor*, 192 Va. 135, 63 S.E.2d 786 (1951) and comments i and h to Restatement of Trusts § 28.

    Answer (C) is correct. Enriching the children without regard to their financial need or any social benefit to the community is merely benevolent. However, mere benevolence is not a charitable purpose. *Shenandoah Valley National Bank v. Taylor*, 192 Va. 135, 63 S.E.2d 786 (1951) and comments i and h to Restatement of Trusts § 28. Thus, **Answer (B) is incorrect.**

220. **Answer (A) is incorrect.** The rule against perpetuities does not apply to wholly charitable transfers. Comment d to Restatement of Trusts § 28.

    Answer (B) is correct. Under UTC § 413, since the trust purposes have become "impracticable, impossible to achieve, or wasteful," the court should modify the purposes of the trust so that it can continue to fulfill the settlor's charitable intentions.

    Answer (C) is incorrect. Whereas older common law statements of the cy pres doctrine required proving the settlor's general charitable intention, UTC § 413 presumes such an intention in situations such as these. Comment to UTC § 413.

    Answer (D) is incorrect. UTC § 413(a) specifically provides that there is no reversion to the settlor or the settlor's successors in interest when charitable trust purposes have become "impracticable, impossible to achieve, or wasteful." Instead, the court is to modify the purposes of the trust so that it can continue to fulfill the settlor's charitable intentions.

221. Yes. UTC § 413(b) provides that a provision in the terms of a charitable trust that would result in distribution of the trust property to a noncharitable beneficiary prevails over the power of the court to apply cy pres to modify the trust only if, when the provision takes effect, fewer than twenty-one years have elapsed since the trust was created (unless

the trust property is to revert to the still-living settlor). Thus, if the cure had been found before twenty-one years had elapsed, the trust assets would be distributed to the intestate heirs. However, since more than twenty-one years have elapsed, the court should modify the purposes so that the trust can continue to fulfill the settlor's general charitable intentions.

222.   **Answer (A) is correct**. While a trust that funds the development and dissemination of information advocating or seeking to improve understanding of a particular set of social, economic, or political views is charitable because it is educational, a trust to promote the success of a particular political party is never charitable—not even to the extent the political party pursues or achieves specific objectives that are undeniably charitable. Comment on clause (f) of Restatement of Trusts § 28. Thus, **Answers (B) and (C) are incorrect**.

223.   **Answers (A) and (E) are incorrect**. Generally, the settlor does not have the right to bring suit against a trustee for breach of trust. Note that even though the trustee has accepted the terms of the trust established by the settlor, this acceptance does not create a contract between the settlor and trustee. Comment a to Restatement of Trusts (2nd) § 200.

         Answer (D) is correct. The beneficiary of a trust or a co-trustee can sue to obtain redress for breach of a trust by a trustee. In some situations, the co-trustee may have a duty to sue. Comment a to Restatement of Trusts (2nd) § 200. **Thus, Answers (B) and (C) are incorrect**.

224.   **Answer (E) is correct**. Unlike the common law, UTC § 706 provides the settlor of an irrevocable trust the right to petition for removal of a trustee. This is an exception to the general rule that the settler has no standing to enforce the terms of the trust. It is not to be construed to give the settlor any other rights, such as the right to an annual report or to receive other information concerning administration of the trust. Comments to UTC § 706. However, while the removal action is pending, the court may order other relief as may be necessary, including compelling the trustee to redress a breach by paying money. UTC §§ 706(c), 1001(a). **Answers (A), (B), (C), and (D) are each incorrect** insofar as they exclude one or more persons who would be entitled to bring the suit.

225.   "A trustee is held to something stricter than the morals of the marketplace. Not honesty alone, but the punctilio of an honor the most sensitive, is then the standard of behavior." *Meinhard v. Salmon*, 164 N.E. 545, 546 (N.Y. 1928).

226.   **Answers (A) is incorrect**. Even a trustee with the power to sell trust property is under a duty not to purchase it personally. Since a self-dealing act is intentional, it is generally immaterial that the trustee acts in good faith in purchasing trust property or that the trustee pays a fair consideration. Restatement of Trusts § 170. Such a sale is voidable by the beneficiary under UTC § 802.

         Answer (B) is incorrect. The general power to sell property is not an authorization for the trustee to engage in self-dealing. UTC § 802 provides that settlors may create trust instruments that authorize self-dealing transactions, but such authorization is not inferred from the mere power to sell because the trustee is given the power to sell by default under the UTC § 816(2).

         Answer (C) is incorrect. Since the settlor has no right to sue the trustee for breach, the settlor's consent is legally irrelevant. Restatement of Trusts (2nd) § 200. Although

UTC § 706 provides settlors the right to petition to have a trustee removed—and self-dealing could fit within the grounds for removal under UTC § 706(b)—the comments to UTC § 706 make clear that it is not to be used to give the settlor any other rights, which would include the right to authorize self-dealing. This is reserved to the beneficiary under UTC § 1009.

Answer (E) is correct. To constitute a valid consent to self-dealing, the beneficiary must consent with full knowledge of all the relevant facts and his or her rights—*i.e.*, the beneficiary must have received full disclosure—and the transaction must be fair and reasonable to the beneficiary. UTC § 1009; Restatement, of Trusts (2nd) § 170(2) and comments k and n to § 216. **Answer (D) is incorrect** because the transaction must be fair and reasonable to the beneficiary.

227.   A duty imposes an obligation on the trustee. Unless waived by the beneficiaries or a court, it requires or prohibits a certain act. The trustee has no choice but to comply with the duty. A power, however, is an option. It is inherently discretionary. A trustee has a choice as to whether or not to exercise the power. The existence of a power is a question separate from whether or not it is prudent under the circumstances to exercise the power. That is, the trustee must fulfill the trustee's fiduciary duties of loyalty, prudence, etc. when determining whether or not (and how) to exercise a power. Thus, a trustee with the power to buy, sell, lease, etc. may only exercise such powers to the extent it is consistent with (or required by) the trustee's duties. Comments to UTC §§ 815 -816.

228.   **Answer (A) is correct.** A trustee has the power to enter into a lease for a period that extends beyond the duration of the trust. So long as the extension is prudent and in Lana's best interest, Benny has the right to extend the lease. The lease will bind not only the lessee but Lana as well. UTC § 816(9). However, if the lease were not prudent or not in Lana's best interest, Benny may be liable for any damages Lana suffered even though the lessee, acting in good faith at the time of the lease, can enforce its terms under UTC § 1012(b). Note that this is a rejection of comment c to Restatement of Trusts § 189 that a trustee could not lease property beyond the duration of the trust. Comments to UTC § 816.

Answer (B) is incorrect. Lana receives the property free-of-trust but subject to the lease. She steps into the shoes of Benny with respect to the rights as lessor, but she is obligated by the lease, if the lessee was acting in good faith when the lease was signed.

Answers (C) and (D) are incorrect. Benny has the right to extend the lease, as explained above.

229.   **Answer (B) is correct.** UTC § 816(21) authorizes a trustee to make payments for the benefit of a beneficiary who the trustee reasonably believes is incapacitated rather than making the payment directly to the beneficiary. The trustee is not required to await a court determination of incapacity. The only requirement is that the trustee's belief

in the beneficiary's incapacity be reasonable and, of course, made by the trustee consistent with the trustee's fiduciary duties of prudence and loyalty. In this situation, Merwan's belief is reasonable, and the indirect payments would be for Faith's benefit.

Answer (A) is incorrect. A trustee is not required to make an imprudent distribution to a beneficiary who the trustee reasonably believes is incapacitated, as explained above.

Answer (C) is incorrect. The relevant issue is the trustee's reasonable belief as to the beneficiary's incapacity. The trustee is not required to have a judicial declaration of incapacity. **Answer (D) is incorrect for the same reason**.

230. **Answer (A) is incorrect.** UTC § 816(15) authorizes the trustee to pay the trustee reasonable compensation. It does not require a beneficiary's consent to the compensation nor to its rate or changes in its rate.

Answer (B) is incorrect. UTC § 816(15) authorizes the trustee to pay the trustee reasonable compensation. It does not require court approval.

Answer (C) is correct. Although UTC § 816(15) authorizes the trustee to pay the trustee's reasonable compensation without the approval of the court or the beneficiary, UTC § 813(b)(4) requires advance notice of a change in the rate or method of compensation to be provided to the beneficiary. Allowing the trustee to pay its compensation without prior court approval promotes efficient trust administration, but places the burden on the beneficiary questioning the amount of the compensation. To provide a beneficiary with time to take action in court against the trustee if the beneficiary believes the compensation is unreasonable, the UTC requires the trustee to give the beneficiary advance notice of any change in the method or rate of the trustee's compensation. Comment to UTC § 813(b)(4).

Answer (D) is incorrect. Neither UTC § 816 nor UTC § 813 (nor any other section of the UTC) requires advance notice of a change in the rate or method of compensation to be provided to the court.

231. In determining whether or not his compensation is "reasonable," Aaron should closely examine not only the responsibilities assumed as trustee but the services actually performed. For example, he should be careful to consider any significant duties he has delegated to someone else (*e.g.*, an investment advisor) to the extent such delegation has reduced the level of services he has needed to render. For the services he did render, Aaron should consider the following factors: the "going rate" of trustees in the community; his personal level of skill and experience; the amount of time he devoted to the trust duties; the amount and character of the trust property; the degree of difficulty in administering the trust property; the degree of risk he assumed in administering the trust property; the nature and costs of services rendered by others for the trust's benefit; and the overall quality of his performance. Comment to UTC § 708. As a practical matter, Aaron should investigate these factors and document them clearly in the event that his judgment as to reasonableness is later questioned. He should also be advised

that, in the event of litigation, the burden of proof will be on him to the prove the reasonableness of the compensation.

232. **Answer (A) is incorrect**. While UTC § 105 provides the general rule that the terms of a trust prevail over any provisions of the code, it makes several exceptions to the general rule. One of the exceptions is the power of the court under UTC § 708(b) to adjust a trustee's compensation specified in the terms of the trust when the compensation is unreasonably low or high. UTC § 105(b)(7).

   Answer (B) is incorrect. The power of the court to adjust specified compensation depends upon the reasonableness of the compensation specified and does not require any allegation that the trustee acted in gross negligence, bad faith, or otherwise contrary to any duties. That is, the trustee may have performed his or her duties satisfactorily, and the compensation level may still be unreasonable. UTC § 105(b)(7); UTC § 708(b).

   Answer (C) is incorrect. A trust is not a contract between the settlor and trustee even though the settlor and trustee may negotiate some or all of its terms.

   Answer (D) is correct. UTC § 708(b) expressly provides that, when terms of a trust specify the trustee's compensation, a court may increase or decrease the compensation if (1) the duties of the trustee are substantially different from those contemplated when the trust was created; or (2) the compensation specified by the terms of the trust would be unreasonably low or high. In this situation, both (b)(1) and (b)(2) are applicable. Given the disparity between the compensation level contemplated and the $2,000,000 and that the duties he actually performed (80 hours of services) were substantially less onerous than those contemplated (800 hours of service) when the trust was created, this compensation is unreasonably high. Thus, a court could lower the level of Francisco's compensation if he does not lower it himself. As to what is "reasonable," see the discussion in the Comment to UTC § 708.

233. **Answer (A) is incorrect**. UTC § 703 rejects the common law rule requiring unanimity among the trustees of an express trust and, instead, adopts the rule long applicable to charitable trusts, which allows for action by a majority of trustees.

   Answer (D) is correct. Since UTC § 706 permits co-trustees to act by a majority, there is always the possibility that there may be a co-trustee who dissents from the majority's decision. UTC § 703(f) provides general protection from liability for those dissenting co-trustees who refuse to join the majority's actions. However, it is not necessary for a dissenting co-trustee to refuse to join the majority's actions in order to avoid liability. UTC § 703(h) protects a dissenting trustee who joined the action at the direction of the majority, such as to satisfy a demand of the other side to a transaction, if the trustee expressed the dissent to a co-trustee at or before the time of the action in question. However, neither of these protections are available if the action is a "serious" breach of trust. A "serious" breach of trust is one for which the trustee could be removed from office under UTC § 706(b)(1). In the event of a serious breach of trust, UTC § 703(g) requires that the dissenting co-trustee take steps to rectify the improper conduct. Comment to UTC § 706. **Thus, Answers (B) and (C) are incorrect**.

234. **Answer (A) is incorrect.** The "legal lists" of appropriate trust investments developed in the 19th century but have been rejected by UPIA. Andersen, § 56[A], Dukeminier, 791-797.

 Answer (B) and Answer (C) are incorrect. Each of these statements reflects the constrained "prudent man rule," which accepted the low returns of low risk investments as inherently prudent while rejecting riskier, more speculative investments even though such investments provide greater return. Andersen, § 56[A], Dukeminier, 791-797.

 Answer (D) is correct. The "prudent investor rule" adopts modern portfolio theory and accepts the correlation between risk and return (*i.e.*, low risk = low return; high risk = high return) and the necessity of diversification as inherent to the concept of prudent investing. Thus, the prudent investor is required to diversify the trust portfolio in an effort to best manage the trade-off between risk and return. UPIA §§ 2-3.

235. In order to invest as a prudent investor, the trustee should consider the following types of circumstances to the extent relevant to his or her trust and its beneficiaries: (1) general economic conditions; (2) the possible effect of inflation or deflation; (3) the expected tax consequences of investment decisions or strategies; (4) the role that each investment or course of action plays within the overall trust portfolio, which may include financial assets, interests in closely held enterprises, tangible and intangible personal property, and real property; (5) the expected total return from income and the appreciation of capital; (6) other resources of the beneficiaries; (7) needs for liquidity, regularity of income, and preservation or appreciation of capital; and (8) an asset's special relationship or special value, if any, to the purposes of the trust or to one or more of the beneficiaries. Uniform Prudent Investor Act § 2(b). Note that Article 9 of the UTC effectively adopts the Uniform Prudent Investor Act even though it does not integrate it into the UTC since some states will have the UPIA as a stand alone statute.

236. **Answer (A) is correct.** The Uniform Prudent Investor Act requires diversification of trust investments unless there are special circumstances in which the purposes of the trust are served without diversifying. "Special circumstances" does not mean the trustee believes the investment is a very good one. Regardless of how sound a single investment is, the Uniform Prudent Investor Act requires diversification. Within a reasonable time after accepting trust assets, a trustee is required to bring the trust portfolio into compliance with the prudent investor rule's diversification requirement. UPIA §§ 3-4. Note that there is an exception for this diversification requirement in the event that tax or other costs of reorganizing the portfolio can be proven to outweigh the benefits of diversification. *See Malachowski v. Bank One*, 590 N.E.2d 559, 565 (Ind. 1992); Dukeminier, 814.

 Answers (B) and (D) are incorrect. While some state laws permit assets received upon the inception of a trust to be retained indefinitely by the trustee, UPIA § 4 requires the trustee to bring the trust investments into compliance with the prudent investor rule's diversification requirement. Initial assets do not have a special status.

Answer (C) is incorrect. Under the Uniform Prudent Investor Act, it is the prudence of the entire trust portfolio rather than single investments that is at issue. UPIA § 2(b). Such portfolios must be diversified. UPIA § 3.

237.   **Answer (A) is incorrect.** All trust *assets* are subject to the prudent investor rule under UPIA § 2(a). There is no distinction between assets with an exclusively financial value and assets that also have emotional or other personal value.

      Answer (C) is incorrect. While some state laws permit assets received upon the inception of a trust to be retained indefinitely by the trustee, the Uniform Prudent Investor Act does not provide any special status for initially-received assets.

      Answer (D) is correct. The only exception from the diversification requirement under the Uniform Prudent Investor Act is with respect to those unusual, special situations in which the very purpose of the trust would be impaired by diversification. This best example is a trust established to hold assets of personal value, such as family homes. This exception is expressed in UPIA § 3 but also reflected in UPIA § 2(a) and (c)(8). **Answer (B) is incorrect** since it reflects only the general rule and not this single exception. A well drafted trust instrument would expressly authorize the trustee to retain the family home without a duty to diversify.

238.   **Answer (A) is incorrect**. UTC § 807 rejects the non-delegation rule of the common law, which prohibited a trustee from delegating responsibilities to an agent.

      Answer (B) is correct. Under UTC § 807 a trustee is not liable for the actions committed by an agent to whom the trustee delegated powers or duties as long as they were powers and duties that a prudent trustee of comparable skills could properly delegate under the circumstances. Further, the trustee is required to exercise reasonable care, skill, and caution in selecting the agent, establishing the scope and terms of the delegation, and periodically reviewing the agent's actions. Since Mariah had no financial expertise and was serving as trustee because she was a family member, it was prudent for her to delegate investment management. See the comment to UTC § 807. Indeed, she may even have a duty to delegate in this situation. Comment j to Restatement of Trusts § 227. Further, the steps described evidence reasonable care, skill, and caution in selecting, hiring, and monitoring the manager. Thus, she is not personally liable for the manager's imprudent investing. **Answers (C) and (D) are incorrect** for the reasons explained.

239.   When one beneficiary is only entitled to income and another is only entitled to principal, whether a particular receipt is characterized as "income" or "principal" determines which beneficiary is entitled to receive it. Thus, the trustee's investment decisions often favor one kind of beneficiary over another. For example, an investment in a stock that does not pay dividends (which would be "income") but has a value likely to appreciate (which would be "principal") favors the principal beneficiary over the income beneficiary. By

allowing the trustee to characterize receipts as "income" or "principal" based upon the trustee's determination of what is appropriate (rather than what is strictly required under the traditional rules), the trustee can make the best trust investments possible without worrying about favoring one beneficiary at the expense of the others.

240. The prudent investor rule adopts modern portfolio theory, which is premised on focusing on the value of an investment in relationship to the other investments in the portfolio. Part of what the modern portfolio theory rejects is analyzing the form of investments. "Income" and "principal" are historical but arbitrary forms for analyzing investments and have no usefulness in modern portfolio theory. A trustee is required under the prudent investor rule to maintain a diversified investment portfolio. To the extent that the trustee's duty to be fair with respect to beneficiaries with conflicting interests requires the trustee to emphasize "income" or "principal" in investing rather than a diverse portfolio, the efficiency of modern portfolio theory is undermined. Thus, it is necessary for the trustee to be free from having to analyze investments in terms of "income" and "principal" if the trustee is going to pursue a diversified portfolio. By allowing the trustee to adjust between the two, the trustee can manage a diversified portfolio and equitably allocate the benefits of such portfolio between the beneficiaries.

241. **Answer (A) is incorrect.** UTC § 105(9) provides that the UTC will prevail over the terms of a trust instrument with respect to UTC § 813(a)'s requirement that a trustee respond to the request of a beneficiary for the trustee's reports and other information reasonably related to the administration of a trust. Thus, the terms of the trust do not override this requirement.

Answer (B) and Answer (D) are each incorrect. The trust instrument cannot override the beneficiary's right to information reasonably related to the administration of the trust. UTC § 105(9). Since the trustee cannot have the power to withhold this information, it is irrelevant whether the trustee seeks to exercise that power in good faith or otherwise consistently with the trustee's fiduciary duties.

Answer (C) is correct. The Uniform Trust Code generally requires the trustee to keep beneficiaries reasonably informed about the administration of the trust and of the material facts necessary for them to protect their interests. Further, trustees are required to promptly respond to a beneficiary's request for information related to the administration of the trust. UTC § 813(a). This right of beneficiaries to request information from the trustee cannot be waived by the trust instrument. UTC § 105(b)(9).

242. **Answer (C) is correct.** Even if the terms of the trust attempt to completely exculpate a trustee for the trustee's acts, the trustee must always comply with a certain minimum standard. UTC § 1008 sets that minimum standard: a trustee must always act in good faith with regard to the purposes of the trust and the interests of the beneficiaries. Trust instruments can reduce the fiduciary standards and other duties of trustees but not below this level. UTC § 105 and UTC § 1008 combine to deny enforceability to any trust provision that would relieve the trustee of liability for breach of trust committed in bad

faith or with reckless indifference to the purposes of the trust or the interests of the beneficiaries

Answer (A) is incorrect because the exculpatory provision cannot entirely eliminate a trustee's liability.

Answer (B) is incorrect because exculpatory provisions can reduce the statutory standards.

Answer (D) is incorrect because UTC § 105 and UTC § 1008 do provide for reducing the fiduciary standard of prudence—reducing it to avoiding bad faith and reckless indifference.

243.   **Answer (B) is correct.** This is a transfer of property by gift. Internal Revenue Code
§ 2501(a). However, since the donee is the donor's husband, it qualifies for the marital
deduction under Internal Revenue Code § 2523, which means it is not a "taxable gift."

Answer (A) is incorrect. Most gifts are between family members. The annual exclusion
provision of Internal Revenue Code § 2503 provides a dollar-based exclusion (but
adjusted for inflation) to cover *de minimis* gifts between family members and otherwise.

Answer (C) is incorrect. Gifts under the annual exclusion amount are not taxable. The
exclusion amount allows the gift to be made without gift tax consequences.

244.   **Answer (D) is correct.** A gift includes property transferred outside the ordinary course
of business for less than full consideration. The amount of the gift is the amount by
which the value of the property exceeds the amount of the consideration paid. Treasury
Regulations § 25.2512-8. In this question, the value of the property is $15,000, and the
amount of the consideration paid is $2,000, so the value of the gift is $13,000. The
amount of the taxable gift is $1,000 (*i.e.*, $13,000 less the annual exclusion amount
of $12,000, if available.) **Answers (A) and (C) are incorrect** for the reasons explained.

Answers (B) is incorrect. Angel has made a gift because he has made a transfer to
Samantha for less than full consideration. Even though some amount of the gift may
be excluded under the annual exclusion, this does not affect the determination of whether
or not a gift was made but rather only the determination of how much, if any, tax liability
arises from the gift.

245.   No. Transfers made in the ordinary courses of business that are free of any donative
intent are not gifts. Treasury Regulations § 25.2512-8.

246.   **Answer (A) is correct.** A donor does not make a gift for federal tax purposes until
he has parted with all dominion and control. His power to revoke is an explicit
reservation of dominion and control to determine what, if anything, Janice is to receive.
Thus, **Answers (B), (C), and (D) are incorrect.** Treasury Regulations § 25.2511-2.

247.   **Answer (C) is correct.** There is no gift when the trust is created because Ramon has
not parted with dominion and control over the trust estate insofar as he has retained
the power to revoke the trust. Treasury Regulations § 25.2511-2. Thus, **Answers (A),
(B), and (D) are incorrect.** However, whenever an actual distribution is made to Ernest
pursuant to the trust terms, a gift is made.

248. **Answer (A) is correct**. Under Internal Revenue Code § 676, the $5,000 is taxable to Ramon because he retained the power to revoke the trust. This is a result of the "grantor trust" income tax rules.

Answer (B) is incorrect. There is no income tax deduction for gifts.

Answer (C) is incorrect. Under the grantor trust rules, the settlor (i.e., the "grantor") is taxable on the trust's income, not the trustee (*i.e.*, not the trust).

Answer (D) is incorrect. The $5,000 distribution to Ernest was a gift to him, and gifts are not taxable to donees. Internal Revenue Code § 102.

249. **Answer (B) is correct**. The annual exclusion is calculated per donee per year. In the current year, Johanna could give up to $12,000 to each of Denise, Greta, Karli, and Heidi. Her $15,000 gift to Karli exceeds the annual exclusion for Karli by $3,000 but the other gifts are each under the annual exclusion amount. Internal Revenue Code § 2503.

Answer (A) is incorrect. The annual exclusion is calculated per donee per year. The $3,000 by which the gift to Karli exceeds the $12,000 limit is not reduced by the $2,000 by which the gift to Heidi is below the limit. Each donee's gifts are independent of the others.

Answers (C) and (D) are incorrect for the reasons explained.

250. **Answer (D) is correct**. Payments to or for the benefit of an adult child are gifts since the parent does not have an ongoing duty of support. However, the $17,000 tuition payment paid to the school is excluded as a tuition payment under Internal Revenue Code § 2503(e), which allows Ali to make an indirect gift to Sara by directly paying her tuition that is excluded from being a taxable gift. The $10,000 gift given directly to Sara is less than the annual exclusion amount under Internal Revenue Code § 2503(a). Thus, **Answers (A), (B), and (C) are incorrect** for the reasons explained.

251. **Answer (A) is incorrect**. Since Clifford and Eve have agreed to split gifts, their combined annual exclusion of $24,000 is available for this gift. Internal Revenue Code § 2513.

Answer (C) is correct. A gift must be of a present interest in order to qualify for the annual exclusion. Since John has the power to withdraw the $20,000 gift (and he was given notice of the gift and a reasonable time to exercise the power to withdraw it), it qualifies for the annual exclusion. Andersen § 62[b]; Dukeminier, 860-868. Thus, **Answers (B) and (D) are incorrect** for the reasons explained.

252. **Answer (A) is incorrect**. Neither Internal Revenue Code § 2033 nor any other provision requires inclusion of life estates created by someone other than the decedent.

Answer (B) is incorrect. Only life estates created by the decedent are included as a result of Internal Revenue Code § 2036. Omar did not create the life estate for himself.

Answer (C) is correct. A life estate created by another person is not included in the gross estate under Internal Revenue Code § 2036 or otherwise. Xavier created the life estate for Omar.

Answer (D) is incorrect. Whether or not Xavier was taxable on the gift to Omar, the life estate is not included in Omar's gross estate for the reasons explained.

253. **Answer (C) is correct**. Mark has not made a *completed* gift because he has the right to withdraw the $50,000. **Thus, Answers (A) and (B) are incorrect**. Treasury Regulations § 25.2511-1(h)(4).

Answer (D) is incorrect. Since the account is a *joint* and survivor account, Elaine has the right to withdraw from the account immediately. She does not need to wait until Mark's death.

254. When Elaine withdraws money from the account for her own personal use, the gift to her is completed. Thus, as a result of Elaine's withdrawal, Mark has made a gift to Elaine of $10,000. Treasury Regulations § 25.2511-1(h)(4).

255. **Answer (A) is incorrect**. Individuals often make reciprocal gifts of comparable value. This has no bearing on whether or not a gift was made.

Answer (B) is incorrect. Elaine has not made a *completed* gift because she has the right to withdraw the $50,000. Treasury Regulations § 25.2511-1(h)(4).

Answer (C) is incorrect because there is not a gift from Elaine to Mark of any amount she deposited until Mark withdraws more than he deposited.

Answer (D) is correct. There will be a completed gift made by the other on the date on which either Mark or Elaine withdraws more than he or she deposited. Treasury Regulations § 25.2511-1(h)(4).

256. **Answer (C) is correct**. Since Mark and Elaine are not married, the portion of the account included in Mark's estate is based on the percentage of the account he deposited. Since Elaine deposited ⅓ of the amount in the account (*i.e.*, $25,000), Mark's estate only includes ⅔ of the account (i.e., $50,000). Internal Revenue Code § 2040(a). **Answers (A), (B), and (D) are incorrect** for the reasons explained.

257. **Answer (B) is correct**. Mark's gross estate includes one-half the value of the account. Internal Revenue Code § 2040(b) provides a special rule for spouses. Regardless of how much was contributed by which spouse to an account held as joint tenants with rights of survivorship, the account is treated as owned one-half by each spouse for estate tax purposes. **Answers (A), (C), and (D) are incorrect** for the reasons explained.

258.   No. Although the $37,500 will be included in his gross estate, the estate will be entitled to the Internal Revenue Code § 2056 marital deduction since the entire $37,500 passes to his surviving spouse as a result of the survivorship provision on the account.

259.   **Answer (A) is incorrect**. The $500,000 will not be included in the gross *income* of Hannah's husband because of Internal Revenue Code § 101. However, that section is an *income* tax section with no relation to the *estate* taxation of insurance policies.

      Answer (B) is incorrect because it is not the best statement. It is true that the $500,000 will be included in Hannah's estate as a result of Internal Revenue Code § 2042. However, it is very important to understand that the inclusion will not generate a tax liability because the payment to the husband will qualify for the marital deduction of Internal Revenue Code § 2056, regardless of the applicable exclusion amount.

      Answer (C) is correct. The $500,000 will be included in Hannah's estate as a result of Internal Revenue Code § 2042, but it will not generate a tax liability because the payment to the husband will qualify for the marital deduction of Internal Revenue Code § 2056.

      Answer (D) is incorrect. The applicable exclusion amount is used in construction with the decedent's tentative tax based and not individual assets included in the gross estate.

260.   **Answer (A) is incorrect**. Whether or not an asset is part of the probate estate is not relevant to determining what is included in the gross estate for federal tax purposes.

      Answer (C) is correct. The assets in the Living Trust will included in her gross estate under Internal Revenue Code § 2038 because she has the power to revoke the trust. However, the assets distributed to Stony Woods College should qualify for the charitable deduction under Internal Revenue Code § 2055. Thus, there should not be a tax liability regardless of the applicable exclusion amount. Note that many times assets included under Internal Revenue Code § 2038 may also be included under Internal Revenue Code § 2036. **Answer (B) is incorrect** for the reasons explained.

      Answer (D) is incorrect because it is not the best statement. While it is true that the assets in the Living Trust will be included in gross estate, it is very important to understand that the inclusion will not generate a tax liability because the payment to Stony Woods College will qualify for the charitable deduction of Internal Revenue Code § 2055.

261.   **Answer (A) is correct**. The amount of any debt legally owed by Natalie and payable out of assets included in her gross estate is properly deducted from the gross estate to determine the taxable estate. Internal Revenue Code § 2053.

      Answers (B), (C), and (D) are incorrect. It does not matter whether the debts are secured or unsecured. However, if Natalie is not personally liable for a secured debt, the debt is subtracted from the fair market value of the asset securing the debt to determine the amount to include in the gross estate. Treasury Regulations § 20.2053-1(a)(1)(iv).

262. **Answer (A) is correct.** In addition to the debts owed by Natalie prior to her death, expenses of last illness, funeral expenses, and administration expenses are also deductible. Internal Revenue Code § 2053. Administration expenses can be deducted on either the decedent's estate tax return or the fiduciary income tax return, not both. Treasury Regulations §§ 1.642(g)-1 and 20.2053-1(a).

Answers (B), (C), and (D) are incorrect. The amounts actually paid for these types of expenses are generally deductible.

263. **Answer (C) is correct.** While the amount devised to Natalie's children is not deductible, the devise to Ahmad qualifies for the "marital deduction," and the devise to the Appaloosa River Valley Hospital qualifies for the "charitable deduction." Internal Revenue Code §§ 2055, 2056. **Answers (A), (B), and (D) are incorrect** for the reasons explained.

264. **Answer (B) is correct.** The $1,000,000 devised to the first described trust would not qualify for the marital deduction because Ahmad was given a "non-deductible terminable" interest in the trust. IRC § 2056(b)(1). The second trust appears to meet the requirements of a "qualified terminable interest property" trust in that Ahmad is entitled to all of the trust's income for the remainder of his lifetime. IRC § 2056(b)(7).

Answer (A) is incorrect. However, if the second trust does not meet the requirements of a "QTIP" trust or if Natalie's executor does not make the "QTIP election," this answer would be correct.

Answer (C) is incorrect. The first trust does not qualify for the marital deduction.

Answer (D) is incorrect. In any event, whatever amount passed to the charity qualifies for the charitable deduction, assuming the devise to the Appaloosa River Valley Hospital meets the requirements of IRC § 2055.

265. The trust estate of the first trust will not be included in Ahmad's gross estate when he dies. At his death, his life estate simply terminates, and the children's remainder interest becomes possessory. Internal Revenue Code § 2033. Whether the trust estate of the second trust will be included in Ahmad's gross estate depends on two factors. First, did the trust meet the requirements of a "QTIP trust"? Second, did Natalie's executor make the "QTIP election"? Internal Revenue Code § 2056(b)(7). If the answer is yes to both questions, the trust estate of the second trust is included in Ahmad's gross estate. Internal Revenue Code § 2044. Any estate taxes attributable to the inclusion of the trust estate in Ahmad's taxable estate are apportioned to Natalie's children, Evan and Madeline, as remainder beneficiaries of the trust. UPC § 3-916. Absent a state statute like UPC § 3-916, the burden of the estate tax may fall on the decedent's residuary estate.

266. **Answer D is correct**. Assuming the trust qualifies as a "QTIP Trust" and Nolan's executor elected to treat it as a "QTIP Trust," the fair market value of the trust at Dalia's death is included in Dalia's gross estate. Internal Revenue Code § 2044.

Answer (A) is incorrect. If the trust does not qualify as a "QTIP trust" or if the executor did not elect to treat it as a "QTIP Trust," no part of the trust estate (other than any income accrued, but not paid, at date of death) would be included in Dalia's gross estate even though Dalia possessed a general power of appointment because the power to appoint to herself was limited by an ascertainable standard.

Answers (B) and (C) are incorrect. The fair market value of the trust estate on Dalia's date of death is included in the gross estate if the trust is a "QTIP trust." Internal Revenue Code § 2044.

PRACTICE FINAL EXAM: ANSWERS

267. **Answer (C) is correct.** Conditions of survivorship are not implied with respect to future interests, like legal remainder interests. *See* Restatement of Property § 165. Faye's interest was devised to Henry.

   Answer (A) is incorrect. Baird only inherited a life estate.

   Answer (B) is incorrect. The remainder interest had been devised to Faye when Adam died and then passed to Henry when Faye died.

   Answer (D) is incorrect. Faye's vested remainder was devised by Faye to Henry.

268. **Answer (B) is correct.** The remainder interest devised to Faye was contingent on Faye surviving Baird. At Faye's death, Faye's remainder interest ceased to exist, and Pennswood Academy's alternative contingent remainder became a vested remainder. Restatement of Property §§ 157, 239.

   Answer (A) is incorrect. Faye's interest was contingent on Faye surviving Baird.

   Answer (C) is incorrect. Baird inherited a life estate.

   Answer (D) is incorrect. Faye's interest was contingent on Faye surviving Baird.

269. Lana and Mitch inherit the remainder interest. At common law, the gift to Faye would have lapsed, and the remainder interest would have been devised to Pennswood Academy. *See* comment to UPC § 2-603. However, most states have enacted "antilapse" statutes which create a substitute gift for the deceased devisee's descendants who survive the testator. UPC § 2-603 is a typical "antilapse" statute. At Faye's death, Faye did not own an interest in the family farm that Faye could devise to Henry.

270. **Answer (D) is correct.** At common law, Faye's equitable vested remainder would have been devised by Faye to Henry. *See* Restatement of Trusts § 55. The result is likely to differ in a state that has adopted UPC § 2-707. UPC § 2-707 would convert Faye's interest into a remainder contingent on Faye surviving Baird, and since she did not, Lela and Mike would take as her substituted takers. **Answers (A), (B) and (C) are incorrect** for the reasons explained.

Answer (D) is incorrect. At common law, Faye's interest passed to Henry.

271. **Answer (A) is incorrect**. Absent an agreement otherwise, when multiple parties consult with a lawyer on a matter, the presumption is that the lawyer represents the clients jointly rather than separately. ACTEC Commentary 1.6. Thus, LaDonna represented David and Chava jointly. Generally, the execution of estate planning documents causes the relationship to transition from an active to a dormant relationship, unless there is a specific communication on point. In a dormant phase of representation, as compared to the active phase of representation, LaDonna has diminished responsibilities to Chava. However, she remains bound by some obligations. ACTEC Commentary 1.4.

  Answer (C) is incorrect. As explained above, the attorney-client relationship between LaDonna and Chava is has moved from the active to the dormant phase of representation. Nevertheless, LaDonna remains bound by some obligations to Chava. That is, the representation need not be active in order for LaDonna to have obligations. ACTEC Commentary 1.4.

  Answer (D) is correct. Chava's and David's interests in the potential trust termination or modification are materially adverse, and LaDonna has ongoing obligations to each of them, even as former clients or clients in a dormant phase of representation. Thus, without the informed consent of Chava, LaDonna may not represent David in this matter. ACTEC Commentary 1.9; Example 1.9-1. Thus, **Answer (B) is incorrect** for the reasons explained.

272. **Answer (B) is correct**. UPC § 2-106 adopts the system of representation called per capita at each generation, which always provides equal shares to those equally related. Shay and Tessie, as grandchildren, each receive an equal ⅓, while Colleen and Martha, as great-grandchildren, each receive an equal ⅙. However, under the older "strict" or "English" per stirpes system of representation, which is used in some non-UPC jurisdictions, Shay would take ½; Tessie would take ¼; Colleen and Martha would each take ⅛. **Answers (A), (C) and (D) are incorrect** for the reasons explained.

273. **Answer (B) is correct**. UPC § 2-803(b) provides that an heir who feloniously and intentionally kills the intestate forfeits the heir's intestate share. It also provides that the intestate's probate estate passes as if the killer disclaimed the killer's interest in the intestate's estate. Accordingly, the interest Edna would have received passes from Clarence to Edna's child, Nellie. A number of states that have not enacted the Uniform Probate Code have similar statutes. *See* McGovern § 2.7.

  Answer (A) is incorrect. Since Edna is deemed to have disclaimed the interest, the interest does not pass to Edna's devisee, Palmer.

  Answer (C) is incorrect. UPC § 2-803(b) provides that Edna's interest passes as if Edna had disclaimed Edna's interest. However, in some states, the applicable "slayer's rule" directs that Edna's interest would be forfeited and Edna's interest passes to

Clarence's other heirs. Accordingly, in those states, Grace and Louis would take Edna's interest, and Nellie is excluded since Edna, in fact, survived Clarence. McGovern § 2.7.

Answer (D) is incorrect. UPC § 2-803(b) provides a legal remedy that avoids having to resort to equitable principles. However, in states that do not have a "slayer's rule" statute, the other heirs may be able to resort to the constructive trust as a remedy to prevent unjust enrichment.

274. **Answer (D) is correct.** UPC § 2-507 provides that a will can be revoked by executing a subsequent will that expressly revokes the previous will. Since the July 2 handwritten note conforms to the requirements for a holographic will under UPC § 2-502, the handwritten note is a subsequent will. The terms of the subsequent will expressly revoke the previous will (*i.e.*, "I don't want my June 1 will. That will is no good anymore.")

Answers (A) and (B) are incorrect. As explained above, the June 1 will was revoked on July 2, so the actions on July 3 and July 4 are superfluous. Importantly, UPC § 2-507(b) provides for revocation by "revocatory act," such as writing "void" on the will, whether or not the cancelling words touch the words of the will. However, if another person takes revocatory action on behalf of the testator, it must be in the testator's conscious presence, which the lawyer was not. Thus, even if the will had not been revoked on July 2, the actions on July 3 and July 4 would not have revoked it because the actions were not taken in the testator's conscious presence.

Answer (C) is incorrect. As explained above, the June 1 will was revoked on July 2, so the actions on July 3 are superfluous. The e-mailed note does not qualify as a holographic will, so it cannot revoke the will under UPC §§ 2-502 and 2-507. That is, revocation by subsequent will cannot be effective unless the subsequent will is valid and the e-mailed note is not a valid subsequent will. The fact that Helena's lawyer had read the e-mailed note is not relevant. Note, however, that UPC § 2-504 is a "substantial compliance" rule. Pursuant to such rules, a court might admit the e-mail to probate even though it has not been executed with statutory formalities and is not a holographic will — if the proponent can establish by clear and convincing evidence that the testator intended the document to be a will.

275. **Answer (A) is correct.** UPC § 2-502(a)(2) requires that the will be signed by the testator or in the testator's name by some other individual in the testator's conscious presence and at the testator's direction. While the UPC has eliminated any requirement that the witnesses sign *as witnesses* in either the testator's or one another's presence, it is necessary that any proxy who signs on behalf of the testator do so in the testator's conscious presence. Although she need not be in his physical presence or within his line of sight when signing his name, requiring "conscious presence" means that Shauna must be within the range of at least one of Manny's physical senses when doing so. As Shauna signed Manny's name when she was inside her car but he was in the back bedroom, there's no evidence that she was within the range of any of Manny's physical senses. Thus, **Answers (C) and (D) are incorrect.**

Answer (B) is incorrect. This answer refers to the more restrictive "line of sight" test, which is not adopted by the UPC for proxy signatures. UPC § 2-502 adopts the more liberal conscious presence requirement.

276. **Answer (B) is correct.** Under the anti-lapse statue of the Uniform Probate Code, since Pasang is a descendant of Nima's grandparents, the gift to her is kept from lapsing in the event she fails to survive for 120 hours. Instead, a substitute gift is made to Sonan as Pasang's surviving descendant. UPC § 2-603(b)(3).

Answer (A) is incorrect. Even though UPC § 2-604(b) abandons the no-residue-of-a-residue rule, the anti-lapse provision UPC § 2-603(b)(3) prevails. UPC § 2-604(b) provides that if the residue is devised to two or more persons and if one share fails to pass for any reason (*e.g.*, death of a beneficiary), the failed share passes to the other residuary devisees in proportion to the interest of each in the remaining part of the residue. That is, under the general rule of UPC § 2-604(b) Tashi would receive 100%. However, since Pasang is a descendant of Nima's grandparents, the gift to her is kept from lapsing and is distributed to Sonan instead.

Answer (C) is incorrect. Pasang's share does not pass pursuant to her will but under the anti-lapse statute of UPC § 2-603(b)(3).

Answer (D) is incorrect. The no-residue-of-a-residue rule would have this result, and the intestate heirs would succeed to Pasang's failed gift. Although this rule remains in effect in some states, it is revoked in the Uniform Probate Code. However, the anti-lapse provision UPC § 2-603(b)(3) prevails so that Pasang's gift does not lapse but instead is distributed to Sonan.

277. **Answer (A) is incorrect.** Hal's bequest was expressly conditioned upon his survival.

Answer (D) is correct. Example 6 to UPC § 2-603 explains that, in a situation such as this, half of the gift goes to the surviving child and the other half goes to the surviving grandchildren who were the children of the deceased child. Because the alternative devise to Hal's children is a class gift and because one of the class members, Golda, failed to survive Fred by 120 hours and left descendants who survived Fred by 120 hours, subsection (b)(2) applies and substitutes Samuel and Zach for Golda. Thus, **Answers (B) and (C) are incorrect.**

278. **Answer (C) is correct.** If the will had not disinherited Blair, he would have taken one-half of the intestate estate (*i.e.*, $50,000). As a general rule, the UPC (unlike many states) authorizes a testator to disinherit an heir for purposes of intestate distribution (as well as, of course, testate distribution.) However, since Blair failed to survive Adair by 120 hours (*see* UPC § 2-104), the disinheriting provision of the will has no effect. Thus, each of Cameron, Euna, Fergie, and Iona would have taken equal ¼ shares under UPC §§ 2-103(3) and 2-106. Comments to UPC § 2-101. **Answers (A), (B), and (D) are incorrect** for the reasons explained.

279. The Uniform Probate Code provides that a multi-party account (*i.e.*, a "joint account") is presumed to belong to the parties in proportion to their net contributions, which is the contributions of the parties plus their pro rata share of interest and dividends appropriately reduced by withdrawals. Thus, as a preliminary conclusion, Aviashai owns $10,666.66 and Ben owns $5,333.33 of the account. Since no more than what Ben owned at the time of his death would be liable, no more than $5,333.33 is available to Ben's creditors. UPC § 6-215(b). However, if Aviashai has clear and convincing evidence that, prior to his death, Ben intended to make a gift to Aviashai of his contributions, then the entire balance would belong to Aviashai as his property. UPC §§ 6-211, 6-206(b), comment to UPC § 6-211. Accordingly, we should consider any evidence that a lifetime gift was intended and, if so, whether or not it was in violation of our then existing rights as Ben's creditors (*i.e.*, whether or not the gift defrauded Ben's creditors.)

280. **Answer (D) is correct.** A trust is created of Theo's equitable contingent remainder interest in the trust previously created by his father, but not of his expectancy in the estate of his mother. A person who expects to receive property in the future by the will of a living person or by intestate succession has no presently existing interest of which to make a declaration of trust or a transfer to another in trust. Such an expectancy is not a contingent future interest but a mere hope or expectation however well founded or likely to materialize. By all traditional and current concepts of property, expectancies are not property interests. Comment a, illustration 1 to Restatement of Trusts § 41. **Answers (A), (B) and (C) are incorrect** for the reasons explained. Note that a spendthrift clause prohibiting the assignment of beneficial interests is very common in practice. Had such a prohibition applied, Theo's equitable contingent remainder interest in the trust created by his father could not have been assigned.

281. **Answer (A) is correct.** The rule against perpetuities is not violated.. All of Carlos's children will attain age twenty-one, if they ever do, within twenty-one years of his death. Restatement of Donative Transfers, Chapter 1 When the first grandchild attains that age, the Red Hook School for the Performing Arts is divested, and that child owns the fee simple title subject to partial divestment if any other of Carlos's children reach age twenty-one. Restatement of Property § 239.

   Answer (B) is incorrect. The grandchildren's executory interests are valid.

   Answer (C) is incorrect. The class of beneficiaries includes any grandchild who reaches the age of twenty-one.

   Answer (D) is incorrect. Javier did not die intestate.

INDEX

INDEX